Leadership Careers in Medical Education

D1428413

Teaching Medicine Series

Jack Ende, MD, MACP
Series Editor

Leadership Careers in Medical Education

Louis Pangaro, MD, MACP
Editor

ACP Press
American College of Physicians • Philadelphia, Pennsylvania

Director, Publishing Operations: Linda Drumheller
Developmental Editor: Marla Sussman
Production Editor: Suzanne Meyers
Publishing Coordinator: Angela Gabella
Cover Design: Kate Nichols
Index: Kathleen Patterson

Printed in the United States of America
Printing/Binding by Versa Press
Composition by ACP Graphic Services

Library of Congress Cataloging-in-Publication Data

Leadership careers in medical education / [edited by] Louis Pangaro.
       p. ; cm. -- (ACP teaching medicine series)
   Includes bibliographical references.
   ISBN 978-1-934465-46-2
   1. Medical college administrators. 2. Leadership 3. Medical education.
I. Pangaro, Louis. II. American College of Physicians. III. Series: ACP teaching
medicine series.
   [DNLM: 1. Education, Medical. 2. Career Choice. 3. Internal Medicine--
education. 4. Leadership. 5. Physician Executives. 6. Teaching--methods.
W 18 L434 2010]
   R833.L43 2010
   610.71'173—dc22
                                        2009053113

10 11 12 13 14 / 10 9 8 7 6 5 4 3 2 1

Contributors

D. Craig Brater, MD, MACP
Dean
University of Indiana School of Medicine
Indianapolis, Indiana

Peter F. Buckley, MD
Associate Dean for Leadership and
    Development
Chairman, Department of Psychiatry
Medical College of Georgia
Augusta, Georgia

Teresa A. Coleman, MD, FACP
Associate Professor of Medicine
Medical College of Georgia
Augusta, Georgia

Steven J. Durning, MD, FACP
Professor of Medicine and Pathology
Uniformed Services University
Bethesda, Maryland

Ruth-Marie E. Fincher, MD, MACP
Vice Dean for Academic Affairs
Medical College of Georgia School of
    Medicine
Augusta, Georgia

**Col Paul A. Hemmer, USAF, MC, MD,
    MPH, FACP**
Vice Chairman, Educational Programs
Professor of Medicine
Uniformed Services University
Bethesda, Maryland

**Capt Eric S. Holmboe, USNR-Ret, MC,
    MD, FACP**
Vice President for Quality and Evaluation
    Research
American Board of Internal Medicine
Philadelphia, Pennsylvania

Joel D. Howell, MD, PhD, FACP
Victor Vaughan Professor of the History
    of Medicine
Professor of Internal Medicine, History,
    and Health Management & Policy
University of Michigan
Ann Arbor, Michigan

David E. Kern, MD, MPH, FACP
Professor of Medicine
Johns Hopkins University School of
    Medicine
Director, Division of General Internal
    Medicine
Johns Hopkins Bayview Medical Center
Baltimore, Maryland

Daniel J. Klass, MD, FRCPC, FACP
Adjunct Professor
University of Toronto
Associate Registrar
College of Physicians and Surgeons of
    Ontario
Toronto, Ontario, Canada

Louis Pangaro, MD, MACP
Chair, Department of Medicine
F. Edward Hébert School of Medicine
Uniformed Services University
Bethesda, Maryland

Barbara Schuster, MD, MACP
Campus Dean
Medical College of Georgia/University of
    Georgia Medical Partnership
Athens, Georgia

Patricia A. Thomas, MD, FACP
Associate Professor of Medicine
Associate Dean for Curriculum
Johns Hopkins University School of
    Medicine
Baltimore, Maryland

To my own models of leadership, James Leonard, Robert Goldstein, and Leonard Wartofsky

Acknowledgments

Each of the authors has the demanding schedule that goes with a successful career, yet their enthusiasm to support this project was inspirational. I am grateful to them for their hard work in preparing this book.

Contents

Visit www.acponline.org/acp_press/teaching
for additional information.

About the *Teaching Medicine* Series

This book series, *Teaching Medicine*, represents a major initiative from the American College of Physicians. It is intended for College members but also for the profession as a whole. Internists, family physicians, subspecialists, surgical colleagues, nurse practitioners, and physician assistants—indeed, anyone involved with medical education—should find this book series useful as they pursue one of the greatest privileges of the profession: the opportunity to teach and make a difference in the lives of learners and their patients. The series is composed of six books:

- *Theory and Practice of Teaching Medicine*, edited by me, considers how medical learners learn (how to be doctors), how medical teachers teach, and how they (the teachers) might learn to teach better.

- *Methods for Teaching Medicine*, edited by Kelley M. Skeff and Georgette A. Stratos, builds on this foundation but focuses on the actual methods that medical teachers use. This book explores the full range of techniques that encourage learning within groups. The authors present a a conceptual framework and guiding perspectives for understanding teaching; the factors that support choices for particular teaching methods (such as lecturing vs. small group discussion); and practical advice for preceptors, attendings, lecturers, discussion leaders, workshop leaders, and, finally, course directors charged with running programs for continuing medical education.

- *Teaching in Your Office*, edited by Patrick C. Alguire, Dawn E. DeWitt, Linda E. Pinsky, and Gary S. Ferenchick, will be familiar to many teaching internists. It has been reissued as part of this series. This book remains the office-based preceptor's single most useful resource for preparing to receive medical students and residents into an ambulatory practice setting or, among those already engaged in office-based teaching, for learning how to do it even better.

- *Teaching in the Hospital* is edited by Jeff Wiese and considers the challenges and rewards of teaching in that particular setting. Hospitalists as well as more traditional internists who attend on the inpatient service will be interested in the insightful advice that this book provides. This advice focuses not only on how to conduct rounds and encourage learning among students and house officers but also on how to frame and orient the content of rounds for some of the more frequently encountered inpatient conditions.

- *Mentoring in Academic Medicine,* edited by Holly J. Humphrey, considers professional development across the continuum of medical education, from issues pertaining to students to residents to faculty themselves, as well as issues pertaining to professional development of special populations. Here is where the important contributions of mentors and role models are explored in detail.

- *Leadership Careers in Medical Education* concludes this series. Edited by Louis Pangaro, this book is written for members of the medical faculty who are pursuing—or who are considering—careers as clerkship directors, residency program directors, or educational leaders of departments or medical schools, careers that require not only leadership skill but also a deep understanding of the organization and administration of internal medicine's educational enterprise. This book explores the theory and practice of educational leadership, including curricular design and evaluation; and offers insightful profiles of many of internal medicine's most prominent leaders.

Jack Ende, MD, MACP
Philadelphia, 2010

Introduction: Views of Educational Leadership in Internal Medicine

This book in the *Teaching Medicine* series addresses leadership careers in internal medicine education. It is written for education leaders—for example, those who direct systems of medical education, whether at the school or department level, such as a clerkship or residency program—and for anyone considering such a career. The chapters are intended to provide those individuals with both information and confidence. What is it like to be someone who makes the success of others possible? What tasks do leaders face? If you are contemplating this kind of career, what do you need to know, and what kind of training do you need? What do you have to do for others, and what do you learn from them? This book has two parts. The first part describes the challenges and responsibilities leaders will face. The second part profiles actual internal medicine leaders, describing how they faced these challenges.

❖ View From the Top

While the *Teaching Medicine* series details the skills all teachers of medicine need—part-time teachers, occasional teachers, or house staff (the base of the pyramid of faculty development) or members of the "core faculty" that does a large percentage of teaching—this book is especially intended for faculty higher up the pyramid: the course, clerkship, and program directors—the "academic directors" (or "academic managers"). It is also for those who are at the top of the pyramid: the chairs, deans, and CEOs of academic medical centers—the "academic executives."

Leaders need a "50,000-foot view," and the first three chapters of this book provide that big picture. Barbara Schuster's chapter 1 describes the theory and practice of leadership and the characteristics of individuals who succeed. In chapter 2, Joel D. Howell provides over a century of historical perspective on the organizational structures of academic medicine, particularly internal medicine, enabling academic leaders to better understand the world in which they work. D. Craig Brater's chapter 3 then describes that world from a contemporary vantage point, including the context and setting in which leaders work—that is, medical schools and academic medical centers (sometimes called the "house of medicine")—along with the cast of characters and their roles, relationships, and responsibilities. He also provides a helpful glossary of the "alphabet soup" of U.S. professional organizations for internal medicine and medical education.

❖ Closer to Ground Level

With chapter 4 the book moves closer to ground level, perhaps the "10,000-foot view." Barbara Schuster and I describe what leaders should generally expect of clinical teachers, clerkship and program directors, and themselves. We are not quite at the level of "in the trenches" detail provided elsewhere in the *Teaching Medicine* series. However, building on chapter 3 we provide a systems perspective of the structures and functions in the educational enterprise—how information flows up and down, and how the system regulates itself. We can use Wennberg's terminology for health systems (1) to characterize faculty development as a process of minimizing unwarranted variation in what and how teachers teach. Chapter 4 catalogues not only what we expect *of* teachers and academic managers but what we want *for* them: the resources, training, and incentives they need to succeed in their work. Although chapter 1 concerns "leadership"—setting institutional goals, picking the right people, inspiring—chapter 4 brings us closer to "management" and the role of faculty development as a way of ensuring quality in the educational system.

In chapter 5, Teresa A. Coleman, Peter F. Buckley, and Ruth-Marie E. Fincher address the professional development of teachers who transition to overseeing the teaching process. What specific mentoring and career incentives do leaders provide as they develop the next generation of leadership? What opportunities and training should aspiring leaders seek out?

❖ Education Leaders' Tool Box

The next few chapters can be considered an introduction to the tools that education leaders need to fulfill their responsibilities as academic managers and leaders. These chapters focus on curriculum evaluation and education research. In chapter 6, David E. Kern and Patricia A. Thomas introduce prospective leaders to the task of curriculum development: How do you do a needs assessment? How do you plan and implement something new? In chapter 7, Steven J. Durning and Paul A. Hemmer provide a detailed and structured approach for academic directors to determine whether the overall program has been successful, and how to detect unwarranted variation across settings. In chapter 8, Daniel J. Klass describes how to plan a comprehensive system to determine whether individual students and residents have succeeded in moving toward independence. Finally, in chapter 9, Eric S. Holmboe describes the practice of educational scholarship and how we use this research to improve our programs and enhance the careers of our potential leaders.

❖ Leadership Profiles

In teaching, we often use the "case method" to reinforce understanding and explore what was just taught. The second part of this book features profiles of outstanding internists who have been wonderful leaders in medical education. Jack Ende, editor of the *Teaching Medicine* series, suggested this idea, and I had the privilege of interviewing a small but extraordinary group of men and women. The purpose and methods are described in more detail in the introduction to that section; the hope is that these "exemplars" will encourage a new generation of leaders.

Louis Pangaro, MD, MACP
Bethesda, Maryland, 2010

REFERENCE

1. **Wennberg JE.** Unwarranted variations in healthcare delivery: implications for academic medical centres. BMJ. 2002;325:961-4.

1

The Leadership Challenge in Internal Medicine

Barbara Schuster, MD, MACP

L eaders in academic medicine are often those who have been successful in director and manager positions in departments and practices. As one rises through the academic ranks from assistant, to associate, to full professor, one usually accepts more managerial positions, such as clerkship director, clinic director, program director, division chief, or chair of a department. Others with a passion for research may have also accepted the position of institute director or laboratory director. As academic physicians accept increasing administrative responsibilities, they require both management skills and more leadership skills to be successful. This chapter explains the roles and styles of leadership, explores the skills needed for leadership, and applies the discussion to the setting of internal medicine.

❖ Defining Leadership

During the 2009 U.S. presidential election, Hillary Clinton and Barack Obama were asked to describe the position of President. Mrs. Clinton was quoted as saying that the President is "a Chief Executive Officer who has to be able to manage and run the bureaucracy." Mr. Obama, however, said that "the Presidency has little to do with running an efficient office; it involves having a vision for where the country needs to go ... and then being able to mobilize and inspire the American people

---

KEY POINTS

- A leader articulates a vision, then provides resources and motivates people to achieve it. A manager deals with immediate issues, such as planning, staffing, and budgeting, to accomplish plans and goals.
- Leadership styles differ. Some leaders gain trust, empower people to achieve goals, and encourage shared innovation; others motivate and reward people toward existing goals.
- Leadership requires courage, stamina, wisdom, passion, and vision.
- Effective leaders communicate with clarity and emotion.
- Risks to leaders include overwork, burnout, and loss of position.
- The rewards can be great, including the fulfillment of a dream and advancing health care as well as the careers of others.

---

to get behind that agenda for change" (1). The latter statement is consistent with John Kotter's definition of leadership and the former with his definition of manager (2).

Kotter, well known for his work on leadership, describes a leader as one who copes with changes and sets the direction for others. The leader aligns people to achieve a vision. A leader motivates and inspires. Kotter contrasts the tasks of a leader with those of a manager. A manager copes with the complexity at hand and, instead of setting direction, does the planning and budgeting for the direction that has been set. A manager organizes and provides staff to achieve the vision that the leader sets but may not take charge of recruiting and aligning the people. A manager ensures that plans are accomplished by problem-solving and organizing.

In academic medicine, as in most professions and business, the junior team member who has accepted his or her first administration position (such as chief medical resident or assistant program director) spends a great deal of time and energy as a manager, scheduling conferences and working the details of the on-call schedule. In parallel with these day-to-day chores, the chief resident is responsible for maintaining the morale of the house staff. In that capacity he or she also begins to develop leadership skills. The chief residency has been described as a fellowship in medical leadership (Schuster R. Personal communication) and is considered a traditional pathway for entrance into the academy of academic medicine. At the senior level, the dean of the medical school, in contrast, should be spending most of his or her day in activities that require leadership skills and fewer hours in management.

All of the above describes things as they *should* be, when things are going well. What about when they are not? The effect of poor leadership has been described an editorial in the *Japan Times*: "the result of poor leadership is not just mismanagement and bad decisions, but a frighteningly widespread apathy. Leadership is not simply about governing but how to inspire. It is often said that people campaign in poetry and govern in prose ... true leadership combines the prose of seasoned understanding with the poetry of energy and vision" (3). In every medical leadership position, the individual must balance the poetry (leadership skill) with the prose (management skill). Leaders need to be prepared to repair damage and, better still, prevent damage before it happens. Generally this requires special qualities and skills, but also an effective leadership style.

❖ Leadership Styles

There may be consensus about tasks of leadership, but much stronger debate surrounds the most successful leadership style. In "traditional" academic medicine, leadership style was most often "top down." Junior colleagues learned by observing senior experts. Questioning the boss was not encouraged. The self-assured professor would lead the younger doctors in rounds, and every decision was based on experience. Paramount in medicine during the late 19th and early 20th centuries was the outstanding clinician mastering and demonstrating the science and art of medicine, with few possible therapeutic interventions. Clinical leadership occurred in a relatively simple environment, and administrators were considered caretakers of an organization (4). The "assertion and control" approach has been much more associated with a masculine style of leading. In contrast, the "consensus" style of leading, which tends to be collaborative and relationally directed, is often considered more feminine.

Those who study leadership suggest that both styles of leadership—directive and collaborative—may be successful depending on the events and environment. More recently, Goleman and colleagues (5) described several styles of leadership: visionary, commanding, affiliative, democratic, pace setting, and coaching. They contend that successful leaders can develop facility in applying each style when appropriate.

James MacGregor Burns (6) described leadership styles as transformational or transactional. Transformational leaders establish themselves as role models by gaining followers' trust and confidence, are willing to state future goals, develop plans to achieve those goals, are open to innovation, and help mentor and empower followers. Transactional leaders are more established in give-and-take relationships that appeal to subordinates' self-interest. Transactional leaders clarify responsibility and reward others for meeting those objectives, correcting those who fail to meet the objectives. Female leaders were found to be more transformational than male leaders. Burns also defined a third leadership category—laissez-faire—a sort of nonleadership that is also more likely to be prevalent in men (7).

Robert Greenleaf propounds the approach of a "servant leader." He states that "the servant leader is a servant first … it begins with the natural feeling that one wants to serve first. This conscious choice brings one to aspire to lead. That person is sharply different from one who is leader first perhaps because of the need to assuage an unusual power drive or to acquire material possessions" (8). Greenleaf sees a servant leader as less narcissistic and driven by the opportunity to serve others.

❖ Qualities and Values of Leadership

Whatever the definition of leadership or differences in the descriptions of leadership styles, there is greater consensus on the qualities and values of great leaders. Whereas skills can be learned, qualities and values are much more likely to define those who emerge as leaders. In an Association of American Medical Colleges monograph (9) written to help search commit-tees evaluate candidates for department chair positions, the leadership characteristics that are brought to the position, such as integrity, are sep-arated from the skills that may be developed after acceptance of a leader-ship position, such as managing difficult employees.

Judith Rodin, former president of the University of Pennsylvania, iden-tified five qualities of leaders: courage, strength, wisdom, passion, and vision (10). Leaders need the courage to stand by their values and to be independent in their thoughts. They must have the courage to take decisive action after considering input from others, even when that action is not supported by the majority view, and they must be consistent. The power of maintaining consistency in one's convictions is enormous, but those who aspire to leadership must understand that strong convictions, even if seen by the majority as correct, may cause conflict with decision-makers and not be without cost. For example, a powerful physician is removed from a position of authority when evidence shows that he demonstrates poor judg-ment. This physician, however, had been responsible for admitting a large number of patients to the hospital. When he changes his hospital affilia-tion, the inpatient census decreases and turmoil among other staff members ensues. Leaders may need to wrestle with the concerns of negative outcomes when they opt to do the right thing.

Leadership, according to Rodin, also requires strength or, phrased differently, stamina. The capacity of an individual to withstand and handle the emotional stressors, along with the physical demands, is a leadership quality. Leadership is not a 40-hours-a-week job; days are long, and evenings and weekends are not sacrosanct. Rodin stated, "it is not the job of a leader to keep everyone happy"—but of course, others' unhappiness may place strain and stress on the leader as she brings people through difficult times, whether budgetary or institutional instability. Although leaders are usually endowed with better than average capacity for hard work, including the ability to juggle and to handle unexpected problems, leaders must understand their physical and emotional limitations. Sensing one's own early warning signs is an important skill that can be developed gradually. The ability to reflect on how one reacts under sleep deprivation, increased pressure, or daily schedules without time for lunch, exercise, or pleasurable activity helps the leader to step back from the edge of burnout. This capacity helps prevent poor decisions, increased risk for physical disability, and general displeasure with their positions. Leaders can also benefit from education on handling difficult and often frustrating personnel issues. The leader will learn how to formulate approaches to a variety of common issues, thus facilitating problem-solving and decreasing the tension that can develop when working with others.

Wisdom, another of the leadership qualities Rodin identified, may have its roots in knowledge, but wisdom flowers through experience and reflection. The wise leader is not someone with the greatest book knowledge or highest academic rank but someone who can reason critically, balance multiple inputs, and accept accountability for decisions. To handle the day-in and day-out work that is less visionary and mission-driven, the leader relies on emotional intelligence—that is, noncognitive skills such as self-awareness, social awareness, self-management, social skills, and common sense.

Rodin also includes passion in her list of leadership qualities. Paired with being passionate is the capacity for relentlessness; leaders should be relentless in pursuing their goals and not yield to the temptation to give in or give up.

Finally, leaders must be able to articulate a vision that is understandable and acceptable. The vision helps to connect those who work to support the leader with an achievable, positive goal. The leader's passion for the mission must inspire those who follow through the pangs of change. Success with transformation requires that the leader continue to repetitively express the vision and demonstrate the continuous small successes that help everyone inch toward the goal.

In a study seeking to define the leadership values considered most important to medical school deans, the one most consistently ranked was integrity (11). Trust and vision came next, followed by excellence, teamwork, respect, and developing people. The unfortunate modeling of the opposite leads to unprofessional behavior. Students and faculty implicitly understand the standards set by the leader. Thus, the environment of academic institutions and the standards of behavior may be leaders' most important responsibilities.

❖ Developing Leadership Skills

During medical school and residency, faculty can coach young physicians in the important basics and prerequisites of leadership: self-reflection, communication, time management and prioritization, and negotiation.

Self-Reflection

Honest self-reflection is a skill necessary for future physicians. Coached self-reflection helps learners to evaluate their knowledge limits and teaches them to monitor their abilities and to understand and accept their areas of deficit. Only after diagnosing one's own limitations can one engage in effective life-long learning, a skill required of all leaders.

Communication Skills

Communication skills vital to leadership can also be perfected as one moves through career positions. From the very early stages of learning to communicate with patients while taking a medical history, through public speaking and giving feedback, one can be coached on how to define a message and communicate with a variety of audiences. Too often, future leaders spend more time optimizing their skill in delivering the message and not enough time perfecting their listening skills. Hearing, absorbing, and accepting input from others are key to preventing leaders from misdirection and losing important followers. Coaches of future leaders need to direct feedback toward listening skills as well as toward speaking and writing skills.

Time Management and Prioritization

Medical education provides opportunities to practice time management and prioritization. Supervisors have the responsibility to model as well as explicitly discuss the balancing and juggling of patient care, self-education, personal issues, and community involvement. On a daily basis, the efficient management of a busy inpatient team is a learning opportunity for students and first-year residents. Mastery of the skill allows the senior resident to then coach the junior resident and student and practice team leadership.

Time management and the need to allocate attention and resources to high-priority issues become even more essential as one rises up the leadership ladder. With each additional administrative position come increasing responsibilities and more meetings with institutional leaders. For deans and hospital CEOs, more time representing the institution with community groups and state and federal legislators complicates scheduling and removes the leader from "home-based" activities. Setting priorities (see also *Teaching in the Hospital* [12], another book in the *Teaching Medicine* series), a skill that students begin to learn in medical school, becomes exceedingly important because the number of days in the week and the number of hours in a day do not change. A key to time management when moving from the manager role to the leader role is to empower one's team with the supervision and fulfillment of defined responsibilities. Helping others to accept ownership and then stepping aside to allow them to execute the plan without close supervision decreases the risk for becoming a micromanager, a negative leadership style that also negatively affects one's own time management.

Negotiation

Negotiation skills are essential for leaders. This skill is practiced from the very beginning of medical education. Working with patients, the student learns to negotiate by helping the patient with medical decisions. The student begins by understanding the therapeutic (or diagnostic) options and the benefits and risks (or costs) of each, and by observing the interchanges between patients and attending or resident physicians. Advanced students and interns present and solicit alternatives to and from patients, learning how patient preference affects the diagnostic and therapeutic plan.

Students who are successful in the core clinical clerkships also learn to negotiate with the nursing staff, the scheduling personnel, and the ancillary services staffs. This skill is further perfected at the program director, chair, or dean level. The program director may be negotiating with the hospital for which services the residents will cover, while the chair is negotiating for space and funds to facilitate the work of the faculty. Meanwhile, the dean is negotiating with the chairs to increase the emphasis on teaching and service to the school and with the provost or president of the university for research and educational support.

Other Skills

Through courses and workshops, emerging leaders can also learn skills in teaching, communication, team leadership, strategic planning, and business management. After a basic introduction, experiential practice followed by reflection and feedback enhances a leader's skills. At every step in leadership, having mentors and coaches to offer feedback and guidance helps even the most senior of leaders to perfect their skills—especially the ability to manage change, one of the core responsibilities of leaders.

❖ Personnel Development

One of the basic but most important and difficult of all leadership skills is personnel development. People have quipped that it would be easy to be a chair if they didn't have to supervise faculty and that it would be easy to be a program director if the residents and attending physicians would "just do their jobs." Working with bright, creative, and talented people is a challenge even for the most respected leader. As a group, medical students and physicians are among the most gifted adults. Gifted adults do not necessarily have better insight or communication skills than anyone else, and they may have less patience with those who cannot think, juggle, or work as quickly as they do.

For those educated in clinical medicine, an excellent approach to handling personnel problems is thinking through a differential diagnosis. By first asking, "Why is this personnel issue surfacing now?" the leader has a routine approach to common or perplexing issues that may occur gradually or suddenly. The differential diagnosis is usually broad, consisting of physical or emotional illness, family illness, family issues, financial problems, and burnout. As most leaders quickly learn, there are at least two sides to every story, and taking a thorough history inevitably yields unanticipated information.

A leader must educate, mentor, and guide a broad array of people with widely divergent skills and capacities. Thus, outstanding leaders not only need psychological insight but also the sensitivity to help every member of the team—from the receptionist to the chief administrative officer—recognize and cope with stress and challenge. The leader must also learn how to relieve employees of responsibility when remediation has failed, as well as guide them to more appropriate positions.

❖ Are Leaders Always Scholars?

In academic medical leadership, the leader must have exceptional expertise in at least one area of scholarship. According to recent tradition, this expertise has been in the scholarship of discovery—that is, independent research. In the past several decades, leaders have come from a successful career in basic science research, during which they added important discoveries to the body of science and medicine. Before the dramatic rise in National Institutes of Health research funding in the 1970s, leaders in medicine had outstanding expertise in clinical scholarship: the clinical care of patients and the education of junior colleagues. Scholarly expertise need not be restricted to basic laboratory discovery. Newer areas of scholarship have expanded, including clinical research and expertise in quality management. Leadership skills and scholarship skills do not overlap completely. An outstanding scholar may or may not be the perfect person to fulfill the modern-day role of dean or chair. However, success in prior scholarship and success in collaborative work that requires planning and managing budgets and delivering work on time are often taken as evidence of the managerial skills that leaders should have developed. Alternatively, leaders who have not excelled in some area of scholarship, be it educational, clinical, or traditional bench science, may not hold the respect of their colleagues and constituents.

❖ Developing New Leaders: Succession Planning

Leaders must engage in succession planning and develop those who will pick up the baton in the next lap of organizational leadership. If the job of leadership is to move the organization to a higher level of accomplishment and to challenge the status quo, it must also inspire a new, shared vision and enable a new group to act. Opening opportunities for those who have been identified (or who self-identify) as potential leaders is an important task for senior administrators. Educating junior colleagues is an accepted responsibility of physician training, and most medical leaders readily and enthusiastically seize this task. The intern and resident have always helped the medical student. The fellow has taught the resident, and the attending physician has supervised the fellow. Senior professors guide and mentor assistant and associate professors through the obstacles and challenges of grant writing, publication, teaching, and medical politics (see *Mentoring in Academic Medicine* [13], another book in the *Teaching Medicine* series). However, faculty mentoring must include helping others to develop leadership skills, which differ from the skills that lead to academic promotion.

Leaders must recognize unconscious bias—in themselves and other faculty—in extending opportunities to emerging leaders in the assistant professor years. It is the responsibility of leadership to support and nurture a diverse faculty. Upon finding a path in internal medicine, whether it be research, education, or clinical care, the promotion to associate professor should also include more responsibility for developing more junior faculty. New associate professors may not have obtained competency in the appropriate mentorship skills; thus, senior leadership must help them perfect those skills. Fostering leadership skills during the associate professor years and offering opportunities to practice these skills through committee membership (and eventually committee chairmanships), program development, and academic management positions (such as clerkship director, program director, or laboratory director) facilitate learning-while-doing and feedback from mentors and advisors. In addition, senior leaders need to identify rising talents and promote their careers with nominations for regional and national leadership positions. A truly effective leader serves the future by promoting the careers of those who will replace them, yet maintains a mentoring friendship even when the opinions of the mentor and mentee begin to diverge.

❖ The Risks of Leadership

A leadership position in academic medicine offers many opportunities for personal growth, but it has its own costs and risks, including stagnation, burnout, and job loss. Many successful academic leaders suggest that one should have a 5- to 7-year strategy for each position accepted. The leader should understand that although institutional change takes time, a person is most likely to fulfill his or her goals for an institution, program, or association within this time frame. Some leaders can continue to spearhead change from a singular position for more than a decade, but most cannot. Once the vision articulated upon beginning a new position has come to fruition, a leader is likely to be enticed by other challenging opportunities in which the leader can begin again with a fresh vision and reinvigorated passion.

Another risk of leadership is job loss. All leaders are also followers, answering to a supervisor or a board of trustees. Circumstances, some not under leaders' control, may cause conflict between leaders and their supervisors; as a result, one of the pair (usually the "follower") must leave (14). Accepting a leadership position is no guarantee of success. Particularly in senior leadership positions, such as department chair, dean, and vice-president of health affairs, the leader serves at the pleasure of the supervisor, often with less position security than members of the faculty. In fact, the more senior the leadership position, the greater the opportunity for influence, but also the greater the risks for position instability. When unexpected position turnover occurs, self-esteem, financial stability, and family support can be significantly affected. Position change is especially difficult when one is balancing family needs and a spouse's career. Reflection on environmental cues and seeking the input of staff, friends, and colleagues may help clarify the desirability or necessity of a career move. The academic leader may need to move not because he or she has faltered but because the institution is moving in a direction unacceptable to the leader or may wish to change leadership given a change in its strategic plan.

Leaders must seek feedback to help them see how they are perceived. Listening to the feedback and self-correcting can help a leader retain a sense of balance and prevent burnout. Because leaders are often protected by one or more administrative assistants, they must regularly "circulate among the troops." Helpful strategies include an open door to those who wish to discuss events, a 360° evaluation with feedback from every member of the team (from the administrative assistant to the senior professor), and active questioning to improve understanding of the day-to-day work environment and the perception of the department and institution. Senior leaders are often isolated and therefore may be the last to know when trouble is brewing. Subtle changes, such as not being included on important decision-making committees; one's emotional responses to meetings (such as anger or decreasing patience); the quality and tone of interactions with supervisors; enthusiasm for going to work; and reactions to feedback on personal behavior are all data the leader can use to complete a self-evaluation of job security and personal contentment. The more senior the leadership position, the greater the opportunity for influence but also the greater the risks for position instability.

❖ Concluding Thoughts

In 1975, Eugene Braunwald, the esteemed leader in academic medicine, stated his concern that "we live in an era when we desperately need true academic leaders, not managers" (15). This concern—that there are not enough true medical leaders, as defined by Kotter—remains. Why has medicine had so much difficulty with developing true leaders? Some have hypothesized that as we have progressed into a more business-oriented era in medicine, the concept of a medical leader has changed: from an outstanding clinician to one who understands the economic and management systems in our medical centers. As a consequence, these less clinically oriented "new medical leaders" may seem out of touch and lack the respect of the profession. It may be difficult for institutional leaders and academic medical centers to have the business expertise needed to cope with today's reimbursement systems and still maintain credibility as a clinician, educator, or teacher. Another hypothesis on the dearth of talented and visionary leaders is that the descriptions for senior leadership positions in academic medicine and the skills required to adequately execute these positions are not congruent; as a result of this mismatch, younger physicians reject or do not admire the leaders as role models. Expectations of those who accept leadership positions may not align with the reality of the positions, increasing distress and inability to achieve the needed outcomes.

Leadership has always been and will always be difficult. Dual-career families, the rapidity of change, and shifting societal values may be additional barriers making the leadership pathway too daunting.

What advice can one give to prospective leaders in internal medicine? How can you handle a job in which the day is never finished, the work is never complete, and the opportunities remain vast? To survive, you must develop a good professional team of individuals who bring skills and a collaborative spirit. Those who aspire to senior leadership should seize opportunities to learn and practice the skills of leadership and, in particular, practice the skills of negotiation, conflict management, and personnel development. Leaders also need to support themselves with a few close personal friends who can anchor them in reality and provide direct and honest assessments. Enjoy the company of many colleagues and acquaintances to prevent isolation. Protect time for activities outside the office that are necessary to refresh your spirit and clear the mind. Leadership, although a serious responsibility, can be fun and creative.

With all of the challenges to being a leader, it may be that Dr. Braunwald is correct—that academic medicine is not tapping those who would be our best leaders, and qualified faculty are shying away from the challenge of leadership. Certainly leadership is not for everyone. But for those who hope to affect the future of medicine and health care, leadership positions are the gateway to fulfilling that dream. Leaders serve others and in return are rewarded with the joy of watching those who succeed them and knowing that they helped develop the individuals who can be entrusted to accept the baton.

REFERENCES

1. **Parker G.** The choice. The New Yorker. January 28, 2008: 29.
2. **Kotter JP.** What leaders really do. Harvard Business Review. 2001;December:85-96.

3. Editorial: A contest for new leadership. The Japan Times. March 9, 2009:10. Accessed at http://search.japantimes.co.jp/cgi-bin/ed20080309a1.html.
4. **Merry MD.** Physician leadership for the 21st century. Qual Manag Health Care. 1993;1:31-41.
5. **Goleman D, Boyatzis R, McKee A.** Primal Leadership. Boston: Harvard Business School Pr; 2002.
6. **Burns JM.** Leadership. New York: Harper & Row; 1978.
7. **Eagly AH, Carli LL.** Women and the labyrinth of leadership. Harvard Business Review. 2007;September:63-71.
8. **Greenleaf R.** The servant as leader. In: Zimmerli WC, Richter K, Holzinger M, eds. Corporate Ethics and Corporate Governance. Berlin: Springer; 2007:79-85.
9. **Biebuyck JF, Mallon WT.** The Successful Medical School Department Chair. Module 2. Washington, DC: Association of American Medical Colleges; 2002.
10. **Rodin J.** The university and public behavior. Address to Penn National Commission. December 8, 1997. Accessed at www.upenn.edu/pnc/rodin.html.
11. **Souba WW, Day DV.** Leadership values in academic medicine. Acad Med. 2006;81:20-6.
12. **Wiese J, ed.** Teaching in the Hospital. Philadelphia: ACP Pr; 2010.
13. **Humphrey H, ed.** Mentoring in Academic Medicine. Philadelphia: ACP Pr; 2010.
14. **Kelley RE.** In praise of followers. Harvard Business Review. 1988;November-December:142-8.
15. **Braunwald E.** Can medical schools remain the optimal site for the conduct of clinical investigation? Presidential address before the 67th annual meeting of the American Society for Clinical Investigation, Atlantic City, New Jersey, 5 May 1975. J Clin Invest. 1975;56:I-VI.

2

The Changing Structure of Medical Education: A Historical Perspective

Joel D. Howell, MD, PhD, FACP

ffective leaders, including leaders in medical education, need to understand the constantly changing structures within which they work. Leaders can more effectively advocate for future change if they understand the process of past changes, which took place within a complex mix of ideas, places, and organizations. Moreover, current medical educational structures were not rationally designed according to a coherent plan and implemented by a blue-ribbon committee. Rather, the central elements of U.S. medical education were created over centuries, as leaders made choices about what to teach, where to teach it, and how to structure medical education. That structure has changed and doubtless will continue to change in response to events both within and outside of the medical system. This process continues, particularly in internal medicine, the specialty that provides residency training for about a quarter of U.S. house officers (1). This chapter provides a historical perspective on the development of the U.S. system of medical education, with particular attention paid to the development of internal medicine. Current and future academic leaders of internal medicine should understand that specialties such as "internal medicine" do not exist in the ether waiting to be recognized and labeled. Rather, internal medicine as a field had to be invented, defined, and established along a wide range of variables by specific people making contingent choices in specific social contexts. To under-

---

KEY POINTS

- From its beginnings in the 19th century, internal medicine education has emphasized an understanding of mechanisms: physiology, pathophysiology, and microbiology.
- An "internist" as certified by the American Board of Internal Medicine in 1936 was intended to denote one of a handful of truly superb diagnosticians, who would consult on difficult cases.
- In 1965 the U.S. Congress passed bills establishing Medicare and Medicaid, which moved public support for graduate medical education to the level of federal policy.
- World wars and national social priorities have influenced the development of specialties.
- The structure of internal medicine education continues to evolve, while remaining firmly embedded in a social context.

---

stand that process leads us to consider the specialty's history. Understanding where internal medicine fits into the larger system of specialty boards and educational institutions can help explain how other specialties fit into that same system. Likewise, an appreciation of the evolution of our system of medical education enables academic leaders to understand the institutions and structures that determine how doctors are educated.

❖ From Apprenticeship to a Revolution in Medical Education

We start with the teaching of clinical medicine in general. Early in the 19th century the handful of U.S. medical schools all sat in the port cities of the eastern seaboard. But very few physicians actually went to medical school. Medical training was generally accomplished through apprenticeship. A person aspiring to become a physician would simply find a more senior physician to accompany on daily ministrations. Because hospitals were essentially nonexistent outside of a handful of larger cities (and were seen more as social institutions than as medical ones in any event), almost all medical care was carried out in people's homes. Apprentices would accompany the mentor to a patient's home. The apprentices would then be expected to carry tools, clean any used instruments, assist in procedures and medicinal preparations, and learn by observing the more senior physician. When apprentices felt that they had learned enough, they would go off on their own and start their own practices. The apprenticeship system could, in theory, be an effective method for teaching the essentials of workaday practice as it existed on the frontier. And it was the educational process that formed the basis for training more than a generation of U.S. physicians.

Having completed an apprenticeship, some ambitious physicians chose to attend medical school. Medical schools in the mid-19th century did not offer much clinical instruction: People who enrolled had already done a clinical apprenticeship. Admission requirements (save the ability to pay) were nearly nonexistent. College education was not required. Medical schools usually lasted 2 years (2). They held a brief term, 12 to 16 weeks, and classes were not graded; students heard the same lectures in their second year as they had during their first year. Investigation was not considered part of the medical school faculty's responsibility. And while we might today see certain elements of instruction as being part of what we would now call "internal medicine," that field as a medical specialty did not exist.

One significant change during the 19th century was the introduction of clinical instruction into the medical school curriculum. To allow this, it helped if medical students and faculty could have regular access to a site of clinical care, a requirement that was difficult to meet when clinics and hospitals were owned and operated independently of the medical school. In 1869, the University of Michigan became the first university medical school to own and operate its own hospital. This was followed in 1874 by the University of Pennsylvania, which was the first to build a university hospital. Over the ensuing years many more medical schools came to run hospitals and clinics, which provided a space for formalized teaching of trainees. Perhaps the most influential, widely emulated early example of the clinical clerkship was the one William Osler created at Johns Hopkins University, which he later regarded as the most useful and important work of his career.

During the early 20th century, U.S. medical education transformed radically, creating a system that persists largely unchanged today. The central features of that reform included an extension of the medical curriculum to 3 and then to 4 years, and the introduction of series of graded courses. As medical educators adopted the educational tenet of "learning by doing," both laboratory and clinical instruction became a central part of the curriculum. Admission requirements were imposed.

One important new concept was the idea that medical knowledge was rapidly changing. In the middle of the 19th century, a medical student might be sent to read Hippocrates, not for historical edification but to learn clinical medicine. By the turn of the 20th century, a medical student at a progressive medical school would more likely be sent to a recent textbook, or perhaps even to the rapidly burgeoning scientific journal literature. The belief that knowledge was quickly changing led medical libraries to subscribe to all the latest journals. It also led to the idea that one of the tasks of medical school professors was to create new knowledge. This reform of medical education was well under way by 1910, but it was given strength (as well as an iconic text) by Abraham Flexner's report to the Carnegie Foundation, the "Flexner Report," which helped to mobilize, strengthen, and fund the forces of reform.

❖ Medicine and Science

German scientists in the latter part of the 19th century started to do innovative work in physiology and especially in microbiology. Wilhelm Koch's 1882 discovery of the organism responsible for tuberculosis opened the floodgates for the discovery of a host of other disease-causing pathogens, and the creation of the new science of microbiology. Clinician Paul Beeson and historian Russell Maulitz trace the term "internal medicine" to the German invention during this period of the new term *Innere Medizin,* meant to convey a new field based on increasing understanding of pathology, microbiology, and physiology and distinct from surgery.

German medicine had an enormous impact on U.S. medicine. Droves of American physicians from the better medical schools went abroad to Germany to learn about the latest advances and to bring those ideas and techniques back to the United States. Many of the leaders of the nascent field of internal medicine gathered in 1886 in Washington, DC, to form the Association of American Physicians (AAP), an event that William Osler called "the coming-of-age party of clinical medicine in America" (3). The AAP anchored a growing group of academic physicians who led the reform of medical education. Most of their research focused on correlating clinical and pathologic findings, often to great effect. For example, the first use of the term *appendicitis* came at the inaugural AAP meeting by the Harvard physician Reginald Fitz, who also described the essential clinical features of the disease and argued for early surgical intervention.

But using clinical-pathologic correlation as the basis for research did not leave much room for some other investigators, who based their work more on laboratory-based techniques. In 1909, feeling a need for an organization of people who were focused more on the newer, laboratory methods of research, a group of physicians formed the American Society for Clinical Investigation (ASCI), also known as the "Young Turks." Like the AAP, this group was open to physicians in all specialties, although it largely consisted of people practicing what we would now term internal medicine. Both the AAP and the ASCI helped to coalesce a nascent group of academic physicians who would lead the transformation of U.S. medical education and form the core of what we now see as internal medicine.

Simply having a new set of ideas and investigative tools, exciting though that may be, doth not a specialty make. Many people opposed the very idea of specialized medicine. A specialist was thought by some to be a "rattlebrained person who, having tried general practice for a year or two and miserably failed, immediately takes up some sub-department of medicine which his inclination may point out as alluring, and becomes a specialist" (4). Attitudes such as these were unlikely to be changed merely by the addition of some new laboratory-based facts to the medical literature.

❖ How to Tell a Specialist

Wars often produce change. World War I started in 1914; the United States entered the conflict in 1917. The apparent value of specialization was enhanced when the Surgeon General decided to divide U.S. Army physicians into sections based on specialties. He included dermatology, neurology, and psychological disease as part of internal medicine, a logical choice. The fact that all three did not later become part of internal medicine illustrates the historically contingent nature of how we define this specialty.

That decision has come to be based on a system of specialty boards. While this approach may seem to make sense, it is hardly the only way that specialties can be defined. Other possibilities were on the table. Each might well have succeeded; had another choice been made, internal medicine and its education might look very different from how it does today.

For example, the National Board of Medical Examiners had been founded in 1915; it had a national constituency and could well have taken up the task of identifying specialists. But it did not. State licensing boards could have been another way to define specialists. Throughout most of the 19th century there was no medical licensure system, but by the turn of the century that began to change. The federal government left medical licensing to the states, and by the time that Flexner issued his famous report in 1910, each state had established its own medical licensure board. Those boards only licensed physicians to practice medicine in general; they did not define a field of practice. But they could have. Indeed, some states formally considered legislation that would have specifically licensed specialists in a particular field. Those bills did not pass. Had they passed, and had states assumed the responsibility for deciding who could practice as a specialist, the states might have taken a far more active role in workforce regulation than they do today.

Another obvious choice for specialty definition might have been through a university education. Much of the change in medicine was being driven through an increased attention to the role of the laboratory sciences in medicine. One can easily envision a situation in which universities would award an advanced degree, perhaps a PhD, which would mark a physician as a specialist. Such a move would have made internal medicine education more focused on research than is the case today. Medical leaders did seriously consider this approach.

Yet another approach would have been to let the primary specialty organization, the American College of Physicians (ACP), decide who was and who was not an internist. Founded in 1915, the ACP considered holding an examination to decide who could become a member. Had it done so, the ACP might well have usurped the role that later came to be held by a specialty board.

All of these ways of defining a specialty make sense. All might have worked, and might have supported the creation of a vibrant and engaged system of medical specialties. Other countries did, in fact, adopt some elements of these alternative ways of defining medical specialties.

But the system that was eventually decided upon in the United States was a series of private specialty boards. The first specialty board to be established was the American Board of Ophthalmology, founded in 1917. By 1936, 10 specialty boards had been established under the umbrella of the American Board of Medical Specialties, which had been founded in 1933. Thus, when the American Board of Internal Medicine (ABIM) came into existence in 1936, it was one of the later boards to be incorporated. The ABIM was formed in time to encompass some fields that had been considering establishing a separate existence, most notably cardiology, gastroenterology, "tuberculosis" (which later became pulmonary medicine), and allergy. However, some candidates for inclusion had established their own board before creation of the ABIM, most notably dermatology in 1932 and neurology (as part of the board in "Psychiatry and Neurology") in 1935.

In 1936, the ABIM saw its role quite differently from what it has come to be today. An "internist" as certified by the ABIM in 1936 was intended to denote one of a handful of truly superb diagnosticians, physicians who would spend most of their energy consulting on difficult cases. The ABIM had no intention that every practitioner of internal medicine should be board-certified, or even that every medical practitioner should be board-certified in anything. Indeed, most board members thought that some 85%

of care would be provided by general practitioners, with internists called in only occasionally to consult about difficult situations.

❖ How to Train a Specialist

Faculty became committed full-time to the medical school, allowing internal medicine faculty to focus their attention on clinical teaching within the medical school. That teaching soon came to include additional training after medical school. In 1893, the Johns Hopkins Medical School opened its doors with a program already in place to train interns and residents.

If postgraduate training was to become an expected part of medical education, the question arose as to how to assure the quality of that education. The American Medical Association (AMA) Council on Medical Education and Hospitals published a list of hospitals with approved internships in 1914. Most of the hospitals that offered internships had no association with a medical school. In 1928, the AMA published its "Essentials of Approved Residencies and Fellowships." But even as specialization was taking hold, the value attached to broad clinical training persisted. During the inter-war period, people who were later to become leading academic internists did not immediately focus on internal medicine after medical school. Rather, they first took 1- to 2-year rotating internships, in which physicians "rotated" through a variety of clinical services. Only later did they start to focus on internal medicine.

In 1940, the AMA Council on Medical Education, the ABIM, and the ACP all collaborated to form the Conference Committee on Graduate Training in Internal Medicine, an early start to some sort of national accreditation of internal medicine residencies. They did so even as war raged in Europe, and not long before the United States was to once again find itself engaged in a massive military effort.

In 1941, the United States formally entered World War II. Even more than had been the case in World War I, this war transformed medicine in important ways that lasted long after the cessation of hostilities. The medical department once again presented an organizational challenge. It quickly grew to almost 50,000 physicians and, when including nurses and corpsmen, had a peak strength of 700,000, three times the size of the entire Army in 1939. How to organize this enterprise? Leaders must use what tools they have, and the Army medical leaders had specialty board certification. Physicians who were board-certified received a higher classification and higher pay. Those who were not board-certified took note of this discrepancy.

Once the war was over in 1945, physicians who wanted to become a specialist found far more residency positions available than ever before. Before the war there had been fewer than 5000 residency positions overall; soon after the war that number was over 12,000, and by 1950 there were 18,669 positions. The numbers for internal medicine residency followed the same pattern—fewer than 1000 in 1941, and over 3700 by 1950. The new Veterans Administration (VA) hospitals provided not only a place to care for wounded veterans but also a place for returning military physicians to obtain specialty training. Board-certified physicians also received a 25% higher salary in the VA system. Not surprisingly, the percentage of U.S. physicians who were board-certified rose rapidly, from only 7.7% in 1950 to 15% in 1950—by the 1980s the percentage was more than 50%.

Before World War II, the federal government had provided very little support for biomedical research, and almost none for research outside of federal laboratories. But by 1940 it had become clear that science both physical and biological was to play a major role in determining the war's outcome. Because there simply was not enough room in existing federal laboratories for the work that needed to be done, the federal government was forced to support research in universities. In 1944, a little-noted legislative act allowed the Public Health Service to award grants for extramural research, and many wartime research contracts were converted to grants after peace came. Public Health Service extramural funding grew more than 10-fold in the first 4 years after the war and since then has continued to grow. Medical schools grew as well, basing much of their existence on the "soft money" of federal research grants. The rapidly expanding system of extramural Public Health Service funding through the National Institutes of Health supported specialists of all types, but probably internists more than others, in addition to reifying elements of the specialty system. The total medical school faculty grew exponentially, far more than the numbers of trainees.

❖ National Organizations, National Challenges

As the number of residency programs rose, coordination among the programs took on added salience. One early issue arose over selection of medical students for house staff programs. Training programs began to pressure medical students to make a commitment earlier and earlier in their medical school career. The average date for finalizing an internship crept from the end to the beginning of the senior year, and by the mid-1940s some internships were being finalized at the start of the junior year, or even in the sophomore year. That sort of early commitment left neither hospitals nor medical students happy, but in the absence of a centralized system any institution attempting unilateral restraint would have been left in a disadvantageous position. The answer came in 1952 with creation of the National Internship and Residency Matching Program and a uniform appointment date. Thus was created the rite of passage in which postgraduate training assignments are announced during the third week in March on a day known today as "Match Day."

In 1965 the U.S. Congress passed bills establishing Medicare and Medicaid, marking a watershed in almost every aspect of medical care. One result was that many more patients acquired access to the health care system. Academic hospitals that had previously run free, explicitly "charity" wards now found that they could be paid for patients for whom they had previously provided free care. Along with payment for patient care came support for education, moving public support for graduate medical education to the level of federal policy. As payment for clinical services expanded, academic centers began increasingly to rely on money generated by clinical practice, practice for which internal medicine trainees were central. Along with this increase in patients came a parallel increase in clinically based faculty.

The year 1965 also saw publication of a report that was to help shape medical education. Informally named after its author, Lowell Coggeshall, dean of the Division of Biological Sciences at the University of Chicago, the report was titled "Planning for Medical Progress Through Education" (5). Commissioned by the Association of American Medical Colleges (AAMC), it called for medical educators to pay increasing attention to national needs. It called for more university-affiliated residency programs; the percentage of residencies in such teaching hospitals went from fewer than 50% when the report was published to over 90% by 1980.

The report also called for a far more active and policy-engaged AAMC. Founded in 1876, throughout the first half of the 20th century the AAMC had remained a relaxed, informal social club for medical school deans. It met yearly around the country at different medical schools, and was, in the words of one AAMC president, "more or less of a family affair." Even immediately after World War II the AAMC remained a small organization with little voice in shaping health policy. Ward Darley, executive director of the AAMC, shaped the Coggeshall committee to encourage transformation of the AAMC. No doubt to his pleasure, the committee called for expansion of the AAMC's mission. That call was not well received by the entrenched power holders, such as the AMA and some specialist societies. Nonetheless, the AAMC moved from Evanston, Illinois, to Washington, DC, to be closer to federal policymakers. It soon became an active participant in national policy debates. The following year the AMA issued a report similar to the Coggeshall report; their version, called the Millis report (6), went over similar ground and also argued for incentives to abate the tide toward subspecialization.

As specialty training became the norm, many specialties began to see the need for oversight committees to evaluate the quality of the rapidly increasing number of residencies. In 1953 the Conference Committee on Graduate Training in Internal Medicine changed its name to the Residency Review Committee for Internal Medicine. To coordinate standards among the various specialties, the Liaison Committee for Graduate Medical Education was formed in 1972. In 1981 this committee was reshaped into the Accreditation Council for Graduate Medical Education (ACGME), a private, nonprofit council. The ACGME established a Residency Review Committee for internal medicine residencies (along with those for 25 other specialties). Today these committees follow policies and procedures that are created by the ACGME.

Throughout the 1970s, patients would stay in hospitals for a long time, allowing for extensive, often leisurely diagnostic evaluation and educational discussions. But in 1982 the Tax Equity and Fiscal Responsibility Act began a move toward prospective payment. This new initiative turned financial incentives on their head. Rather than there being a financial incentive to keep patients for long periods, shortening lengths of stay became the goal. The implications for internal medicine education quickly became apparent. Diagnoses were often made before the patient entered the hospital, and patients would be discharged as soon as they were medically able to be sent home (or to another health care facility). While this change in practice patterns may have reduced expenses, it also reduced opportunities for clinical teaching and increased the pace and turnover rate on hospital wards.

❖ Libby Zion and House Staff Work Hours

Medical education has always been a part of the larger social fabric. Even though it was widely known that house staff in internal medicine (and perhaps even more so in other specialties) worked extremely long hours, a sad event in 1984 led to a series of changes that dramatically reshaped the nature of internal medicine education. On the evening of March 4, an 18-year-old college student, Libby Zion, was admitted to the New York Hospital with a high fever and shaking movements of unclear cause. Her condition rapidly deteriorated and she died the next morning. The unexpected death of anyone is a tragedy, perhaps even more so when the person who dies is someone so young and apparently healthy. But in this case Libby Zion's father, a journalist named Sidney Zion, decided to make her death a signal event to produce reform in the system. While the exact cause of Libby Zion's death was never entirely clear, what soon became clear was that the house staff caring for her, like house staff all over the country, routinely worked shifts of 36 hours (or longer). As Sidney Zion put it in an op-ed piece in the *New York Times* (7), "You don't need kindergarten to know that a resident working a 36-hour shift is in no condition to make any kind of judgment call—forget about life-and-death."

The Manhattan district attorney convened a grand jury to consider murder charges against the physicians involved in treating Libby Zion. While the grand jury did not indict anyone (a malpractice case subsequently assigned shared blame to New York Hospital and to Libby Zion, for allegedly concealing her drug use), it was highly critical of the hospital. This led to the creation of a state commission to consider improvements to the graduate medical education system. In 1987, that commission issued a report, sometimes known by the name of its chair, Dr. Bertrand Bell (8), which recommended that house staff work no more than 80 hours a week, no more than 24 hours in a row, and get increased supervision from attending physicians. In 2003 the ACGME made these recommendations mandatory for all residency training programs. Other rules have come to limit the number of patients a house officer can admit, as well as the total allowable size of the service. Subsequent reports have suggested even more reductions in allowable work hours.

The ultimate consequence of these reforms is yet to be seen. House officers are clearly better rested. But fewer hours worked mean, as it must, fewer patients seen by each house officer, and thus less opportunity for education. It also means that formal teaching sessions may be less well-attended than before. With the need for more hand-offs of patient responsibility from person to person, it may open the likelihood of increased errors. These reforms may change the nature of professionalism, but in what direction remains to be seen (see chapter 1 of *Mentoring in Academic Medicine*, another book in the *Teaching Medicine* series [9]). On the one hand, physicians of days gone by might have felt themselves obligated to stay with a patient as long as necessary. On the other hand, physicians today might be forced to go home but might also realize that after many hours without sleep their patients would be better cared for by a well-rested physician.

❖ New Challenges for a New Century

As we move into the 21st century, we confront new questions. One of the most important is: What sorts of physicians should we train? The 1960s saw a dramatic expansion of the number of U.S. medical schools, based largely on the perceived need for more primary care physicians. However, many of the additional physicians wound up training in subspecialties. To rectify this imbalance Congress required that programs produce more primary care physicians. However, as always, the devil is in the details, and the final legislation measured the numbers of physicians in the primary care fields of internal medicine, pediatrics, and family medicine in the first year of residency training, a time when almost no residents have formally begun to subspecialize. Thus, medical schools found themselves already in compliance and had no reason to want to change. Later in the 1970s, the Health Resources and Services Administration funded residency programs specifically in primary care internal medicine. These new programs offered additional training in the outpatient setting for gynecology, dermatology, orthopedics, otolaryngology, ophthalmology, psychiatry, and preventive and occupational medicine, as well as twice as much continuity-of-care experience. Primary care tracks in internal medicine remain, but increasingly more internal medicine residents choose categorical tracks as a path toward subspecialty fellowships.

An influential 1980 workforce study by the Graduate Medical Education National Advisory Committee (10) concluded that the United States would soon have too many physicians, especially too many specialists. In 1986 the U.S. Congress authorized formation of the Council on Graduate Medical Education, which has continued to analyze workforce trends. Early in the 21st century, as Baby Boomers age and move toward retirement, we again appear to be facing a shortage of primary care physicians to care for adult patients.

The idea that internists ought to be primary care physicians reflects an important change. The first model internists were seen as master diagnosticians, consultants for only the sickest and most complex patients. Now, board certification is seen as an obligatory rite of passage for almost all practicing internists in the United States. General practitioners made up 28% of U.S. physicians in 1963, 13% in 1977, and are almost nonexistent today (11).

As noted earlier, most trainees in internal medicine will go on to become subspecialists. There are many potential reasons for the low numbers of trainees wishing to go into primary care. One is rising medical school tuitions and increasing debt. Subspecialists today simply make higher salaries than primary care physicians, often much higher. At the same time, subspecialists often spend a fair amount of time delivering primary care outside of their area of subspecialization. Another reason for the relative lack of interest in general internal medicine (primary care) as a career path among internal medicine trainees may reflect the nature of the training experience. As hospital stays become even shorter, and as those patients are less representative of internal medicine as a whole, it is hardly surprising that time spent on the traditional hospital ward rotation rarely leads to excitement for primary care practice.

One response has been to shift more education to the ambulatory setting. If more training took place away from the large, tertiary, academic health center, it might allow trainees more exposure to "real world" practice. However, that move would also make it difficult to enforce some sort of consistent curriculum, a situation reminiscent of the early apprenticeship model for medical education. In addition, if the internists with whom trainees work are unhappy, the trainees are less likely to be attracted to internal medicine.

On the other hand, the hospitalist movement appears to be here to stay. Rather than having many ward physicians, each attending only 1 to 2 months a year, a cadre of dedicated inpatient hospitalist physicians could be truly focused on the mechanics and intellectual content of inpatient care. In theory, this could allow them more time to focus their attention on inpatient teaching. But this approach may also lead to the primary teachers of inpatient internal medicine being people who have little experience in the continuum of care, including office-based practice, or additional training in or attention to the academic mission. This is especially a concern as work hour restrictions lead programs to off-load some care to nonteaching services, which will often be staffed by the same group of hospitalists. By contrast, many academic centers have built their quality improvement programs around hospitalists, who have become, at many institutions, the guiding force of the "new disciplines" of patient safety and system-based practice. Residents now view hospitalist medicine as a career option, and program directors and indeed organizations of internal medicine education are weighing whether medical residencies should be split into different tracks, including hospitalist, subspecialist, and outpatient tracks.

Meanwhile, educational theory has moved in ways that reflect both a desire to see education as a continuum and a wish to assess competency in defined areas, rather than merely adding up trainees' "time served." During 2000–2002, ACGME identified and endorsed six general competencies with which to assess residents; later, the American Board of Medical Specialties endorsed the same competencies in practicing physicians. Specialty recertification is a means of focusing education and evaluation on sustaining skills over time. Recertification was introduced in 1969 and adopted as policy by the American Board of Medical Specialties in 1973. The ABIM instituted mandatory recertification starting in 1990 (although older certificate holders were grandfathered in and do not need to participate). Related is state-mandated continuous medical education (CME), which applies to all specialties (see chapter 6 in *Methods for Teaching Medicine*, also part of the *Teaching Medicine* series [12]). Some states mandate the format for CME; some mandate that specific topics be covered (such as HIV and AIDS, or domestic violence).

In 2002 the AAMC established the Institute for Improving Medical Education to improve education in medical school and residency, as well as CME. A 2004 report, "Educating Doctors to Provide High Quality Medical Care: A Vision for Medical Education in the United States" (13), outlines key goals for medical education and offers a set of recommendations not only to medical schools and teaching hospitals but also to the organizations that accredit and license physicians.

Calls for change continue, including those to refocus the residency experience on education and to emphasize the central tenets of evidence-based medicine and quality improvement (14, 15). New technologies enable educational initiatives to be shared throughout the world, with consequences that are not yet clear. Amidst the seemingly constant discussions about redesigning the curriculum at all levels—all too often leading to what the medical sociologist Samuel W. Bloom has called "reform without change"—some constants remain. Sick people come to us for care. We attempt to teach trainees at all levels how best to care for them. And the structures within which we train, as well as the answers that we give to our patients, will doubtless continue to change in ways that are and will remain firmly embedded in the social context in which we all work and live.

REFERENCES

1. **Brotherton SE, Rockey PH, Etzel SI.** US graduate medical education, 2003-2004. JAMA. 2004;292:1032-7.
2. **Ludmerer KM.** Learning to Heal: The Development of American Medical Education. New York: Basic Books; 1985.
3. **Osler W.** The coming of age of internal medicine in America. Int Clin. 1915;4:1-5.
4. **Van Zandt HC.** Specialists. Trans N Y State Medical Assoc. 1887;4:347-51.
5. **Coggeshall LT.** Planning for medical progress through education; a report submitted to the Executive Council of the Association of American Medical Colleges. Evanston, IL: Association of American Medical Colleges; 1965.
6. **Millis JS.** The graduate education of physicians: Report of the Citizens Commission on Graduate Medical Education. Chicago: American Medical Association; 1966.

7. **Zion S.** Doctors know best? New York Times. May 13, 1989.
8. **Bell BM.** House staff supervision and working hours [Letter]. JAMA. 1990;264:2738-9.
9. **Humphrey H, ed.** Mentoring in Academic Medicine. Philadelphia: ACP Pr; 2010.
10. **Graduate Medical Education National Advisory Committee.** Summary Report of the Graduate Medical Education National Advisory Committee to the Secretary, Department of Health and Human Services. Washington, DC: U.S. Department of Health and Human Services, Public Health Service, Health Resources Administration; September 30, 1980. Publication HRA 81-651
11. **Weisz G.** Divide and Conquer: A Comparative History of Medical Specialization. Oxford, United Kingdom: Oxford Univ Pr; 2006.
12. **Skeff KM, Stratos GA, eds.** Methods for Teaching Medicine. Philadelphia: ACP Pr; 2010.
13. **Institute for Improving Medical Education.** Report of the Ad Hoc Committee of Deans. Educating Doctors to Provide High Quality Medical Care: A Vision for Medical Education in the United States. Washington, DC: Association of American Medical Colleges; 2004.
14. **Fitzgibbons JP, Bordley DR, Berkowitz LR, Miller BW, Henderson MC; Association of Program Directors in Internal Medicine.** Redesigning residency education in internal medicine: a position paper from the Association of Program Directors in Internal Medicine. Ann Intern Med. 2006;144:920-6.
15. **Weinberger SE, Smith LG, Collier VU; Education Committee of the American College of Physicians.** Redesigning training for internal medicine. Ann Intern Med. 2006; 144:927-32.

3

The Organization of Medical Education: A Brief Guide

D. Craig Brater, MD, MACP

A cademic medical centers are large, complicated entities with many moving parts and multiple missions. These institutions are committed to education, research, and service, but the three missions themselves are broad and complex. For example, service includes service not only to patients but also to the profession and to the community. Medical education encompasses a spectrum from middle school and high school students through practicing physicians; thus, its setting is both within and beyond the confines of the academic medical center. All the missions and their component parts are interlinked and dependent on one another. As a result, issues in patient care can adversely affect the educational milieu; a paltry research or scholarly enterprise can severely compromise the breadth of education by not immersing learners in a culture of inquiry and of using critically reviewed evidence as the basis for clinical decision-making. For the young academician who seeks a career focused on medical education, the complexity of academic medical centers can be daunting.

This chapter defines and describes the major elements and roles in the system. It also clarifies the tasks involved and the human, interpersonal dimensions so that new and aspiring medical educators can more confidently navigate the environment. The chapter concludes with a discussion of the "alphabet soup" of medical education; this section includes a glossary of the common acronyms and abbreviations to help novices become more comfortable with the large 'house of medicine."

KEY POINTS

- Internal medicine education largely takes place in academic medical centers, which are complex organizations that integrate the tripartite missions of patient care, education, and research.
- Internal support for education within each school radiates from the office of the dean. Through divisions for education and student affairs, the dean provides resources and direction to ensure institutional compliance with accreditation requirements.
- Education in internal medicine is managed departmentally under the direction of chairs by course, clerkship, and program directors across the continuum from undergraduate to graduate to continuing education.
- National organizations within internal medicine provide support for student education (Clerkship Directors in Internal Medicine), resident education (Association of Program Directors in Internal Medicine), and continuing education (American College of Physicians). The American Board of Internal Medicine provides certification in the specialty and subspecialties of internal medicine.
- Externally, the Liaison Committee on Medical Education, the Accreditation Council for Graduate Medical Education, and the Accreditation Council for Continuing Medical Education support the interest of the public in the quality of medical education through review and accreditation of educational programs.

❖ Interacting Dimensions and Components

At most academic medical centers, medical education has many dimensions extending well beyond medical students per se. The reason for this is logical: Many components within the broad definition of medical education are interdependent and amplify one another. For example, graduate medical education (GME)—the training of residents and specialty fellows—is synergistic with medical student education because residents and students frequently serve together on clinical teams on which they assist one another. Accreditation of residency programs requires that the curriculum include a component for residents as teachers. This fact emphasizes that residents in training are expected to be teachers of other learners; most residents would also tell you that students are also a stimulus for their own learning because students' inquisitive natures quickly expose gaps in a resident's knowledge—what better motivation for learning!

❖ Medical Education: A Broader Definition

A broader definition of the medical education than has traditionally been considered recognizes that a continuum extends from middle school and high school (1) through the continuing medical education of practicing physicians. In any systems approach, the inputs into the process—the raw materials—are critical. Reaching into middle school and high school makes sense because this is the period during which young people may begin to consider medical careers. Medicine in general and medical education in particular must be considered part of a larger social structure. We are used to thinking of this framework in terms of our social obligation to care of patients, but the concept also applies to medical education; we need to emphasize and reinforce an educational approach at all levels that focuses on critical thinking and problem-solving in distinct contrast to rote memorization. If that is the case, and if we always want to attract the best, the brightest, and the most humanistic young people into medicine, then the discipline of medicine should take responsibility for helping people in their formative years learn about medicine. Although most medical schools do not yet have an established mechanism for outreach into precollegiate education, there are many ways to do so, including working with teachers to develop curricula that are inspiring, organizing "show and tell" sessions, hosting tours of clinical and laboratory settings, and offering summer experiences.

A particular need in this setting is to inspire more minority youngsters to pursue medicine. Minority representation in medicine has been and continues to be woefully inadequate and accounts in part for the health care disparities in the United States. Thus, medical schools have a moral obligation to reach back to early years of education to help young minority students and their families realize that a medical career is not only an exciting prospect but also an attainable one.

❖ Selecting the Right Students

Medical education also entails working at the undergraduate (college) level in a variety of forums. It is critically important that medical schools work with college advisors to make sure they give good advice to students hoping to pursue careers in medicine. Being admitted to medical school is highly competitive, making it easy for college advisors to fall into the trap of counseling students to be singularly focused on grades and Medical College Admission Test scores. But it seems safe to say that we want people pursuing medical careers who are in it for the right reasons (2). We should look for students whose experiences have allowed them to get a better idea of what medicine is about and have shown attributes essential for being a true medical professional. Advisors need to encourage college students to pursue volunteer work—so-called service learning—so that students can determine whether they have the altruism and humanism necessary for a career in medicine. Students should explore real-world experiences that will help them decide whether they really want to pursue a medical career (3). Medical schools should also try to provide as many summer opportunities as possible, both clinical and research, for interested students. A major challenge is funding for such experiences. Some students can volunteer and receive no compensation, but in the ideal world stipends would be provided. A few grants are available for some programs like this, including ones that focus on experiences for minority students, but resources are scarce. As a result, there are usually far more people who want to pursue these experiences than there is funding.

❖ The Terms We Use: UME, GME, and CME

Medical student education is also called UME (undergraduate medical education). This nomenclature can be confusing because this step occurs after college and shares the same timeline as graduate work in other fields. But since "GME" (graduate medical education) is claimed by residency education, UME has become the label for medical students. Both UME and GME are discussed in more detail later in this chapter. The last segment of medical education is CME, or continuing medical education, which refers to physicians' life-long learning.

Discussed more fully in chapter 6 of *Methods for Teaching Medicine*, another book in the *Teaching Medicine* series (4), CME responds to practitioners' need for new knowledge and continuous improvement of their practices. The fundamental question becomes, How can the explosion of new knowledge be sifted for relevance and then condensed into "digestible" packets of information that best allow a busy practitioner to assimilate and incorporate the new information into treatment of patients? No one should be better able to sift, condense, and disseminate information than faculty of a medical school. But in this author's opinion, shared by the authors of the cited chapter, we do a less than acceptable job of this. Too much CME still uses approaches that lead to unsuccessful assimilation of new knowledge into practice. The hope is that medical educators of the future can advance the field and turn CME into something that is truly effective and affords more patients the benefits of new discoveries. Moreover, undergraduate (medical school) and graduate (residency training) education needs to prepare students and residents for life-long learning and make them more sophisticated consumers of CME.

In summary, medical education is a big tent that ideally stretches from middle school to the practicing physician—almost a cradle-to-grave approach. Not only are there many components (corresponding to a horizontal time line from middle school to ongoing practice), but within each component there is a vertical dimension that comprises, at a minimum, a curriculum, ways to evaluate learners, ways to evaluate teachers, and faculty development to help teachers be as effective as possible. These vertical dimensions are the concrete tasks of medical education, and the organizational components described next are the way that medical schools and academic medical centers manage them.

❖ Key Positions in the Medical School

The Dean and the Dean's Office

As discussed previously, academic medical centers and medical schools have broad missions and responsibilities. The dean is where the "buck stops" for almost all of these activities, raising the question, Where does education fit into a dean's list of responsibilities? In fact, medical education is *the* primary responsibility. If a school had severely limited resources and was forced to cut missions, the one that would remain would be education—after all, our institutions are medical *schools*. The main responsibility is to train future generations of physicians. This is not to say that education is not enhanced and enabled by performing research and taking care of patients; it is, but the question concerns which area is primary.

Another reason for the primacy of education in the dean's responsibilities is that the dean sets the tone for the entire school. If the dean gives short shrift to medical education, the faculty as a whole gets the message and will do the same—the net effect is obvious. This does not mean that deans should be expected to actively manage all the educational activities; that is probably impossible in terms of today's demands on a dean. But deans must make certain that they continually and consistently reinforce that education is valued and primary.

Senior Associate Dean for Educational Affairs

Of course institutions differ in how medical education is organized, but similarities are great. Most schools appropriately designate a senior dean with responsibility for educational affairs. Common labels for such an individual are senior associate dean, executive associate dean, or vice-dean. This individual should report directly to the dean and be a member of an executive leadership team of the dean and senior deans. This senior dean is typically very experienced as both a teacher and a manager of educational programs.

Assistant and Associate Deans

Reporting to the senior dean, with responsibility for education, should be a collection of individuals dedicated to education. These individuals might be MDs, PhDs, and EdDs who should be formally trained in medical education. Those selected have usually distinguished themselves as teachers rather than having been formally trained in the science of education. Any institution will be well served to specifically recruit those who, in addition to their devotion to students, also have formal educational training. Such individuals may be credentialed educators or proven expert teachers; in addition, they have developed specific knowledge and skill sets in the principles, theory, and application of educational methods (see chapter 4 of this book for more details on the differing levels of the educational hierarchy). Otherwise, these potential leaders are making recommendations and decisions on the basis of notions rather than data. Medicine is rich in data on missions of research and service; the same rigor should be applied in education.

Within the dean's office, medical education roles and responsibilities can be allocated in many ways, in terms of the "divisions" that report to the senior dean for education (Box 3-1). Within each of these areas, an infrastructure is needed. In smaller schools, some of these divisions would probably be merged or have the same individual be responsible for more than one area.

❖ Divisions of Medical Education

The following are the key roles and functions that usually reside in the dean's office.

Student Affairs

Medical student affairs encompass a broad range of functions that include clerical, financial, and emotional. They may be grouped in different offices with different names, but the activities are consistent across schools.

The Registrar's Office and Scheduling

At the risk of stating the obvious, the amount of record-keeping required in a medical school is immense. Academic institutions, hospitals, and

---

Box 3-1. "Divisions" That Report to the Senior Dean for Education

▶ Premedical education—namely, education at the middle school, high school, or college level
▶ Medical student education:
  • Medical student affairs (the personal lives and counseling of students)
  • Curricular affairs
▶ Graduate medical education
▶ Continuing medical education
▶ Diversity
▶ Advocacy/"events"

---

insurance companies will be seeking verification data on a student for decades after they graduate. An infrastructure to support this need is a mandate. Increasingly, much of this can be done electronically, but the reality is that people are still vitally needed and the more compulsive they are, the better. The same applies for the residency programs.

Scheduling is a nightmare—literally hundreds of individuals are rotating here and there throughout the system, and one event after another is occurring. To stay on top of this requires an infrastructure that has both electronic and human components—the latter consisting of hard-working, dedicated individuals.

Student Support
Students have a variety of ever-changing needs that fall under the general heading of "support." Financial counseling is continuous—particularly in this era, where more and more of the costs of education are borne by students and their families because of the paucity of public support. It is instructive that at the author's institution, the staff person who regularly receives high praise from students is the one responsible for scholarship and financial counseling.

Individual students at times need encouragement, nudging, discipline, an empathetic conversation, cheerleading, parenting, guidance, and a general sense that they are valued and cared for as individuals. It may be instructive that in one school, student satisfaction as measured by the

Association of American Medical Colleges' questionnaire was for many years well below the national average. In an intentioned effort to address this deficiency, students were interviewed; they revealed that for many reasons they did not feel valued or cared about. The school initiated a wide variety of student support efforts. For example, workshops for students in leadership positions were conducted; there were "no holds barred" luncheons for students, the dean, and the senior dean for educational affairs; and students were assigned to all relevant school committees (and soon students started competing to be included). Within a few years this school was well above the national average in student satisfaction and remains there. The bottom line is that students need support services, and each institution must decide how to prioritize this need among competing demands and limited resources. Medical school leaders should note, however, that satisfied students have a positive ripple effect throughout the entire institution, leading to the recommendation that student support should be a high priority for any academic medical center.

The individuals who provide all the medical student affairs services are often behind the scenes. More often than not they see their work as far more than a "job"—they know of the impact they have on the development of young professionals and understand how important that is to the profession of medicine. Thus, they have a sense of purpose. This cannot be taken for granted; these individuals need to know that they are appreciated. Ignoring them or low-balling their needs will eventually extract a high cost; it is best to make sure the infrastructure is adequate and that efforts expended on support of students are much appreciated.

Curricular Affairs

Curricular affairs, or the Office of the Assistant/Associate Dean for Curriculum, monitors, maintains, and updates the curriculum (including oversight of so-called reform when there is a major undertaking to fundamentally revise a curriculum). This office is often responsible for preparing the accreditation documents for the Liaison Committee on Medical Education. In addition, curricular affairs should be committed to and empowered to perform what might be called educational continuous quality improvement. This office should be charged with monitoring quality throughout the educational continuum. For example, it should develop methods for evaluating the quality of lectures and small-group learning sessions, as well as individual teachers in any educational venue, including clinical settings. This group should collate this quality information and disseminate it as feedback to school and department leaders and the faculty themselves. Moreover, this information should become an integral component of the annual performance review and compensation setting for each individual; the relevant department chair; and course, clerkship, or program director. The importance of capturing such data and linking compensation to it cannot be overstated. The only way an institution demonstrates that quality of education is important is by measuring it and compensating individuals for it.

Faculty Development

It is also vitally important that some office, perhaps the curricular affairs group, be responsible for faculty development programs in medical education. If an institution is serious about the quality of education, in addition to monitoring and providing incentives for it, it will also provide its faculty members with methods to enhance their personal teaching skills. (This topic is also discussed in chapter 4 of this book and in three other books in the *Teaching Medicine* series: *Methods for Teaching Medicine* [4], *Teaching in Your Office* [5] and *Teaching in the Hospital* [6].) For example, pretend your institution does not now gather feedback from learners on the quality of teaching, as measured by any of several techniques. Then, an effort is launched to provide data to individual faculty on the quality of their teaching. Your dean and department chair are committed to linking compensation to these measures (not necessarily in a formulaic fashion), so you know that faculty members are going to pay more attention to the quality of their lecturing than they might have in the past. And suppose one faculty member has poor scores. What do you do? You can simply accept the data and allow the faculty member to suffer the consequences. Or you can assume that most people are motivated to do better—particularly if compensation or advancement might be at stake. Thus, this situation presents an opportunity to help an individual be a better teacher (see chapter 4 in *Theory and Practice of Teaching Medicine*, another book in this series [7]). Faculty members deserve at least one "strike"; the vast majority have never had any opportunity to learn how to teach. Some are good by nature, but many are not. Thus, it is incumbent on the institution to identify faculty members who need help in their teaching skills and then provide them with training.

Assessment and Evaluation

The curricular affairs office or group develops evaluation methods for individual students, individual teachers, and the curriculum as a whole. It disseminates the measurement instruments, collects and collates the data, provides feedback to faculty members and their chair, and designs faculty development opportunities to help individuals improve. In addition, of course, curricular affairs "babysits" the curriculum. A curriculum is tricky business. Its objective is to provide learners with the knowledge base, skill set, and competency to be good physicians. Everyone looks at elements of the curriculum through a different lens. The biochemist may think the world revolves around the Krebs cycle, while the physiologist feels the same about the Nernst equation. As biological science within different basic science departments becomes more similar than different, departments are differentiating themselves through the courses their faculty members teach. All this means that developing consensus across the entirety of a faculty is a challenge. It is vitally important to have consistent input from faculty about the curriculum, in particular when a major curricular overhaul is to occur. That having been said, many faculty members do not spend all day every day worrying about the curriculum. It is the "pros" in the curricular affairs office who should lead the charge in modifying the curriculum and keeping the process on track, all the while making certain the faculty has an opportunity for input.

Graduate Medical Education

Graduate medical education comprises all the clinical training programs after medical school and before independent practice. Older terms for what to call trainees sometimes coexist with newer or administrative terms. At times, the first year of training has been called an internship (a term now in less use), or sometimes PGY1 for postgraduate year 1 (in which case it means post–*medical school* graduation, and not education that occurs after GME). The several remaining years (length depending on the specialty) are almost always called residency. Subspecialty training may follow; this stint occasionally is also called residency but at other times postdoctoral training or fellowship. (These terms can be confusing; for example, how does one distinguish the postdoctoral training of a PhD scientist in a clinical department from that of a physician gaining subspecialty expertise?) For simplicity, today one refers to initial training in the "primary specialty" and then to "subspecialty" training. The primary specialty entails a residency (including the first post–medical school year) that requires 3 or more years to complete. Subspecialty trainees are sometimes also called residents by institutional documents (for example, in the Veterans Affairs system) but more often are called subspecialty fellows.

The GME Office

The GME office is usually in the dean's office, and often separate from UME infrastructure, although they communicate closely. There is usually a centralized function that coordinates the different GME programs, exerts quality control, manages periodic reviews, sets policy, determines pay and benefits packages for trainees, and exerts discipline on individual trainees or programs. There is also a distributed network in departments in which the different training programs "reside." For example, internal medicine has a primary residency that is based in the department per se, but the department also has subspecialty programs in a host of disciplines. Each of these also has a program director and local infrastructure, usually within a subspecialty section or division.

Graduate medical education is sufficiently large and complex that there is usually a senior physician leader who also holds the title of assistant or associate dean, although at some medical schools this position may be accorded the title vice-dean. Many of the same functions described for UME are also needed in GME. For example, accreditation requirements for most if not all programs require that there be a well-defined curriculum, that trainees provide input on the quality of faculty members and their training overall, that there be programs in teaching residents how to teach, and that there be dedicated faculty who have time available to focus on the GME program. It should be obvious that synergies and efficiencies are possible when the UME and GME offices work well together.

GME Funding

The GME programs are "sponsored" by hospitals, and their funding derives from same. At academic medical centers, the school of medicine is usually the coordinating center for GME, with funds flowing from the hospitals to the school for doing so. Many hospitals not affiliated with a medical school also sponsor residency programs. These are usually led by senior accomplished practitioners who are dedicated to education and are willing to commit a percentage of their time to GME leadership.

The federal government provides billions of dollars each year to hospitals to support GME to increase the number of physicians available to provide care under the Medicaid and Medicare programs (8). Medicare provides direct medical education funds to pay the salaries and benefits of residents, and indirect medical education money to reimburse the hospital for extra costs, such as longer patient stays in training hospitals.

The money that goes to a particular hospital is managed by the hospital's financial structure (see the section on the chief financial office for more details) rather than by the program director of the residency or by the dean's office in the medical school. But this money is one determinant of how many training positions can be offered by the hospital in the specialty or subspecialty.

Continuing Medical Education

Continuing medical education was briefly discussed earlier (and in greater detail in chapter 6 of *Methods for Teaching Medicine* [4]). Suffice to say that the CME office has both internal and external reach. Internally, it is involved with ensuring that staff physicians have opportunities for life-long learning. This takes on many forms, such as regular conferences, symposia, and simulation centers. Many of these activities overlap with student and resident venues, so again CME should not be disjointed from UME and GME. Externally, the CME office is usually responsible for approving educational offerings to faculty but also to practitioners outside of the institution, whether individual lectures or series of conferences. These offerings provide continued health education credits that can be applied by faculty and practitioners to maintenance of licensure within a state, or to maintaining credentials and privileges within an institution.

Diversity

Diversity is an important initiative throughout all aspects of the academic institution and health system. It is so important that it deserves special mention. The percentage of minority physicians is highly discrepant from the percentages of minorities in the overall population (see chapter 6 in *Mentoring in Academic Medicine*, also part of the *Teaching Medicine* series [9]). Faculty representation is even worse. Data show that minority patients fare better when they have a minority physician caring for them (10, 11). Thus, issues of diversity are not simply philosophical convictions about social justice; they have ramifications for the well-being of our friends and neighbors. As noted previously, there is a huge "pipeline" problem in that the numbers of minority students seeking medical careers are inadequate. Thus, the profession's efforts described at the start of this chapter to reach into the earlier years of schooling should have special focus to help attract minority applicants. The recent campaign to increase diversity in the physician workforce is another way to do this (www.aspiringdocs.org). Regardless of strategy, increasing the numbers of minority physicians will require an institutional investment in programmatic infrastructure and a clear statement of the importance of diversity coupled with expectations for improvement.

Advocacy/"Events"

Special events, be they scheduled celebrations or unforeseen projects, stream across the academic calendar. These range from the white coat ceremony for beginning students, to graduation, to public recognition of student leadership, to meetings of different student interest groups. Such events can be arranged in an ad hoc fashion, but if done in a coordinated manner, students receive a strong message from the school that it cares. Thus, a small investment reaps substantial dividends.

❖ Key Positions in the Departments

Apart from the important roles played by individuals aligned principally with the medical school, there also are individuals whose work occurs at the level of the department and hospital. Following is a brief description of key educational and institutional leadership roles. More detailed expectations for each are discussed in chapter 4 of this book.

Chair of the Department: Just as the senior dean for education must be empowered by the dean, such is the case within individual departments. The chair must also stress the importance of education to those within the department. This is critical for those who work within the department and whose careers are centered on education.

Vice-chair for Education: This role is the department-level analogue for the senior dean for education. This individual is usually senior, with broad education and leadership experience—for example, distinguished service as a program or clerkship director. This person interfaces "up" with the school educational structure and across all aspects of education for the department, such that program directors, clerkship directors, and other similar administrators report to him or her for their educational responsibilities.

Clerkship Director: The clerkship director is responsible for the student experiences within a required, departmentally based, clerkship in which all medical students participate. This core clerkship, typically in the third year, may last 6 to 12 weeks. Additional required clinical rotations (such as subinternships/acting internships) or in subspecialty rotations chosen by a few students (electives) may be run by the clerkship director or in some schools by a director of fourth-year programs.

Program Director: The program director has a function similar to that of the clerkship director, but for the GME program. The period covered by the GME program could be the 3 years of internal medicine specialty training or the 2 to 4 years of subspecialty training of fellows (12).

Clerkship Administrator: Each clerkship usually and ideally has a dedicated, full-time person to support planning, curriculum, and assessment.

Residency Administrator: Similar to the clerkship administrator, this individual broadly supports the administrative needs of the residency programs.

❖ Key Positions With the Hospital

Hospital Chief Executive Official (CEO): Just as is the case with the dean, the hospital CEO has broad responsibilities, one of which is medical education. The health system (inpatient and outpatient) provides numerous venues for medical education. Because it is impossible to properly train learners without these venues and it is impossible for a health system to have doctors without schools of medicine, the health system and the school are interdependent. Also as occurs with the dean, if the health system CEO does not support education, that attitude ripples through the entire organization and results in a difficult environment for the academic enterprise. It is critically important, therefore, that the CEO of a health system who is partnered with a school of medicine be knowledgeable about, and committed to, medical education. Some systems have an executive leader to whom both the dean and the health system CEO report (for example, a vice-president for health affairs). In this structure, a debate over education can be adjudicated by the vice-president. In the absence of such a structure, the quality of the interaction between the dean and the CEO depends on the two of them as individuals, as they both must maintain the educational mission as their principal priority.

Designated Institutional Official: Accreditation bodies, such as the Residency Review Committees of the Accreditation Council for Graduate Medical Education, will hold this individual responsible for maintaining documentation of compliance with regulations. (This person may also be the associate dean for GME within the school of medicine.)

Chief of Staff (Chief of Medical Services): This individual has broad responsibilities on policy within the physician staff. His or her commitment to medical education will have a profound impact on the selection of physicians practicing in the system and whether each is similarly committed to medical education.

Chief Financial Officer (CFO): Because most residency slots and stipends are funded through hospitals or health systems with Medicare funds, as opposed to schools, the money actually flows into the health system and is managed by the CFO (8). Thus, it is important that the person with oversight of system funds be supportive of medical education.

❖ Leadership, Governance, and Accreditation

National Interdisciplinary Organizations
An alphabet soup of organizations monitor and accredit the different elements of medical education; similarly, many professional organizations encompass those working in the different areas of medical education (Table 3-1).

Association of American Medical Colleges
The Association of American Medical Colleges (AAMC) is the overarching organization that represents the 131 accredited medical degree–granting U.S. medical schools and the 17 accredited Canadian medical schools. It

Table 3-1. The Alphabet Soup of Medical Education*

Acronym	Full Name	Description	Web Address
Organizations			
AAIM	Alliance for Academic Internal Medicine	Comprises APM, APDIM, ASP, CDIM, and AIM (see below for explanation of these 5 groups) to serve as the unified voice for academic internal medicine	www.im.org
AAMC	Association of American Medical Colleges	Organization that represents all U.S. and Canadian medical schools and teaching hospitals	www.aamc.org
ABIM	American Board of Internal Medicine	Accrediting body for individual internists	www.abim.org
ABMS	American Board of Medical Specialties	Coordinating organization for the two dozen boards that certify specialties	www.abms.org
ACCME	Accreditation Council for Continuing Medical Education	Organization that accredits continuing medical education programs	www.accme.org
ACE	Alliance for Clinical Education	Coordinating council for all eight national specialty-based organizations of course and clerkship directors	www.alliancefor clinicaleducation.org
ACGME	Accreditation Council for Graduate Medical Education	Organization that accredits residency training programs	www.acgme.org
ACP	American College of Physicians	Organization that represents internal medicine	www.acponline.org
AIM	Administrators of Internal Medicine	Professional society for administrative staff in internal medicine departments	www.im.org/About/ AllianceSites/AIM/
APDIM	Association of Program Directors in Internal Medicine	Professional society for directors of residency programs in internal medicine	www.im.org/About/ AllianceSites/APDIM
APM	Association of Professors of Medicine	Professional society for chairs of departments of internal medicine	www.im.org/About/ AllianceSites/APM

continued

Table 3-1. The Alphabet Soup of Medical Education* (continued)

Acronym	Full Name	Description	Web Address
ASP	Association of Specialty Professors	Professional society for subspecialty section chiefs in internal medicine	www.im.org/About/AllianceSites/ASP
CDIM	Clerkship Directors in Internal Medicine	Professional society for directors of internal medicine clerkships and other undergraduate programs	www.im.org/About/AllianceSites/CDIM
ECFMG	Educational Commission for Foreign Medical Graduates	Oversees licensure of international medical graduates (IMGs) when they come to the United States; since so many internal medicine residents are IMGs, this organization is important to GME in internal medicine	www.ecfmg.org
LCME	Liaison Committee on Medical Education	Organization that accredits medical schools	www.lcme.org
SACME	Society for Academic Continuing Medical Education	Professional society for individuals with interest and involvement in continuing medical education	www.sacme.org
SGIM	Society of General Internal Medicine	Specialty society for general internists	www.sgim.org
Other			
GME	Graduate medical education		
MCAT	Medical College Admission Test		www.aamc.org/students/mcat/start.htm
NRMP	National Resident Matching Program		www.nrmp.org
RRC	Residency Review Committee		www.acgme.org/acWebsite/navPages/nav_180.asp
UME	Undergraduate medical education		

*Please see text for definitions not given here.

has a diverse set of responsibilities, including advocacy for issues important to medical schools and their affiliated hospitals. The AAMC has leadership courses for deans, chairs, and educational leaders and venues for a wide variety of groups to meet and learn from one another—for example, those with business leanings, those interested in faculty development, those responsible for information technology, and educators. The AAMC has no direct accrediting responsibilities. It administers the Medical College Admission Test (MCAT) and the National Resident Matching Program (NRMP).

Liaison Committee on Medical Education

The Liaison Committee on Medical Education (LCME) is the accrediting body for U.S. and Canadian medical schools. It is sponsored by, and has members from, the AAMC and the American Medical Association. It sets accreditation standards that determine whether an institution or program meets those standards for function, structure, and performance. Any new medical school must gain approval from LCME. Existing medical schools are reviewed no less frequently than every 7 years. Such reviews are highly detailed and require extensive, months-long self-study by the school, followed by a site visit that may last close to a week, culminating with a report to the LCME, where an accreditation decision is made. Decisions may range from removing accreditation to probation to full reaccreditation for 7 years. Often, questions and clarification are sought by LCME before a final decision is made.

Since the internal medicine clerkship and other internal medicine rotations are always key elements of medical student education, faculty and staff involved in this segment of UME, notably clerkship directors, are critically important for the school's success in the LCME evaluation.

Accreditation Council for Graduate Medical Education

Residency programs and subspecialty fellowships, namely GME, are accredited by the Accreditation Council for Graduate Medical Education (ACGME). Accreditation can be for a maximum of 5 years. Each graduate training program in an institution must be accredited. Rules and expectations for the different disciplines are developed in collaboration with the academic community by the Residency Review Committee for each training discipline. Members of these committees are appointed by the American Medical Association Council on Medical Education and the appropriate medical specialty boards and organizations. Thus, the committee for internal medicine sets standards (always seeking input from the programs), performs site visits, and reports to the ACGME as a whole for accrediting decisions.

Accreditation Council for Continuing Medical Education
Continuing medical education is accredited by the Accreditation Council for Continuing Medical Education (ACCME). Like other bodies discussed, the ACCME conducts periodic site reviews and determines accreditation standards. Programs can be accredited for a maximum of 6 years.

National Internal Medicine Organizations

American Board of Internal Medicine

The American Board of Internal Medicine (ABIM) is a nonprofit, independent evaluation organization that certifies physicians in internal medicine and its subspecialties (about one of every three practicing physicians in the United States). Internal medicine is one of 24 approved medical specialty boards that work with the American Board of Medical Specialties in the development and use of standards in the ongoing evaluation and certification of physicians.

American College of Physicians

The American College of Physicians (ACP) is a national professional organization of internists, and is the largest medical specialty organization and second-largest physician group in the United States. Its membership of 129,000 includes internists; internal medicine subspecialists; and medical students, residents, and fellows. The ACP's mission is to enhance the quality and effectiveness of health care by fostering excellence and professionalism in the practice of medicine.

Alliance for Academic Internal Medicine

The Alliance for Academic Internal Medicine (AAIM) is a consortium of five academically focused specialty organizations described below. Through these organizations, AAIM represents department chairs and chiefs; clerkship, residency, and fellowship program directors; division chiefs; academic and business administrators; and other faculty and staff in departments of internal medicine and their divisions. Because all are part of "academic" internal medicine (in contrast to the practice of internal medicine), the five organizations banded together can speak with one voice, amplifying and in partnership with ACP and ABIM.

Clerkship Directors in Internal Medicine

The Clerkship Directors in Internal Medicine (CDIM) is the national organization of those responsible for teaching internal medicine to medical students. Each medical school may have one institutional member and many other individual members. CDIM meets annually for members to present educational innovation and research and to attend lectures and workshops.

CDIM members note the importance of this organization in advancing their careers. The key administrators who support the clerkships also meet annually with their clerkship directors.

Association of Program Directors in Internal Medicine
Just as clerkship directors have a professional organization, so do residency program directors. The Association of Program Directors in Internal Medicine (APDIM) represents internal medicine training programs in general. It is a vibrant group whose members learn from one another. It has active leadership development programs, is a highly regarded voice for training issues and standards both within and outside internal medicine, and interacts with the Residency Review Committees for internal medicine in periodically revising standards.

Association of Specialty Professors
The Association of Specialty Professors (ASP) is an organization of division chiefs who are often also subspecialty program directors. Members also include program directors who are not division chiefs. Similar to APDIM, ASP convenes those invested in subspecialty training programs.

Administrators of Internal Medicine
The Administrators of Internal Medicine (AIM) is the national organization of those who administratively support departments of medicine within each medical school.

Association of Professors of Medicine
The Association of Professors of Medicine (APM) is the organization of departments of internal medicine represented by chairs and appointed leaders at medical schools and affiliated teaching hospitals in the United States and Canada. Members of the APM provide the primary leadership and direction to academic internal medicine, including education, research, and patient care. Most educational leaders within departments of medicine report to the chair or vice-chair for education. The APM meetings now include members of the Association of Chairs and Chiefs of Medicine (ACCM), the organization of physicians responsible for the academic mission of departments of internal medicine at teaching hospitals, whether or not they are chairs of a medical school department.

❖ Conclusion

In the complicated, demanding realm of medical education, internal medicine often plays a central role in both schools and hospitals. There are senior leaders (deans, chairs, and hospital CEOs) to provide direction, resources, and incentives, and educational managers (associate deans; vice-chairs; and course, clerkship, and program directors) to provide management, support, and inspiration. These individuals and the offices they oversee provide the infrastructure enabling departments, schools, and hospitals to function smoothly and to offer students, trainees, and practitioners the educational experience they deserve. Finally, there are national organizations that serve the public, the profession, and the specialty through education, oversight, networking, and a forum to present research and new ideas.

This chapter is written for those already in or planning a career in medical education. It should help them understand all the parts and players so that they can succeed within their current roles, consider the different roles they may want to play, and learn about others with whom they will interact. This chapter should increase their confidence and sense of excitement at taking on the work of educating future physicians.

REFERENCES

1. **Fincher RM, Sykes-Brown W, Allen-Noble R.** Health science learning academy: a successful "pipeline" educational program for high school students. Acad Med. 2002; 77:737-8.
2. **Albanese MA, Snow MH, Skochelak SE, Huggett KN, Farrell PM.** Assessing personal qualities in medical school admissions. Acad Med. 2003;78:313-21.
3. **Mann K, Gordon J, MacLeod A.** Reflection and reflective practice in health professions education: a systematic review. Adv Health Sci Educ Theory Pract. 2009;14:595-621.
4. **Skeff KM, Stratos GA, eds.** Methods for Teaching Medicine. Philadelphia: ACP Pr; 2010.
5. **Alguire PC, DeWitt DE, Pinsky LE, Ferenchick GS.** Teaching in Your Office: A Guide to Instructing Medical Students and Residents. 2nd ed. Philadelphia: ACP Pr; 2008.
6. **Wiese J, ed.** Teaching in the Hospital. Philadelphia: ACP Pr; 2010.
7. **Ende J, ed.** Theory and Practice of Teaching Medicine. Philadelphia: ACP Pr; 2010.
8. **Salsberg E, Rockey PH, Rivers KL, Brotherton SE, Jackson GR.** US residency training before and after the 1997 Balanced Budget Act. JAMA. 2008;300:1174-80.
9. **Humphrey H, ed.** Mentoring in Academic Medicine. Philadelphia: ACP Pr; 2010.
10. **Cooper-Patrick L, Gallo JJ, Gonzales JJ, Vu HT, Powe NR, Nelson C, et al.** Race, gender, and partnership in the patient-physician relationship. JAMA. 1999;282:583-9.
11. **Hausmann LR, Ibrahim SA, Mehrotra A, Nsa W, Bratzler DW, Mor MK, et al.** Racial and ethnic disparities in pneumonia treatment and mortality. Med Care. 2009;47:1009-17.
12. **Meyers FJ, Weinberger SE, Fitzgibbons JP, Glassroth J, Duffy FD, Clayton CP; Alliance for Academic Internal Medicine Education Redesign Task Force.** Redesigning residency training in internal medicine: the consensus report of the Alliance for Academic Internal Medicine Education Redesign Task Force. Acad Med. 2007;82:1211-9.

Understanding Systems of Education: What to Expect of, and for, Each Faculty Member

Barbara Schuster, MD, MACP

Louis Pangaro, MD, MACP

The education of students and residents offers many opportunities for physicians who seriously consider the pledge in the Hippocratic Oath to teach the next generation. Teaching is one of the basic expectations of being a physician, whether or not one has a full-time position on the faculty. Whether offering a single lecture to the first-year medical school class, supervising a preceptorship in an office setting, or accepting responsibility for the internal medicine clerkship, every physician can participate in fulfilling the mission.

This chapter, however, is written not for all teaching faculty but for those entrusted with responsibility for educational programs. Accordingly, it focuses on the organizational structures of the teaching faculty. The "levels" of responsibility for teaching and education are explained, and specific expectations are formulated by level of responsibility. The chapter then details what support should be given to help educators fill those expectations. It is not enough to specify what we want of teachers; support for them must be provided. This support is generally the responsibility of those who are higher in the hierarchy of medical education and administration. In short, this chapter will specify not just what to expect *of* educators but also what to expect on their behalf—that is, what to expect *for* them. Chapters in other books in the *Teaching Medicine* series describe specific skills used in clinical teaching; this chapter compares and contrasts what

---

KEY POINTS

- Each level of teaching and program responsibility in the pyramid of faculty development has its own expectations and its own need for support and faculty development.
- House staff and occasional teachers must know what to expect of their students, and have basic skills in setting a learning climate, communicating goals, and giving feedback.
- Core teachers do most teaching for fellows, residents, and students. They must have more and better skills, and be consistent in assessment of trainees.
- Course, clerkship, and program directors are academic directors who need the training and time to manage a system with consistency in teaching and evaluation across teachers and sites. They must communicate closely with those above and below them.
- Academic executives (chairs, deans, CEOs) must understand what is expected at each level of teaching and provide inspiration, time, training, support, and resources.

---

each group of educators needs depending on their level of responsibility (Table 4-1). The hope is that this chapter will be a useful guide for education leaders and directors (see chapter 3 of this book) and will facilitate institutional planning for an effective faculty and, therefore, for an effective educational program.

❖ The Pyramid of Educators

A pyramid (Figure 4-1) can be used to depict the roles and numbers of educators in the medical education system. Responsibilities intensify and also become more supervisory and administrative as one moves "up" the pyramid. The pyramid is broadest at its base, and the number of teachers for whom some faculty development must be provided is greatest at the base. Referring to this as the "base" is preferred over calling it the "bottom" of the pyramid because many teachers are needed to support the entire teaching enterprise. The base consists of house staff and occasional teachers, and the idea of "the base" allows consideration of what is expected of *all* teachers, however small their role.

Table 4-1. Expectations for Level of Educational Role*

Skill	House Staff	Occasional Teachers	Core Teachers	Academic Directors	Institutional Leaders
Knowledge of education					
Learning goals and objectives	x	x	xxxx	xxxx	xx
Expectations of teachers	xxx	xxx	xxxx	xxxx	xxx
Teaching methods	x	x	xxx	xxxx	x
Evaluation methods and tools	x	x	xx	xxxx	x
Accreditation standards	x	x	xx	xxxx	xxx
Legal precepts	x	x	xxx	xxxx	xxxx
Educational literature			xx	xxx	x
Adult and life-long learning	x	x	xxxx	xxxx	xxx
Advising/mentorship	x	x	xxx	xxxx	xxx
Teaching skills					
Establishing learning climate	xxx	xxx	xxxx	xxxx	xx
Supervising	xx	xx	xxx	xxx	xx
Facilitating small groups	xx	xx	xxx	xxx	xx
Lecturing	x	x	xx	xxx	x
Giving feedback to learners	xx	xx	xxxx	xxxx	x
Giving feedback to teachers	x	x	xx	xxxx	xxx
Assessing learners	x	x	xxxx	xxxx	x
Skills in "bedside" observation	xx	xx	xxxx	xxxx	x
Evaluation methods and tools	x	x	xx	xxxx	x
Assessment construction	x	x	xx	xxxx	xx
Curriculum development/evaluation	x	x	xx	xxxx	x
Faculty development	x	x	xx	xxxx	xx
Financing of medical education	x	x	xx	xxx	xxxx

*The numbers of Xs indicate the authors' judgment of importance.

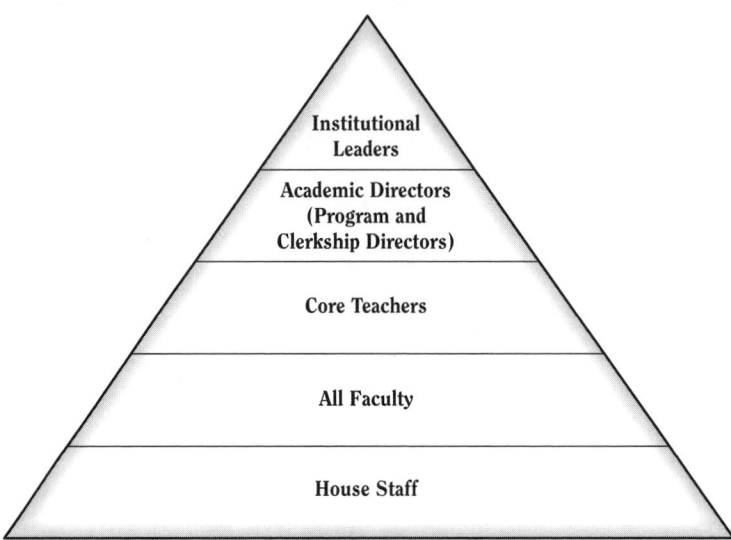

Figure 4-1 The pyramid of faculty development. The breadth of the figure illustrates the number of faculty at each "level." Institutional leaders (chairs, deans, hospital CEOs) have unique responsibilities for providing resources.

As one moves up the pyramid, the number of educators in each role is smaller. Each department or hospital service typically has a smaller cadre of "core teachers" who do the heavy lifting in undergraduate and graduate medical education; they are often but not always primary care specialists. Higher up still are the academic managers: the course, clerkship, and program directors who oversee a major part of the curriculum. They do a lot of teaching on their own, but supporting and mentoring the larger number of teachers closer to the "base" becomes a major endeavor. It is the responsibility of those higher up to provide guidance and resources for those in the trenches. Finally, at the top of the pyramid are institutional leaders who may now only teach occasionally but who have a major role in providing support and incentives for everyone else.

The Base of the Pyramid: House Staff and Occasional Teachers

Entry Into the Academy of Educators

Many physicians remember that since their fourth year of medical school, they have taught those more junior in the profession, and that as early as the first year of medical school, they learned to teach patients through the questions they answer. Later, during residency, it is expected that trainees will teach formally, mentor informally, and through their actions model the expertise and sense of duty required in the profession. Finishing residents and fellows should not just be managers in patient care but also educators.

House officers (residents and fellows) are large in number, and are often the daily teachers for a majority of medical students. The need to train them in curricular goals for students is now expressly articulated in the medical school accreditation standards of the Liaison Committee on Medical Education (LCME) (1): "The objectives of the educational program must be made known to all medical students and to the faculty, residents, and others with direct responsibilities for medical student education." The Accreditation Council for Graduate Medical Education (ACGME) requires that internal medicine residents are trained in teaching and evaluation with specific focus on medical students (2).

During subspecialty training, fellows often teach students and residents while consulting on patients. In fact, fellowship may be a transitional step to a faculty position, and although this group of trainees is often busy developing clinical expertise and performing research, their training in the basic educational skills should not be neglected.

Occasional Teachers

As has long been the tradition in medicine, a new physician, whether in practice or appointed to a faculty, should think about teaching. Because of other commitments—to practice, administration, or research—some physicians work with students only "occasionally." Although each does only a few hours per year, in the aggregate these teachers may provide education for a large part of the student body.

Early opportunities for all physicians to teach include offering preceptorships for first- or second-year medical students in their offices (see *Teaching in Your Office*, another book in the *Teaching Medicine* series [3]). Some physicians accept a third-year student for a half-day a week or biweekly in their offices, and thus support the core medicine clerkship. Other occasional teachers present a lecture or lead a small-group student session on a topic in the physician's area of expertise, such as smoking cessation or domestic violence. A specialist may be asked to formally lecture on a specific topic or be the clinical consultant on a patient case being discussed as a clinical correlation experience. A physician may also be considered an occasional teacher if he or she accepts the responsibility for teaching on the inpatient or subspecialty service several weeks a year. Most occasional teachers volunteer their time and expertise and, in so doing, fulfill their Hippocratic Oath to pass on their knowledge. Medical education is indebted to this large group of dedicated teachers.

Core Teachers

In any institution, there is often a smaller group of teachers who do a large percentage of the teaching. These are "core teachers." The Residency Review Committee (RRC) for Internal Medicine mandates that there be a specified number of core teachers depending on program size. Each core teacher must contribute 10 to 15 hours weekly to the education of residents. Core teachers may be responsible for an area of subspecialty teaching, a permanent ambulatory supervisor in the resident outpatient practice, or a regular attending on the inpatient resident service. Intensivists and other subspecialists who regularly accept students on their service become core teachers. Whereas occasional teachers may or may not receive fiscal reimbursement for their educational contributions, core teachers will usually receive a partial salary, or "protected time" for teaching.

Academic Directors

The term "academic directors" (or "academic managers") is used for those who have explicit responsibilities for oversight of educational programs, including specific medical school courses and postgraduate programs. These are the program directors for residencies and fellowships, the clerkship directors for the core clinical clerkships, the course directors for individual or integrated medical student courses, and the overall coordinators for individual years of undergraduate medical education curriculum. Each residency or fellowship program, each core specialty clerkship, and each "introduction to clinical medicine" course typically has one such person per medical school. However, affiliated hospital systems may require "on-site" assistant program directors and assistant clerkship directors; thus, the number of faculty considered an academic director can be greatly expanded. Academic director positions that are medical school or hospital based usually require substantial professional effort, and are usually reimbursed by percentage time of a full-time educator's salary. If a highly paid specialist chooses to accept an academic director position, his or her fiscal support would generally be lower than if the time were spent in clinical work. The ACGME and LCME do not specify what is considered appropriate financial support for program directors or clerkship directors, and course directors in medical schools are even more variably paid.

In addition to administrative responsibilities for the organization, delivery and assessment of the curriculum, and the evaluation of learners, academic directors usually spend considerable time teaching in multiple settings. They have often accepted their positions after achieving personal success in core teaching arenas, and are often superb teachers gathering energy for the administrative aspects of their positions by continuing their contributions as hands-on educators. Most academic directors also continue to provide clinical care in their specialty or subspecialty and continue scholarly pursuits in an area of personal interest.

What should be expected of academic managers in addition to the things expected of core teachers? As seen in Table 4-1, this group must not only be highly skilled (effective and efficient) themselves but must be able to develop these skills in others. In addition to giving feedback to learners, they must be able to give feedback to teachers. Their knowledge of assessment methods must go beyond direct observation at the bedside. In addition to being able to assess a learner's fund of knowledge through their own questioning, they must be familiar with the use of multiple-choice tests and other, more sophisticated assessment modalities (see chapter 8 of this book for more information). They must be conversant with the educational psychometrics and the feasibility of test methods (cost and difficulty of implementation).

Institutional Leaders

At the top of the pyramid are those who are spending less time teaching students but more time allocating resources and funds within the department, the medical school, or the hospital system and setting the environment for learning and high-quality care. These are the departmental chairs, deans, vice-presidents for health care, and chief executive officers (CEOs), who are ultimately responsible for the success of education, as well as patient care and research. The specific perspectives and educational skills that they need are somewhat different from those for all the other educators. Senior leaders may have been chosen for their skills in research, management, or business. However, most senior leaders have served in the core of teachers, and their understanding of and appreciation for the unique skills of educators is essential for the success of the academic medical center.

❖ All Teachers

Basic Expectations *of* All Teachers

As described in other books in the *Teaching Medicine* series (3–6), as a foundation, all teachers must have a significant knowledge of their clinical area of expertise and feel confident in their knowledge. Effective teachers are not those who can recite the textbook or the current journal articles but those who can model and explain how we gather and synthesize clinical information, consider an appropriate differential diagnosis, and develop a diagnostic workup or therapeutic plan in collaboration with their patients.

The art of transmitting the skills and knowledge of the accomplished clinician is the mark of the skilled educator. However, we cannot assume that as they increase their knowledge of their own specialty teachers will develop the skills of the educator. Skilled educators must also develop knowledge of educational goals and objectives, expectations of their own teaching role, educational modalities, evaluation techniques, and accreditation standards. Where one sits in the pyramid of educators will determine the extent of the educational knowledge base required.

Knowledge of the Program's Goals and Objectives

All teachers must be familiar with the specific expectations for students or residents with whom they work on a specific rotation. The accreditation bodies have appropriately insisted that the institution—typically through the academic directors—familiarize all teachers with the goals and expectations for their learners. Residents, in particular, "must be familiar with the educational objectives of the course and clerkship and be prepared for their roles in teaching and evaluation" (1). Strategies for familiarizing faculty with programmatic goals and objectives will be discussed later. The point here is that consistency in expectations of students and residents is required to ensure institutional performance standards and is essential for trainees to perceive that the educational system as fair.

Within the private office setting, the practitioner should be allowed to set clear expectations about dress, patient interactions, and office procedure (see Appendix A in *Teaching in Your Office* [3] for an example of a "contract" with learners in the office). The institution sending the student must support the practitioner in setting office standards consistent with the rotation and course goals. The institution should also help educate the practitioner to deliver clear expectations and directions to the student and educate the student that the standards set by the practitioner will be institutionally supported. Learning to deliver a clear message facilitates learning and allows clear feedback. Setting standards and conveying them to the learner can be developed and practiced in sessions held in mutually acceptable settings, including the office of the practitioner, a practice called academic detailing. Educating the entire office staff to be consistent in maintaining standards for student and resident performance is important in developing excellent teaching placements.

Setting Specific Learning Goals

Adult learners are motivated to learn what they can use now. So, in addition to having the generic competency expectations in mind, all teachers need to be flexible, and encourage learners to ask questions. When a topic of interest is unexpected, and especially if it is complex, they should help the learner allocate time to find an answer, and allocate time for them to report back what they have learned.

A Supportive Learning Climate

Few teaching skills are as important as the ability to establish a learning climate in which learners can recognize and address their limitations, and so improve (see chapter 3 of *Theory and Practice of Teaching Medicine* [4] and chapter 1 of *Methods for Teaching Medicine* [5] for additional information on setting the learning climate). This is the first of seven teaching categories in the Stanford Faculty Development Program (7). It could be argued that no skill is more important than this one in fostering a humanistic attitude in students and residents because how they feel treated may affect how they treat others.

Teaching Methods

All teachers should be comfortable with interactive discussions in which learners are expected to do more than listen to a lecture or to repeat or report a patient's findings. Active learning methods help the learner move toward independence. It is probably not enough that teachers understand that teaching is listening as much as it is talking, and they need to practice and be intuitively comfortable with this approach.

Certainly, those who teach occasionally in a given format—such as in a lecture or a small group (see chapters 3 and 4, respectively, in *Methods for Teaching Medicine* [5])—should be fluent in the methods that are typical for these settings. In a small group, this means encouraging all learners to participate and doing as much listening as talking. In a lecture, teachers should speak audibly and avoid hyperdensity of information.

Direct Observation, Evaluation, and Feedback

It is axiomatic that trainees require feedback to improve their performance, and not just of skills (interpersonal, manual, or analytic)—feedback is also needed on the efficacy of their reading and the ability to reflect and grow on their own. All teachers should understand and practice direct observation (8) and feedback (see chapter 3 of *Theory and Practice of Teaching Medicine* [4]). At a minimum, all teachers should understand the importance of critiquing learners' behaviors (what they were observed to do) and to avoid personal, ad hominem comments on "who they are." It also desirable for teachers to practice being specific and even concrete in the advice they give to students, especially those who do not seem to pick things up quickly.

Many teachers are not comfortable with using a program's expectations, and cannot grade accurately; and just as many teachers are uncomfortable giving low grades. However, all should be expected to report their observations to the clerkship or program director (either in person or on an evaluation form); it is desirable that teachers give unequivocal feedback to a student or resident when performance has been substandard, even though this may require more effort and system resources.

For students, evaluation and grading are a clear demonstration of the values of the institution and the faculty. Transparency and consistency are essential to fairness and, to some extent, the process of evaluation represents professionalism.

Recognizing a Learner in Distress

Medical school and residency are stressful, and at times learners can be overwhelmed. Whether or not all teachers are skilled in managing such situations, all should be able to recognize warning signs and red flags—recurrent absence, depressed mood, inappropriate coping, alcohol on the breath—and know how to refer such a problem to the appropriate institutional contact (see chapter 6 in *Teaching in the Hospital* [6]).

Expectations *for* All Teachers

New teachers and occasional teachers are a major challenge for academic managers and department leaders. New house officers and occasional faculty may have the least experience with students and typically have the least familiarity with the goals and objectives of their own institutions. Yet, the needs of the learners that they supervise are no less important, and no less challenging, than for the core teachers who see many more students. In addition to having less experience with learners and goals for their own learners, teachers at the "base" of the pyramid may also have less time available to participate in faculty development. Moreover, these occasional teachers do not often have an opportunity to quickly incorporate feedback from students into their teaching practice. So for occasional teachers the benefits of feedback from their own learners may be somewhat dilute. If they are interested, they might be offered a possibility of workshops on specific teaching skills, such as direct bedside observation and feedback, including the use of "standardized students" who might provide a variety of experiences in an afternoon (see chapter 4 in *Theory and Practice of Teaching Medicine* [4] for further details). This means that special attention needs to be given to ensuring they understand what to expect of their learners.

Time to Teach

The tension between time to teach and time for clinical patient care (productivity) can prevent some teachers from teaching at all, and prevent others from being truly learner-centered when they do. It is a principal responsibility of academic directors to accurately quantify the time expectations for specific teaching roles (such as 30 minutes devoted to a student in each half-day in clinic), and to be sure the department chair, service chief, or CEO endorses the teacher's efforts.

Orientation to Goals

As already noted, that accreditation bodies have insisted that the medical school familiarize all teachers with the goals and expectations for their learners. At a minimum, this is done through handouts or e-mails. Optimally, it is done through direct contact with the course, clerkship, and program directors, not just through orientation but through ongoing training in the framework for expectations established by the school or department. This is preferably done through face-to-face discussions with teachers about their own students, so that goals can be reinforced, evaluations calibrated, and feedback planned (9).

Simplicity of Goals and Objectives

Practicing clinicians and residents are often busy with patient care and other tasks, and teachers should not be overwhelmed by elaborate statements of objectives for students and residents that are written by those heavily invested in the educational process. Practicing clinicians, per the message of Kern and colleagues (10), should be spared the expectation that they master details of learning objectives for trainees (see chapter 6 for more details). Academic managers and deans should guard against proliferation of such lists. Whenever the educational jargon is not intuitively obvious to teachers, the system must invest more effort to amplify the expectations, or more time to explain them to the faculty to be sure that teachers are comfortable with the goals and objectives, and grading learners.

Recognition

Teachers should be recognized for their contributions. Often this is with a faculty appointment in the school of medicine; for board-certified physicians, their position would be instructor or assistant physician (typically with a "clinical" prefix if they are occasional teachers). In some institutions residents are given a title, such as "teaching fellow." The dean's office and the department chairs will set policies for such appointments, and the academic directors will have to make sure that the policies are applied consistently and fairly.

Most institutions have awards for outstanding performance as a teacher, and these may be designated for different settings (for example, ward attending, clinic attending, community preceptor). The office of the chair or program or clerkship director typically provides the resources to propose candidates and determine awardees. In addition to recognition in a public forum, there might be a small financial award.

Feedback
Most programs ask trainees to fill out end-of-rotation evaluation forms, or critiques, on the program and their teachers. Teacher-specific forms should be shared with the teachers, and we also recommend that the program or clerkship director initial them, and perhaps write comments that thank the teacher or on occasion ask whether the teacher wants to discuss a "negative" comment from a learner.

It is also satisfying for teachers to know how their own students and residents finished up, after all the grades are in and the examinations calculated. We recommend providing this information to teachers as a form of feedback and quality control. It can help them reflect on their own observations about their trainees' fund of knowledge and skills.

❖ Core Teachers

What should we expect of core teachers in addition to everything we expect of the larger group of "all teachers"? For everyday tasks, such as observing interviewing skills and physical examination skills in learners, this group of teachers should be proficient in the accuracy of their observations and the precision of their feedback. They should be not just effective and accurate but efficient. They should know what specific skills and knowledge areas tend to be problematic for learners at a particular level, and so can save time and focus quickly.

Because by definition they bear a great deal of responsibility in a program or clerkship educational system, core teachers must meet the expectations for all teachers described above and have the needed support given to them.

Expectations *of* Core Teachers
Goals and Objectives
Core teachers need to be familiar enough with the terminology that guides curriculum and assessment that they can communicate it, clearly and quickly, to students and residents. At the graduate medical education level, this typically means a detailed understanding of the six general ACGME competencies that are used for measuring outcomes at the end of training: medical knowledge, interpersonal and communication skills, professionalism, patient care, system-based practice, and practice-based learning and

improvement. In addition, many medicine clerkships use the reporter-interpret-manager-educator (RIME) framework (11), and core teachers should be calibrated to use this system in describing the level of the student's (or resident's) performance with a particular patient.

Fostering Understanding and Self-Directed Learning

Core teachers need to be skilled in teaching methods, such as explaining things to learners, whether in a lecture setting or in a small group; they also must be skilled in fostering independence through self-directed learning, reflection, and self-analysis. To some extent they need to model these behaviors as well.

Core teachers have to be flexible in responding to the needs of different kinds of learners. Whether or not they are versed in educational theory and terminology, they cannot always do things one way. Core teachers need to be able to run many kinds of teaching sessions: one-on-one, small group, and so forth (described in *Methods for Teaching Medicine* [5]). They need skills in working with the same learners over time, and in planning learning activities over days, weeks, and months. Finally, they need skills in team-building and in fostering trainees' collaboration with nurses and others on the health care team (see chapter 3 in *Teaching in the Hospital* [6]).

Assessment and Evaluation; Grading and Feedback

Learning is often driven by what is graded, so those with frequent student/resident contact must be especially consistent in what they observe and how they interpret it. Core teachers should be skilled in discriminating between acceptable and substandard performance, and probably between acceptable and outstanding performance as well. Not only should they be able to identify learners who are clearly outstanding or clearly deficient but they must also have the skills to help a wide variety of learners and help the "pass" student get to "high pass." To summarize, core teachers should do more than the basics. Program directors and clerkship directors need to count on them for observations and teaching interventions that are equivalent to their own. Basically, they should be the program's or clerkship's evaluation framework as fluently as the program director or clerkship director would, and give the same kind of feedback.

Core teachers should clearly be able to determine that a student or resident is progressing satisfactorily or not; for instance, that an intern is a reliable reporter but is not making progress toward becoming an interpreter, much less a manager. Whether or not they have the time or skill to diagnose the underlying reason that a student or intern is failing to progress—cognitive, emotional, or social—they should be able to recognize the problem.

Advising and Mentoring
All teachers have responsibility for giving learners feedback on their own patients, but some are called upon to advise students and residents in their longer-term choices, such as what rotations to consider or how to plan for career options. Core teachers have close contact with many students over a year, and there will probably be many occasions for advising students and residents. Some teachers will be given a special gift of trust by students and residents and have the chance to be mentors (see *Mentoring in Academic Medicine*, also part of the *Teaching Medicine* series [12]). This more sustained relationship can center on a research project, or it may simply be a part of a relationship developed over a year or more, such as in a small fellowship program.

Expectations *for* Core Teachers
In addition to the same kind of support as all teachers and residents, core teachers need other things.

Time for Teaching
The internal medicine RRC specifies 20 hours per week for associate program directors. The Association of Professors in Medicine and the Clerkship Directors in Internal Medicine have endorsed 25% full-time equivalency for clerkship administration and 25% full-time equivalency for teaching and scholarship as a target expectation for protected time for clerkship directors (13).

Faculty Development
To achieve what we expect of them, core teachers need more intensive faculty development. To some extent, faculty development is a strategy for minimizing unwarranted variation in teachers' performance. The core faculty deserve a deep investment in their core skills so that in all circumstances, certainly critical ones, they behave as the program director or clerkship director would. The department of medicine (or the medical school) should provide the resources for all core teachers to participate in a formal teaching skills program. The department and its service chiefs should provide the time for this to happen. In particular, core teachers may need training for the specialty skills needed for evaluation, advising, and mentoring, and certainly will need time to work with learners in developing their own careers.

Academic Progression
Core teachers may aspire to academic careers, particularly as clinician-educators. Planning for their development and progression is an essential

interest of department chairs, and can be directly fostered by academic managers. They should be encouraged to take on responsibility for lectures or lecture series, to participate in local educational conferences and journal clubs, and to join research projects. They should be encouraged to attend— and perhaps be subsidized to attend—professional meetings that feature educational workshops and research, such as those of the Society of General Internal Medicine, Clerkship Directors in Internal Medicine, and the Association of American Medical Colleges. Career development such as this is discussed further in chapter 5.

❖ Academic Directors

Course, clerkship, and program directors are the pivotal leadership and information hubs for the educational system. They have a critical role in looking "up" the pyramid by briefing the institution's leadership and in looking "down" the pyramid by providing guidance, support, and resources for all teachers, including the "core." In other words, they must function as both managers and educators for the entire department.

Under the aegis of the Alliance for Clinical Education (the coordinating council for the national specialty organizations with required medical student clerkships), expectations "of and for" clerkship directors have been defined and agreed upon (14). The internal medicine RRC specifies roles and responsibilities for graduate medical education *program* directors. Academic directors must "know the rules" for program accreditation, and for certification and licensing of their individuals trainees.

Expectations *of* Academic Directors

Expectations at this level of the pyramid include all those already mentioned for all teachers and core teachers. In particular, academic directors must be very skilled in articulating goals for trainees, directly assessing progress, and in giving feedback. This section highlights some additional key expectations.

Assessment of Individual Trainees

Course, clerkship, and program directors must be skilled in observing students and residents, in evaluating their progress, and in helping them improve, if needed. In other words, they must do more than report what they observe a student do; they must be able to interpret their findings and manage any deficits. They must also observe, evaluate, and give feedback to faculty.

Described in greater detail in chapter 8, academic directors must have facility with the "tool chest" of assessment methods available for describing the progress of students and residents toward eventual independence, and for measuring achievement in each of the six aforementioned ACGME competencies. They should be personally skilled in observing and evaluating their students and residents and be well calibrated in making even the finer grading distinctions the department uses, such as between "pass" and "high pass" for students, or between "6" and "8" on the American Board of Internal Medicine evaluation form.

Although they do not need to be experts in designing individual assessment tools (such as writing multiple-choice test questions or scripts for standardized patients), they do need to be able to converse with such experts, to know the reliability and validity of their tools, to know the resources needed and costs of these tools, and to know when and how to sample skills and competencies during their clerkships and programs. Most important, they must be able to develop a comprehensive plan of assessment that supports learning now, and fosters independent learning and self-correction in the future.

Clerkship and program directors must be efficient and effective in collating evaluations from multiple teachers with results from specific tests of knowledge and skill into a summative evaluation at the end of the clerkship, or periodically during residency (at least annually).

It is especially important for academic directors to know the resources required to meet the standards of the ACGME and LCME and to track the progress and achievement of individual residents and students. As part of their "talking upward," they should be able to describe the needs in faculty time and dollars to their chairs, and if necessary to the CEO of a hospital, for what it takes to deploy a multimodal assessment strategy for each dimension in the competency framework that they use.

Finally, academic managers should be very familiar with the legal issues involved in grading students and residents, especially in giving students failing grades or putting residents on probation.

Curriculum Development and Evaluation
Academic directors must be able to design (see chapter 6) and evaluate (see chapter 7) the curriculum as a whole, and any new elements as they are introduced. They must be alert to changes in the practice of medicine and able to perform updated "needs assessments" to respond effectively. They must be able to work with stakeholders inside and outside of their department to define and enable needed changes.

Clerkship and program directors are responsible for many "products" each year, such as schedules; a series of lectures, teaching exercises, and demonstrations; or a series of examinations. It is reasonable to use these products as an indication of achievement—efforts happening as planned can be taken as a clear sign of success, and improvement through research and development can be seen as outstanding.

Leadership Qualities

Academic managers should be trusted by trainees and by their own superiors in the academic hierarchy. Students must recognize them as being fair and consistent, and chairs must regard them as having judgment and not being whiners. Clerkship directors and program directors must be able to negotiate with leadership above them, and take the lead in conflict resolution between trainees and, if necessary, between departments and hospital services. In that sense, academic directors must be able to earn the respect of and represent the interests of the core faculty.

Expectations *for* Academic Directors

What should we do for this critical hub in the educational system? Having selected the course, clerkship, and program directors and the vice-chair for education, the chair of the department should ensure that they all have the resources and training necessary to fulfill their roles and responsibilities. In addition to the support given to core teachers, academic directors need special mentoring from the chair (or vice-chair) (see the introduction and chapter 13 of *Mentoring in Academic Medicine* [12]).

Academic Advancement and Development

It is especially important for chairs to be sure that academic directors have a defined path for academic promotion, typically in a clinician-educator pathway, and usually in a non–tenure track (see chapter 5). There should be time for personal scholarship (writing articles and doing educational research) and support for attending professional meetings where innovations and research are presented and where educational and research skills may be developed (see chapter 9).

When possible, academic directors should be encouraged to take advanced training in educational and research methods, such as a masters degree (for example, a Masters in Public Health or a Masters of Health Professions Education degree). At the least they should be funded to attend formal courses related to their education role, such as courses for new program directors (from Association of Program Directors in Internal Medicine) or new clerkship directors (from Clerkship Directors in Internal Medicine), or structured in-residence courses, such as those offered for clinician-educators or educational leaders by Harvard Macy Institute (www.harvardmacy.org).

Clerical and Administrative Support

Clerkship and program directors must have support from dedicated, full-time clerical and administrative personnel in proportion to the number of trainees, the number of faculty evaluating each student, the number of program sites and rotations, and the importance of the evaluation process (that is, whether the process is a "high stakes" one).

❖ Institutional Leaders: Chairs, Deans, and CEOs

Educational expectations for those at the "top" of the pyramid include roles quite different from those for teaching full-time, or managing academic programs full-time. These are included in this chapter because anyone wishing to understand the big-picture system of medical education must clearly understand the role of the tip of the pyramid well enough to include it in a larger strategy for the department or institution—especially to justify and provide the resources needed.

Many chairs and deans have been active teachers and have come up through the ranks. As a result they do understand what it means to supervise students and residents. On the other hand, many of the rules of accreditation and certification have changed considerably. Many chairs and deans are not personally familiar with evaluating residents using the six competencies, or with the increased workload demanded by the LCME's requirement that clerkships establish specific diagnoses and patients to be seen by each student. Because they are often the providers of resources and are in a position to demand information and reports on educational process and quality, the expectations "of" and "for" them are discussed together.

Goals, Objectives, and Assessment of Individual Trainees

It is the role of the dean's office, in collaboration with the departments, to establish and articulate what is expected of each student or resident by the end of the curriculum. Typically, the Designated Institutional Official or an associate dean for undergraduate or graduate medical education is acting on behalf of the dean, and a vice-chair for education or a clerkship director is acting on behalf of the chair (see chapter 2 for a fuller discussion).

Chairs, deans, and CEOs do not themselves need to be intimately familiar with educational terminology or theories or, for example, how to calculate the reliability (stability of measurement) for an objective structured clinical examination (OSCE) using standardized patients. On the other hand, they do need to know that these activities must take place and require resources to meet expected standards of reliability and validity. It is the role of the academic directors to explain what resources are needed, and it is the role of the institutional leader to be receptive.

Institutional leaders do, however, have a compelling interest in the legal aspects of evaluating individual trainees, especially when academic probation or even dismissal is a possibility. Clerkship directors and program directors should be able to quickly summarize for them how goals and objectives are conveyed to students and teachers, and how consistency in the assessment process is achieved. Once assured that the process has been neither arbitrary nor capricious, chairs, deans, and CEOs should be comfortable in supporting their academic directors, and not override grading decisions.

Curriculum, Teachers, and Time for Teaching

Institutional leaders should understand the continuum of undergraduate, graduate, and continuing medical education and of how within their system one stage prepares for the next. They must recognize that the higher stages need "protected time" to support those still in training. Ultimately, it is the senior leadership—chairs or hospital chiefs, deans and CEOs—that may allocate the resources of time, or rather protected time, and money that make the educational mission possible. In the world of clinical teaching, teaching is often done in small groups or one-on-one. This is relatively inefficient compared with a large lecture, so academic directors are occasionally called upon to justify, or at least quantify, the time it takes for specific educational tasks (for example, small-group tutorials, precepting a student in a clinic, or teaching physical diagnosis). More granular measures, such as educational value units (analogous to clinical relative value units) are not routinely used in most schools, but chairs and deans should work with clerkship and program directors to determine how many hours of teaching, and from that how many teachers, are needed per year.

In addition to the time to teach is the time needed to learn how to teach; this allows consistency across teachers, across rotations, and across hospitals as teaching sites. It is essential for academic directors to explain to institutional leaders the importance of consistency in curriculum and assessment, not only for legal reasons but to foster a sense of fairness.

When newer ways of teaching are available (or needed), such as using standardized patients or teaching associates to teach physical diagnosis, the course director should be able to detail the direct costs of training and, for example, paying the standardized patients, and the number of faculty hours offset if the innovation were to be adopted.

Mentoring: In Both Directions

It is clearly the role of chairs to mentor their course, clerkship, and program directors. They provide encouragement, a planned set of academic expectations leading to promotion, and resources necessary to fulfill the mission of education. But who mentors or informs the chairs about recent developments in educational practice, educational requirements, and perhaps even educational theory?

Chairs may attend the annual meeting of their national organization. The Association of Professors of Medicine meets at least once a year, and educational issues are usually on the program. In addition, the Association of Professors of Medicine may meet jointly with Association of Program Directors in Internal Medicine and Clerkship Directors in Internal Medicine, giving the chairs a chance to hear about educational research and development. The national and regional meetings of the American College of Physicians may feature educational sessions and tracks. New chairs may attend courses specifically designed for them, such as those given annually by the Association of American Medical Colleges and by the Harvard School of Public Health. These are intensive programs, lasting more than a few days, and educational issues are usually included in the program, if not prominently.

Leadership

Teachers and academic directors do not expect chairs, deans, and CEOs to be experts in educational theory or current assessment technology, but they do expect unambiguous support for the educational mission of the school or hospital, both in words and, when required, in funding (see chapter 3 of this book). Academic directors can assist institutional leaders in this role. Providing annual, brief reports on the success of the curriculum, and the teaching hours used, can build leaders' trust. Most leaders have been managers and so like to see data. Offering specific data, especially on outcomes for individuals (such as success in passing the U.S. Medical Licensing Examination or certifying examinations) or outcomes for innovative curriculum (such as in patient safety), is one way the clerkship and program directors satisfy the desire to manage through metrics.

At times there is a tension in the appointment-promotion-and-tenure committee between the collective view of the committee, which may be dominated by externally funded physician-scientists, and the accomplishments of the clinician-educator who is being considered for promotion. It is here that the dean or the university vice-president for health affairs (or whoever selects members for the appointment-promotion-and-tenure committee) has a chance to make a clear statement about how the institution values educational work. It is the institution's support for teaching that often determines whether a faculty member stays or leaves. Recruiting and training new faculty is time-consuming and can be expensive if one adds in the extra faculty orientation and development that is needed. Leaders need to be sensitive to this, and efforts from the clerkship and program directors to enrich the clinician-educator portfolio with credible data on teaching, both quantitative and qualitative, will be very helpful in this regard.

❖ Conclusion

This chapter has outlined the skill sets and competencies expected of teachers at different levels of educational responsibility within an institution. As suggested by the image of the pyramid, there are fewer teachers at each level as one moves upward. While time devoted to teaching may actually decline at the highest reaches of the pyramid, *responsibility* for the teaching that takes place "below" increases substantially. For faculty who are more regularly involved in teaching, more is expected of them, and more must be invested in them in both training and resources. All teachers, including house officers, require some basic skills in working with students. Core teachers do more for the institution; they need more skills, and more must be invested in them. Course, clerkship, and program directors are the academic directors who power the educational mission. Finally, it is the institutional leaders (chairs, deans, and CEOs) who provide the resources and, importantly, the vision needed to accomplish the teaching mission. Like their directors, core teachers, and faculty, they too need to understand what is required if the educational mission is to succeed. In the end, this is a team effort, and everyone involved has an important role to play.

REFERENCES

1. **Liaison Committee on Medical Education.** Functions and structure of a medical school. Accessed at www.lcme.org/standard.htm#current.
2. **Accreditation Council for Graduate Medical Education.** ACGME program requirements for residents education and internal medicine. Accessed at www.acgme.org/acWebsite/downloads/RRC_progReq/140_internal_medicine_07012009.pdf.
3. **Alguire PC, DeWitt DE, Pinsky LE, Ferenchick GS.** Teaching in Your Office: A Guide to Instructing Medical Students and Residents. 2nd ed. Philadelphia: ACP Pr; 2008.
4. **Ende J, ed.** Theory and Practice of Teaching Medicine. Philadelphia: ACP Pr; 2010.
5. **Skeff KM, Stratos GA, eds.** Methods for Teaching Medicine. Philadelphia: ACP Pr; 2010.
6. **Wiese J, ed.** Teaching in the Hospital. Philadelphia: ACP Pr; 2010.

7. **Skeff KM, Stratos GA, Berman J, Bergen MR.** Improving clinical teaching. Evaluation of a national dissemination program. Arch Intern Med. 1992;152:1156-61.

8. **Holmboe E.** Direct observation by faculty. In: Holmboe ES, Hawkins RE. Practical Guide to the Evaluation of Clinical Competence. Philadelphia; Mosby Elsevier; 2008:119-29.

9. **Pangaro LN.** Evaluation forms and formal rating scales. In: Holmboe ES, Hawkins RE. Practical Guide to the Evaluation of Clinical Competence. Philadelphia: Mosby Elsevier; 2008:24-41.

10. **Kern DE, Thomas PA, Hughes MT, eds.** Curriculum Development for Medical Education: A Six-Step Approach. 2nd ed. Baltimore: Johns Hopkins Univ Pr; 2009.

11. **Pangaro L.** A new vocabulary and other innovations for improving descriptive in-training evaluations. Acad Med. 1999;74:1203-7.

12. **Humphrey H, ed.** Mentoring in Academic Medicine. Philadelphia: ACP Pr; 2010.

13. **Pangaro LN.** Expectations of and for the medicine clerkship director. Am J Med. 1998; 105:363-5.

14. **Pangaro L, Bachicha J, Brodkey A, Chumley-Jones H, Fincher RM, Gelb D, et al; Alliance for Clinical Education.** Expectations of and for clerkship directors: a collaborative statement from the Alliance for Clinical Education. Teach Learn Med. 2003; 15:217-22.

5

Developing a Career in Academic Medicine

Teresa A. Coleman, MD, FACP
Peter F. Buckley, MD
Ruth-Marie E. Fincher, MD, MACP

M anaging an academic career can be a tricky business. Navigating
the academic waters requires understanding of the culture and
"rules." Purposeful, self-directed professional development is a
key to academic success. Many institutions are taking meaningful steps
to articulate and implement processes to support career development.
Nonetheless, every faculty member must accept responsibility for, and
take the lead in, his or her professional career development. Forging a
successful career requires interdigitating personal career goals and preferences with department and school expectations and needs. Failure to
align the two may result in falling short of institutional or personal
expectations, stagnation, personal frustration with the work environment, and even attrition. A faculty member may leave by personal choice
or the institution's decision; either way, it is a loss for both.

❖ Two Scenarios

Consider two junior faculty. We will be returning to them throughout
the chapter. Both are general internists with enough time in rank to be
promoted to associate professor, and both are excellent teachers. Both
attended the school's "Career Development-101," a 1-day "getting started" program; are well liked in the division of general internal medicine;
and are respected clinicians and teachers. Now, consider the differences.

KEY POINTS

- Effective career development is in the best interest of both the faculty member and the institution. It is in the school's best interest to limit costly attrition and to "grow" the next generation of effective senior faculty leaders.
- Leaders should help junior faculty plan for and understand the expectations of their promotion "track" as early as possible.
- Mentors should encourage future leaders to accept teaching roles in line with their career goals, and help them learn to control their own time.
- Career development and formal leadership development programs may be quite helpful.
- Career setbacks can be opportunities for gaining insight and redirecting career paths.

Dr. "All Over" does everything she is asked to do and does it well, but has flitted from activity to activity without developing a thread or niche; she has rave teaching evaluations ("a 'born' teacher") and has won awards, but has little to no scholarship (publications or otherwise). She is not known outside the institution except as an excellent clinician to whom to refer patients. She has not been promoted after 6 years as an assistant professor because of a failure to demonstrate mastery and scholarly activity related to a focus area. As a result, she leaves in frustration.

Dr. "Straight Track" has been more proactive. She took the "Career Development-101" advice, read the guidelines from the promotion and tenure committee, created a career plan, and participated in local faculty development workshops to become a more effective teacher. She began to establish her niche early by volunteering for education-related assignments preferentially over additional clinical assignments, and documented the outcomes of her endeavors. She adopted a "two-fer" philosophy and tried to publish or present variations on as many of her internal projects as possible (for example, see a rare clinical problem, then present a student case conference and write a case report). She applied for and received the position of clerkship director when her predecessor left the institution; in addition, she asked him why he left and what he learned from his experience. After 3 years as clerkship director, she was offered the position of director of student education. She accepted the position and excelled at it; now she is being considered for the position of associate dean of curriculum. A competing institution is wooing her for the same position, and for much higher financial compensation, but she doesn't want to pull her children out of school.

Although there are parallels and differences between these scenarios and the outcomes experienced by Dr. "All Over" and Dr. "Straight Track," neither represents the clear "win-win" scenario that each faculty member and the chair had envisaged a few years ago when they sat together during recruitment. Dr. "All Over" is a great teacher and clinician, but was unfocused and lacked clear career goals. She met the department's needs, but not hers. Therefore, she became frustrated and left. Dr. "Straight Track" had a clear vision and implemented it, and is enjoying great job satisfaction and success at her parent institution. But she is now weighing the opportunities presented to her by competing institutions and the temptation to take on more responsibility at her current institution. If she leaves, her department will sustain a significant loss, not to mention the costs of recruiting and developing her replacement. Family issues raise the stakes of whatever decision she makes.

Take-home message: Effective career development is in the best interest of both the faculty member and the institution. It is in the school's best interest to limit costly attrition and to "grow" the next generation of effective senior faculty leaders. Development is in the faculty member's interest because professional satisfaction may result in a long-term commitment to the institution and in immense personal and professional satisfaction.

An academic career can develop for all faculty members without planning, advising, mentoring, or formal training, but it is unlikely to be the career the individual would have liked to have had. This chapter identifies the factors and processes that influence academic career development, provides guidance to prospective leaders in medical education on career may serve as a guide to career development for, and enumerates pertinent resources that can assist the multifaceted process of academic maturation. The chapter focuses on the particular aspects of career development that are relevant for faculty in the educational track.

❖ Understanding Promotion: The Sooner the Better

Academic promotion is not automatic. Junior faculty should begin planning for promotion at the time of academic appointment. Time in rank is only one, and probably the least important, indicator of readiness for promotion. You must understand the expectations of your particular promotion "track."

Promotion and tenure committees evaluate faculty performance on the basis of the expectations of the faculty member's career track. Typically, tracks are tenure-eligible or non–tenure-eligible. Increasingly, clinician faculty are on nontenure tracks, and researchers (PhDs or MD clinician-scientists) are on tenure tracks. The former tend to be for clinician-educators/educator-clinicians and the latter for funded researchers. However, variation among schools is considerable; therefore, understanding the local expectations is key. At many institutions, there are pathways in tenure track (researcher and clinician-investigator) and pathways in nontenure track (clinician-educator and educator-clinician). Tenure tracks often require extramural, overhead-bearing grant funding. The clinician-educator pathway is the most common MD pathway in most medical schools and includes clinicians who engage heavily in clinical care, often with learners, and who teach primarily in clinical settings. The educator-clinician pathway is appropriate for faculty who devote substantial time (usually more than 50%) to teaching and other educational activities. Course and clerkship directors, and other educational administrators (such as associate dean for curriculum), often take this path. Institutional promotion and tenure committee guidelines usually define expectations for each track. Most medical schools require scholarly work for promotion on all pathways. Many schools have embraced a definition of scholarship that includes research, but also other peer-reviewed and publicly disseminated work.

Within each track, guidelines typically document 1) years of service necessary for promotion and 2) expectations for research, teaching, institutional service, and demonstration of attainment of a professional reputation. As you progress from assistant, to associate, to full professor, expectations for achievements increase.

For example, at the authors' institution, a clinician-educator seeking promotion to associate professor would be expected to have 4 years of service as an assistant professor at the institution, in addition to showing the following:

- 50% to 80% of time devoted to clinical care activities
- Evidence of a commitment to mentoring and advising learners
- Evidence of participation in and attainment of teaching excellence, as demonstrated by excellent evaluations or the attainment of awards
- Authorship of peer-reviewed research or other scholarly publications; typically this means at least one to two first-authored and one to two additional coauthored peer-reviewed publica-

tions or peer-reviewed and publicly disseminated education materials

- Administrative or service leadership in the section, department, or school
- Attainment of a regional reputation, as manifested by speaking engagements, participation in professional organizations, and presentations at regional meetings

To achieve full professorship, the same individual will need to later demonstrate progressively increasing engagement within the academic educational community, attainment of a national or international reputation, attainment of leadership positions in national organizations, and ongoing significant contributions to educational literature.

Junior faculty often do what they are asked to do but are reluctant to approach their chair proactively to discuss responsibilities and career development. However, it is essential that even the most junior faculty become proactive in guiding their career development early on to avoid career missteps or wasting time. You should talk to your division chief or department chair about career goals, opportunities desired, useful and important future contacts, teaching opportunities that will result in evaluations, and relevant committees in which to participate. The bottom line: All faculty, but particularly those who are in the early phases of their academic career, need to understand promotion expectations and document accomplishments.

❖ Choosing the Appropriate Career "Track"

Hard as it may be, planning for the future is essential and requires the early development of clear professional career goals. Reflect on desired 5- and 10-year goals and on potential pathways to get there. This may be more difficult than it sounds. Finding a model faculty member who has achieved your aspirations may help identify concrete steps to lead toward your goals. Contact the person and arrange a time to talk about the career pathways he or she took. You will probably be surprised to learn that he or she did not have his or her entire career planned out as an assistant professor and first took advantage of opportunities as they arose. On the other hand, the person also probably did not just do everything he or she was asked to do without proactive planning to create future opportunities congruent with desired future goals.

To avoid being a Dr. "All Over," you can take the following steps:

- Write down what you think you would like to be doing in 5 and 10 years. Do you want to become a course or clerkship director, program director, division chief, department chair, associate dean for education, or even a dean?

- Identify a faculty member, not necessarily from your institution, who has followed the career trajectory you desire; contact and talk with the person about his or her career development.
- Read the literature, not just in your clinical specialty but also the education literature (if you want to be an educator) and the faculty development/leadership literature (if you aspire to leadership roles).
- Negotiate for professional activities that will facilitate reaching your goals.

❖ Documenting Progress: The Curriculum Vitae and Educator's Portfolio

Documentation is critical and often underemphasized. The progress of the faculty member's goals and achievements should be chronicled in both a curriculum vitae (CV) and an educator's portfolio.

The Curriculum Vitae as a "Living Document"

A CV should be developed carefully, kept current, and used to display accomplishments and to guide future career development. Most schools have a required format that should be followed when preparing for promotion. The organization of a CV should be clear and easy to follow (Box 5-1). Dates should follow in sequence (consider putting the most recent first). A carelessly organized CV suggests a faculty member who is disorganized and does not pay attention to detail.

Use the CV to assist in your desired career development. Determine what it should look like to attain the desired goal (for example, to become clerkship director). It may be helpful to create "white space" that defines what should be filled in before the next step. Your CV should demonstrate disproportionate accomplishments in the domain of greatest interest. For example, if the desired goal is to become a clerkship director, there should be evidence of considerable teaching experience, participation on education-related committees, excellence in teaching (such as high ratings on evaluations or receipt of awards), and evidence of mentoring students or residents. Document attendance at and participation in meetings relevant to medical education, and demonstrate engagement in scholarly work related to education.

Box 5-1. Key Elements of a CV

- ► Name
- ► Academic rank
- ► Administrative title (if applicable)
- ► Office address
- ► Contact information
- ► Education
  - • Institution(s)
  - • Date(s) of attendance
  - • Degree(s) awarded
  - • Board certification/recertification: Board and date
- ► Professional (experience in chronological order)
  - • Academic appointments
  - • Administrative responsibilities/appointments (e.g., editorial boards, professional societies)
  - • Committee assignments: major institutional committees; national committees (with dates)
  - • Research and training grants awarded
  - • Awards/honors
  - • Scientific and professional societies (include offices held)
  - • Community activities (include offices held)
- ► Presentations
  - • National, regional, and state meetings
- ► Publications
  - • Abstracts
  - • Peer-reviewed journals
  - • Books and chapters
  - • Nonrefereed journals

The CV of Dr. "All Over" documents numerous local committee assignments that are thematically unrelated. She has only one publication to date (middle author on a case report), but she has many teaching accolades. It occurs to her late that some of her committee time may have been better spent on scholarly work related to her chosen but undefined area of interest (a point for her to later negotiate with her division chief). She is not promoted, and does not understand why—she is unfamiliar with the promotion and tenure guidelines and the expectations of her academic "track."

In contrast, the CV of Dr. "Straight Track" is clearly organized and meticulously constructed. She serves on several thematically related institutional committees. She has several publications achieved through collaboration with others of interest whom she met at local, then regional, then national organizations. She is a member of several national committees, and expects to become chair of one of them soon.

Update your CV frequently and promptly. It just takes a minute to keep it up to date, but can be frustrating to update a year later. While updating your CV, look for opportunities in areas that are underdeveloped, but are important to fulfill your aspirations. Carefully "building" your CV will help you be ready to take advantage of opportunities: for example, to assume a larger administrative role, become a clerkship director, or even change tracks. Ask yourself, "Does this CV look like the CV of a person who would be selected to become a clerkship or program director, or an associate dean for curriculum?" (Box 5-2).

As your career develops, some entries that seemed important early in your career may no longer seem important. Consider consolidating or even

---

Box 5-2. Developing and Maintaining Your CV

- ► Follow the school's format.
- ► Keep it up to date.
- ► Remember that visual appearance is important (e.g., make sure there are no typos and that the same format is used for all bibliographic entries).
- ► Use the CV as a guide for "readiness" for next steps in career development.

eliminating them. For example, you may reach a point where you delete all regional presentations, leaving only national and international presentations, or include abstracts only from the past 5 years. Although you cherish the thought of "a big CV," packing it with redundant or not-so-important entries (such as the names of lectures you give repetitively, local presentations, and local committees) may obscure your important accomplishments so they are missed.

Develop and Maintain an Educator's Portfolio Even If It Is Not Required

Why Create an Educator's Portfolio?

Educator's portfolios are increasingly being used in the medical school promotion process. In 1990, five medical schools used educator's portfolios in the promotion process; in 2003, 76 schools used them (1). An educator's portfolio is a useful way to document educational contributions for purposes of helping to guide career development.

What Is an Educator's Portfolio?

This systematic collection of information documents accomplishment in the domain of education. It should include multiple sources of information to document quantity, quality, and impact and should be collected over time. Documentation of educational contributions includes five areas: teaching (quality/quantity), curriculum development (quality/quantity), advising and mentoring activities (quality/quantity), education leadership/administration (quality/quantity), and assessment of learner performance (quality/quantity) (2). The document should focus on the quantity, quality, and scholarship resulting from your teaching activities. Common educator's portfolio elements include the following:

- Statement of purpose of preparing the educator's portfolio
- Percentage of time devoted to educational activities
- Reflective statement of teaching philosophy
- Documentation of educational contributions, divided into categories

Regarding this last point, all educator's portfolios include the direct teaching category. Separate learner levels if you teach at multiple levels (for example, medical students, graduate students, residents/fellows, peers) to document quantity. In addition, faculty may contribute to additional categories. Each category should include documentation of contributions (quantity and quality), and evidence of engagement in the academic community (taking a scholarly approach or engaging in scholarship related to the activity).

What Should Be Included?

An educator's portfolio should be as long as necessary to paint a picture of the domains, quantity, and quality of your work. There is no set page limit, but an educator's portfolio should not be longer than necessary to present important information concisely and completely. For most, this can be accomplished in approximately five to seven pages (Box 5-3).

Attaching supporting documents as appendices to supplement or illustrate the body of the educator's portfolio is optional. However, an educator's portfolio without appendices should stand on its own. Members of the promotion and tenure committee are inundated with large packets of information on faculty members under consideration for promotion or tenure. Do not include an exhaustive list of all lectures and presentations given. Of note, the educator's portfolio format may vary between institutions, and an institution may prefer the document be prepared in a standardized format particular to that institution. Excellent examples of documentation in each of the five categories are available (1) (Box 5-4).

Knowing what to include in the portfolio prompts the question, What is the definition of "scholarly work"? All faculty should strive to take a scholarly approach to their educational activities by drawing from and building on the work of others, with the goal of improving their educational work, whether teaching, curriculum development, or other activities. Faculty with a special interest in education should also engage in scholarship related to educational activities. Like all scholarly work, educational scholarship must be presented in a format that allows it to be reviewed by peers for quality and made public for others to use (Box 5-5).

Educational scholarly works may be peer-reviewed by multiple venues:

- Publications: Journals such as *Academic Medicine, Medical Education, Medical Teacher, Evaluation and the Health Professions,* and *Teaching and Learning in Medicine* or specialty journals that publish educational work (such as the

---

Box 5-3. Recommended Content Categories of an Educator's Portfolio

► Direct teaching (quantity)

► Assessment of learner performance (quality)

► Mentoring/advising (quantity and quality)

► Curriculum development (a scholarly approach)

► Educational administration/leadership

Box 5-4. Assessment Domains and "Evidence" of Accomplishments

► Quantity
  • Narrative or tabular display of who, what, when, where, how much, how many
► Quality
  • Summary of student and, if available, peer evaluations
  • Comparative data to show change in your evaluations over time or your performance compared with peers who teach in the same setting
  • Invitations of presentations outside department or school
  • Repeat invitations to present to the same group or course
  • Teaching awards, including criteria
► Engagement with the community (scholarly approach and scholarship)
  • A scholarly approach requires drawing from relevant literature and best practices in the field; using this information to improve one's teaching; assessing outcomes (e.g., student learning), and using the results to continuously improve teaching, curriculum development, and so forth.
  • Scholarship builds on a scholarly approach and involves contributing to, not just learning from, best practices and educational literature. Scholarship is demonstrated by creating an educational product that is peer-reviewed and publicly disseminated for others to learn from or build upon.

Journal of General Internal Medicine or *Journal of the American Medical Association*).
• Peer-reviewed repositories, such as MedEdPORTAL, Health Education Assets Library (HEAL), Multimedia Educational Resource for Learning and Online Teaching (MERLOT), or Family Medicine Digital Library

- Peer-reviewed presentations, such as the Association of American Medical College's Group on Educational Affairs

A school's decision to embrace these standards—quantity, quality, and engagement with the education community—should occur in parallel with development of an infrastructure to support educators. This includes sustained faculty development for educators, access to educational resources and journals, peer review mechanisms, and consultation and support specific to each activity category (2). Take advantage of the school's resources, such as the following:

- Academy of Medical Educators
- Faculty development office and resources
- Educational experts on your campus or elsewhere
- Grant-writing assistance
- Curriculum development committees

❖ Developing a "Reputation"

Most medical schools require faculty to document a regional reputation for promotion to associate professor and a national or international reputation for promotion to professor (Box 5-6). Start by becoming an excellent, highly regarded educator at your own school. Get involved in relevant institutional activities as you develop your niche locally. Express interest in, and take advantage of, opportunities to become involved in department, school, and institutional activities and committees that help foster your career development. However, realize it is easy to become involved in too many time-consuming activities that are not congruent with your professional development. It may be difficult or inappropriate to tell your division chief or department chair "no," but avoid over-volunteering or acquiescing too quickly if you have concerns.

Returning to our two faculty members:

Dr. "All Over" seems to excel in volunteering. Her CV includes pages of committees and she is only an assistant professor. Yet, these committees are "all over" and do not indicate a clear career pathway. Committee work may have precluded time for activities that would have been more academically productive.

Dr. "Straight Track" does not really place much of a premium on committees. She has been on several education-related committees, which were congruent with her career desires, but has avoided nonfocused assignments. She has become well known and recognized in her own school as an excellent teacher. She has been invit-

---

Box 5-5. Three "Ps" of Educational Scholarship

Product

Peer review, to assess quality

Public, for others to learn from or build upon

---

ed to speak at regional meetings, where she performed well, result-
ing in additional invitations to speak. She has attended educational
leadership conferences, become known, and has collaborated on
several publications related to teaching. She is now serving on sev-
eral Association of American Medical College (AAMC) committees,
including a graduate medical education (GME) committee.

A clinician-educator who aspires to leadership roles in education should seek a variety of opportunities, such as:

- Teaching medical students in years 1 and 2 (teaching clinical skills and small-group facilitation, advising, mentoring)
- Giving lectures or conferences for students and house staff in your department
- Speaking in other departments in the institution when invited
- Volunteering to give Grand Rounds (consider an educational topic)
- Seeking "two-fers" by converting a lecture into a workshop, abstract, or manuscript
- Accepting invitations to speak at regional or national meetings
- Attending regional and national educational meetings and participating in an "education track" at specialty meetings
- Developing collaborative relationships with educators to improve your educational program and becoming involved in scholarly work related to education

See Box 5-6 for tips on expanding your reputation.

❖ Accepting Opportunities as an Educator

As soon as you realize a strong career interest in education, start working on projects that are related to education. For example, try collaborating with faculty who are engaged in activities to which you aspire (such as a clerkship or program director). Read the relevant literature and learn about similar programs nationally so that you learn the "state of the art" of

---

Box 5-6. Developing a "Reputation"

▸ Review your CV for evidence that you are known outside your department; set goals for extending your reputation

▸ Let your wishes be known. Tell your division chief or department chair whether you want to be nominated to attend a particular meeting (e.g., Association of American Medical Colleges Early Career Women in Medicine conference, regional Group on Educational Affairs meeting)

▸ Introduce yourself at meetings. Seek colleagues as mentors and collaborators.

▸ Attend a meeting the first time just to learn; by the second time you attend, try to be on the program or a committee

---

your area of emerging interest. Soon you will be an asset to your colleagues and will contribute not only a fresh perspective but also new directions and ideas related to educational projects. Again, take the lead. Suggest an idea for improving a course or program, design an assessment or outcome plan, and evaluate the result of your intervention. By doing this, you are taking a scholarly approach that will generate data to improve the program and, potentially, to be presented at least locally. Seek colleagues with similar interests and expand your project to include another department or school. Participate in the "educator track" at noneducation meetings (such as educator sessions at a meeting of the Society of General Internal Medicine or American College of Physicians) to begin building a network of colleagues with similar interests to foster further collaboration. Strive to present your work at meetings. Expanding your sphere of colleagues and collaborators will pave the pathway to leadership in medical education. Great teachers are recognized locally, but great educators may become innovators who are recognized nationally. Think strategically. Dr. "All Over" rarely does! See Table 5-1 for clinical and educational resources for junior faculty.

❖ Faculty Attrition and Why It Is Undesirable

Why Faculty Leave

Faculty members are the most valuable resource of any successful academic medical center. Yet, recent data indicate that 42% of current academic faculty are considering leaving academic medicine, and not just their cur-

Table 5-1. Clinical/Education Professional Associations and Resources for Junior Faculty

Organization	Web Address
American College of Physicians	www.acponline.org
Harvard Macy Institute	www.harvardmacy.org/programs/overview.aspx
Association of American Medical Colleges	www.aamc.org
Association of Directors for Medical Student Education in Psychiatry	www.admsep.org
Association of Professors of Gynecology and Obstetrics	www.apgo.org/home
Association of Program Directors in Internal Medicine	www.im.org/About/AllianceSites/APDIM
Association for Surgical Education	www.surgicaleducation.com
Clerkship Directors in Internal Medicine	www.im.org/cdim
Consortium of Neurology Clerkship Directors	www.aan.com/go/education/clerkship/consortium
Council on Medical Student Education in Pediatrics	www.comsep.org
Central Group on Educational Affairs	www.aamc.org/members/gea/regions/cgea/start.htm http://shaw.medlib.iupui.edu/cgea/cgea.html
Northeast Group on Educational Affairs	www.aamc.org/members/gea/regions/negea/start.htm
Southern Group on Educational Affairs	www.aamc.org/members/gea/regions/sgea/start.htm www.mededu.miami.edu/SGEA
Western Group on Educational Affairs	www.aamc.org/members/gea/regions/wgea/start.htm
Society of Teachers of Family Medicine	www.stfm.org
Society for Executive Leadership in Academic Medicine	www.selaminternational.org
Executive Leadership in Academic Medicine	www.drexelmed.edu/Home/OtherPrograms/ExecutiveLeadershipinAcademicMedicine.aspx

rent institution, altogether (3). The reasons faculty consider such a major career change include difficulty balancing life and work, lack of recognition of clinical work and teaching in promotions considerations, absence of faculty development programs (3, 4), and inadequate mentoring (3).

The loss of faculty from academics has at least two negative consequences: an undesired career change for the faculty member and a significant replacement cost for the institution. The cost of replacing a single faculty member in an academic institution is estimated to be approximately $125,000 to $250,000 (5, 6). Attrition may be caused by many factors; one of these, as mentioned above, is dissatisfaction with work–life balance. Bickel (7) has written:

> Among the most disadvantageous structures and practices are tenure and promotion policies that force unnecessary choices, either advancement or family, during the decade following residency training when most female and male physicians have young children. Since female physicians tend to be most productive between the ages of 50 and 60, they do not fit the career trajectory assumed by promotion policies, and they often do not strive for promotion to senior rank as a result.

This inequity has contributed to inadequate progress in women's leadership in academic medicine. Nationally, women make up only 14% of tenured faculty, 12% of full professors, and 8% of medical school department chairs (7).

Imbalance of life and work, lack of recognition of clinical work and teaching in promotion considerations, and a lack of mentoring are foundations of professional dissatisfaction. Faculty development programs address these issues proactively.

The Balancing Act

There are strategies junior faculty may employ to balance career and family responsibilities in academic medicine, in addition to the short-term remedy of parental leave. These strategies include part-time appointment, non–tenure-track selection, tenure rollback ("stop-the-clock"), and a prorated tenure track option. The availability of these options varies widely among medical schools (8). Even if your school does not offer a specific strategy, present a plan that you think would work for you. This is an expected part of negotiating with your division chief or chair. The worst that can happen is that your recommendation will be declined.

The literature addressing work–life balance is recent, beginning in the mid-1990s. Tips from a prominent female physician successful in the balancing act (9) provide guidance about the importance of career planning and "taking the lead":

- Set personal and professional goals and plot a course toward achieving those goals. Look in the mirror and ask yourself, Who am I and who what do I want to be? Do I want to be a department chair? Do I want to have a national reputation? Do I want to be a parent? Do I want to work full- or part-time? Do I want to do research? Do I want to live in a rural or urban area? There is no right or wrong answer to any of these questions; they are personal decisions.
- Once you have established your goals, surround yourself with people who share these goals to include your life partner, professional colleagues, and mentors. To achieve balance among the various responsibilities of family and career, it is essential to have competent and trustworthy support people, such as secretaries, technicians, and child care providers, to whom you can delegate responsibility.
- Strive for geographic proximity—that is, have all your activities close together. Establish priorities in your life, being careful not to sacrifice personal priorities over professional priorities because such decisions will more likely lead to regret.
- Get up 1 to 2 hours earlier than you have to each morning. That extra time in the morning, when your mind is fresh, allows you to complete tasks and arrive at work feeling like you have already accomplished something. Use this time to attack some significant project.
- Take care of yourself. If your health fails, it is a stress on the entire family. Maintain a sense of humor. The most frustrating or irritating situations at work or home, when reframed, can also be the funniest.

Faculty Development Programs

General Overview

Academic institutions increasingly have formalized processes and resources for mentoring to develop the careers of junior faculty (see *Mentoring in Academic Medicine*, another book in the *Teaching Medicine* series [10]). Definitions of faculty development include the following:

- A planned program to prepare institutions and faculty members for their academic roles, including teaching, research, administration, writing/scholarship, and career management. Offerings include the following focus areas: 1) professional,

including individual scholarship; 2) instructional; 3) leadership; and 4) organizational (such as time management) (11).
- Six types of career development activities: 1) organizational
strategies, 2) fellowships, 3) comprehensive local programs,
4) workshops and seminars, 5) continuing medical education,
and 6) individual activities (12).
- An orientation to the academy that includes faculty roles and
responsibilities and the values, norms, and expectations of the
university; ongoing mentoring and development in clinical
and research domains (13).

Although these examples provide a conceptual basis for distinguishing
among programs, actual programs often contain elements of more than
one type. Programs vary in focus, content, and resources. All aspire to
assist faculty toward planned and well-executed professional growth. Some
focus on educational attainment (such as educators' academies), some on
research (such as a junior faculty research colloquium), and some on
broader administrative and executive leadership development.

Outcomes of Career Development Programs
Career development program outcomes are difficult to assess, but for the
most part, they appear to be successful. One way to conceptualize the outcomes of a program is to use the four levels identified by Kirkpatrick (14):
- Level 1: the participants' reaction to the program (such as satisfaction)
- Level 2: the learning resulting from the program—changes in
knowledge, attitudes, and skills
- Level 3: behavior change—performance of learned skills back
in the job setting
- Level 4: organizational impacts (such as better patient care
and job retention)

Kirkpatrick points out the value at each level but encourages evaluators to strive for higher levels. The following are examples of successful
career development programs.

A primary care faculty development program at the University of
Wisconsin featured a year-long series of five weekend workshops focusing
on preparing preceptors to teach curricular areas relatively new to medical
education, such as evidence-based medicine, teaching skills, technology
tools, doctor–patient communication, quality improvement, and advocacy.
Program participants thought the program resulted in improved teaching
and clinical skills; intrapersonal growth; and increased self-confidence,
interdisciplinary networking, and mentoring (15).

In 2000, the Vanderbilt School of Medicine established the institutionally funded Vanderbilt Physician-Scientist Development program to provide centralized oversight and financial support for physician-scientist career development. In 2002, Vanderbilt developed the National Institutes of Health (NIH)–funded Vanderbilt Clinical Research Scholars program using a similar model of centralized oversight. Physician-scientists who entered these programs from 2000 through 2006 were compared with Vanderbilt physician-scientists who received NIH career development funding during the same period without participating in programs. Seventy-five percent of the Vanderbilt Physician-Scientist Development program and 60% of Vanderbilt Clinical Research Scholars participants achieved individual career award funding at a younger age than the comparison cohort. This shift to career development award funding at a younger age among those program scholars was accompanied by a 2.6-fold increase in the number of new NIH K awards funded and a rate of growth in K-award dollars at Vanderbilt that outpaced the national rate of growth in K-award funding (16).

In 2000, only 20% (16) of 76 medical schools surveyed had offices devoted to career development, and no school had a comprehensive faculty development system (17). According to Kanter (18), several ingredients are necessary to create workplace empowerment: access to opportunities, information, support, resources, and relationships. Achieving workplace empowerment leads to retention, job satisfaction, and improved performance. These concepts, developed to describe work in corporations, were tested with nursing faculty; a positive relationship between work empowerment and job satisfaction, retention, and work performance was demonstrated (19, 20).

Career development programs, which emphasize mentoring, career planning, performance feedback, establishing colleague networks and connectedness and acculturation to one's school and university, are effective interventions that improve faculty satisfaction, productivity, institutional loyalty, and retention. Even when fully funded to serve hundreds of faculty members, they are also less expensive than the costs of faculty turnover. Unfortunately, faculty development offices and programs are underdeveloped or underused in many medical schools (3) (Box 5-7).

Developing a Successful Mentoring Relationship

Why Seek Mentoring?

Mentoring in Academic Medicine (10) explores in detail the importance of mentoring, especially for junior faculty. Several recent studies have identified benefits of mentoring programs for career development in academia. In one study, faculty who participated in a collaborative, peer-based mentoring program were more likely to decide to remain in academic medicine (3). A recent

---

Box 5-7. Faculty Development

▶ Identify faculty development options available at your school, and take advantage of them.

▶ Attend workshops offered by a faculty or career development center.

▶ Strive to become a member of an academy of medical educators if your school has one.

▶ Identify mentors from your institution or elsewhere—you may have several for different aspects of your career development.

▶ Be proactive: Don't wait to be asked if you want to participate; volunteer, sign up, express interest.

---

study of clinician-researchers demonstrated a decrease in faculty attrition through the use of formal mentoring programs supported by the institution (21). Yet, a study of faculty vitality at the University of Minnesota Medical School found that only 52% of faculty felt they had a network of supportive colleagues in their own department, and fewer than half reported having even one "weekly substantive teaching or research conversation" with colleagues (4). A meta-analysis of mentoring programs found that less than 50% of medical students and less than 20% of faculty members had a mentor. Yet, mentorship was reported to have an important influence on personal development, career guidance, career choice, and research productivity, including publication and grant success. Mentoring is perceived as an important part of academic medicine, but the evidence to support this perception is not strongly literature based. Practical recommendations on mentoring in medicine that are evidence-based require studies using more rigorous methods, addressing contextual issues, and using cross-disciplinary approaches (22).

How to Seek Mentoring
While finding a good mentor might seem intuitive, it is not an easy task, particularly for young faculty intent on launching an academic career. Mentors need to be senior enough and established in their own career to be able to effectively assist a junior colleague. The mentor and protégé should share interests and a mutual vision of the desired goals of mentorship. Effective mentoring relationships may be hard to achieve if they are geographically separated. However, being at different schools does not preclude developing an effective relationship. Brilliant scholars are not inher-

ently brilliant mentors. Some are too busy, have little interest, and may even be ineffective in their interpersonal skills for the task of mentoring junior colleagues. Of course, this is not a one-way street; the protégé must also possess key attributes and aspirations that will ensure that the mentoring relationship is successful (for example, being enthusiastic, working hard, asking good questions, not missing appointments).

While an ideal mentor may be in the department or in another department on campus, it is also important to seek mentors outside the institution. Distant mentors provide a different perspective, and they can be particularly helpful with "the big picture." In addition, they may be receptive to a junior colleague from another department or school whom they could invite to participate in panels and related academic opportunities. Outside mentors, collaborators, and colleagues are key to becoming a national leader in medical education.

❖ Leadership Opportunities in Academic Medicine

As discussed in chapter 1 of this book, leadership does not emanate from an innate or endowed skill set. In academics, leadership and academic advancement typically result because of academic accomplishments, rather than administrative experience. For example, a department chair is likely to have obtained his or her position on the basis of academic rather than administrative success. This means it is important to establish sound academic credentials beginning early in one's career. Leadership attributes of chairs include being a motivator; being knowledgeable in conflict management, negotiations, finances, and academic organization; being a mentor and educator; having the desire to lead; being a good communicator; tolerating role ambiguity; and being a visionary with the ability to plan strategically (23).

If you aspire to a leadership position, seek opportunities to prepare for the next step in your career. As a junior faculty member seeking a career as an educator, become an exemplary teacher, build your academic credentials, and develop administrative and leadership experience incrementally. Begin by taking advantage of first-step leadership roles, such as becoming chair of a committee, becoming a course director, or developing a project (for example, curriculum) that involves several people. Then, seek opportunities to develop leadership skills within your institution. These may be as simple as attending workshops on topics such as leading a meeting or negotiation.

When you attend regional or national meetings, meet people to help form a network of colleagues who share common interests and can serve in mentoring roles to assist in your skill set development. The principles for success as a residency program director also apply to faculty aspiring to become clerkship directors or associate dean for curriculum. If you aspire to be or are a clerkship director, become involved in your discipline's clerkship director organization (for example, Clerkship Directors in Internal Medicine) and aim to get on the program at national or regional AAMC meetings. The Group on Educational Affairs is an excellent venue for peer-reviewed presentations, workshops, and meeting experts. The American College of Physicians' national and chapter meetings are valuable opportunities to present educational work resulting from collaboration with students or residents. As you learn the structure of an organization, identify a committee on which you would like to serve and let your interest be known. Plan to attend a particular meeting once just to learn, and try to be on the program the next time you attend. Seek opportunities for special training, but do not underestimate the value of long-term mentoring relationships and learning by "trial and error." Connections you make locally and nationally will help position you to participate in a formal leadership program. Table 5-2 shows examples of roadmaps for career development.

After developing an early track record of leadership skills, seek external opportunities that are geared toward your interests. Several programs are available, including the following formal training opportunities for which data are available to support their value:

- The National Institute for Program Director Development (NIPDD), begun in 1994, is a 9-month fellowship that provides instruction, education, and formative experiences for family medicine physician educators to hone the knowledge, skills, and attitudes to be effective leaders as directors of residency programs. The knowledge domain focuses on the accreditation process, trainee certification requirements, institutional GME and non-GME policies, federal guidelines for GME, and trainee assistance resources (24).
- The Harvard Macy Institute Fellowship program, established with a grant from the Josiah Macy Jr. Foundation, is designed to advance health care education through professional development. The major objective of the programs is to help participants develop the strategies and skills required to lead organizational change and drive innovation. The program combines the themes of learning and teaching, curriculum, evaluation, leadership, and information technology (25, 26).
- The Robert Wood Johnson Clinical Scholars Program trains young physicians to be scholarly research leaders in health services research and policy (27). Seventy-five percent of the nearly 1000 graduates since 1972 have taken academic jobs right out of the program.

Table 5-2. Sample Steps to Success as a Leader in Medical Education

Desired Position	Activities to Do			Desired Outcomes	
	This Year	Next 2–3 Years		Products	Collaboration Opportunities
ICM director (usually a year 1 and 2 course)	Participate in teaching and learn new teaching skills (e.g., lecture, small-group leader)	Volunteer to help with ICM curriculum development, improve assessment; attend/participate in CDIM or AAMC		MedEdPORTAL peer-reviewed product; work adopted by school, other department	Seek collaborators at national meetings (e.g., GEA, CDIM)
Clerkship director	Become ICM director or play key role in ICM or standardized patient program; strive to attend CDIM meeting	Conduct studies of curriculum; become an important contributor to the clerkship; volunteer for extra activities		Peer-reviewed product related to clerkship; appointment as associate clerkship director	Seek collaborators at meetings, especially CDIM; become committee member
Program director	Be a member of resident interview committee; become a "most effective" in ACGME; become member; learn RRC standards	Attend and become active in APDIM; become active in ACGME; become involved with work to meet ACGME competency-based objectives		Success of program (years of RRC accreditation); high ABIM pass rates	Chair national committee

continued

Table 5-2. Sample Steps to Success as a Leader in Medical Education (continued)

Desired Position	Activities to Do		Desired Outcomes	
	This Year	Next 2–3 Years	Products	Collaboration Opportunities
Vice-chair, education	Express interest in educational administration; strive to become an important education leader in department	Chair (or co-chair) education committees in department and school; become the "go to" person for education in department	Engage in educational scholarly work related to ICM, clerkship, and/or residency; produce 2 peer-reviewed products/year	Use national meetings as opportunity to identify collaborators and mentors; seek educational grant funding
Associate dean for curriculum	Express interest in educational administration (i.e., curriculum committee); strive to become an important education leader at the school level	Become a key member of curriculum and other school-level education committees; strive to become chair; seek collaborators in other departments and schools; become active in GEA; become a "go to" person for education in school; express interest in position	Become a "regular" on regional and national GEA programs; be "prime mover" behind an educational advancement in school	Use national meetings as opportunity to identify collaborators and mentors; seek educational grant funding

AAMC = Association of American Colleges; ABIM = American Board of Internal Medicine; ACGME = Accreditation Council for Graduate Medical Education; APDIM = Association of Program Directors in Internal Medicine; CDIM = Clerkship Directors in Internal Medicine; GEA = Group on Educational Affairs; ICM = Introduction to Clinical Medicine; RRC = Residency Review Committee.

- The Executive Leadership in Academic Medicine (ELAM) is a year-long program designed to help women develop the professional and personal skills required to lead and manage in today's complex healthcare environment, with special attention to the unique challenges facing women in leadership positions. The program has been successful, as indicated by a recent study comparing accomplishments of ELAM fellows to matched AAMC members and nonmembers (28).
- The American College of Physicians developed its Leadership Enhancement and Development (LEAD) Program in 2008. The program is designed for internists early in their careers and offers a variety of activities designed to provide participants with the skills, resources, and experiences necessary to become effective leaders in any setting (www.acponline.org/education_recertification/resources/leadership_development).

❖ If It All Goes Wrong: Rescuing and Restarting a Career

Not many people give much thought to this aspect of an academic career—and even fewer write about it. Nevertheless, it is important to acknowledge that mistakes and career setbacks can, and do, happen. People experience professional disagreements, and professional relationships may not evolve as expected. For example, your boss and you are like oil and water, a mentor–protégé relationship doesn't blossom, the service you are working on is shut down and you have to start all over again, or the department is financially in crisis and you put your career objectives on hold to help with more clinical work. A desire to develop a new career trajectory is not necessarily a bad thing or an indication of failure. After success on a given trajectory for a number of years, one might want to learn new skills. For Dr. "All Over," it may be that she is taking on too many tasks and is unable to succeed and finish any. For Dr. "Straight Track," it might be seeking new challenges. Whatever the reason, some things just don't evolve as planned, and you need to be prepared for this.

Should you find yourself in an untenable position, try to avoid getting unduly frustrated. Rather, review the situation in which you find yourself. Identify and learn from the causes so you can avoid them in the future. Talking with senior colleagues and mentors outside or even inside your institution can be helpful. Often, they can provide a more objective analysis of your situation than you can. Avoid making decisions in anger or in haste. While you may end up leaving your institution, the decision should be the result of a carefully planned and contemplated strategy. Alternatively, you may choose not to leave but rather pursue a different career trajectory at your institution. List the pros and cons of each option that you have at this stage and share this list (confidentially) with your mentor or senior colleague. A midcareer "crisis" does not have to be a "crisis"; instead, it can be used as an opportunity for introspection and regrouping. Five or 10 years from now, decisions made today could be turning points toward a successful career as a medical educator.

❖ Conclusion

Although not to be taken for granted, when it occurs, career advancement is highly satisfying, especially in medical education, where the educator truly has a love and gift for teaching. It is important, however, that an aspiring leader in education takes care of his or her career. Careers don't just happen. It is important to pursue one's career in a thoughtful and progressive manner. Avoid being Dr. "All Over," and strive to emulate Dr. "Straight Track." Be balanced, remain open to suggestions and opportunities, and consider the bottom-line tips described in Box 5-8.

Box 5-8. Tips for Educational Career Advancement

1. If you aspire to a career with education as a "centerpiece," become an excellent teacher.

2. Develop career goals early on and select the appropriate clinical track based on what you want out of your career. The "right" track is the track on which you will be successful.

3. Know expectations for promotion: Read your faculty handbook and promotion and tenure committee guidelines carefully and consult with knowledgeable people to be sure you understand how your activities will be interpreted.

4. Identify individuals within your institution (or others) with similar career trajectories. Are these people you can develop formal or informal mentoring relationships with?

5. Take advantage of opportunities. Accept positions, appointments, and speaking engagements in line with your career goals.

continued

6. Document your progress. Regularly update your CV and educator's profile. Your calendar can be an excellent resource for recalling specific times and dates.

7. Learn to control your time. Studies suggest that work–life balance has more to do with how well an individual schedules than the actual job itself.

8. Become involved in scholarly work early—choose projects in which you have a sustained interest and build upon them.

9. Take advantage of career, teaching, and education skills development programs at your institution; negotiate to participate in similar programs outside your institution.

10. Have the courage to discuss your career desires with your division chief or department chair. Be proactive in career planning; don't just do what you are asked to do.

11. Find "your" organization and become active (e.g., Clerkship Directors in Internal Medicine, Association of American Colleges, National Board of Medical Examiners).

12. Network within "your" organization to establish a support network and future collaborators.

13. Continue your own education as a learner to become a better educator.

14. Recognize, learn from, and, most important, appreciate opportunities given to you by your mentors. Translate what you learn into opportunities you can give to your learners and to others who also may hope to advance their careers.

REFERENCES

1. **Simpson D, Hafler J, Brown D, Wilkerson L.** Documentation systems for educators seeking academic promotion in U.S. medical schools. Acad Med. 2004;79:783-90.
2. **Simpson D, Fincher RM, Hafler JP, Irby DM, Richards BF, Rosenfeld GC, et al.** Advancing educators and education by defining the components and evidence associated with educational scholarship. Med Educ. 2007;41:1002-9.
3. **Lowenstein SR, Fernandez G, Crane LA.** Medical school faculty discontent: prevalence and predictors of intent to leave academic careers. BMC Med Educ. 2007;7:37.
4. **Bland CJ, Seaquist E, Pacala JT, Center B, Finstad D.** One school's strategy to assess and improve the vitality of its faculty. Acad Med. 2002;77:368-76.
5. **Pololi LH, Knight SM, Dennis K, Frankel RM.** Helping medical school faculty realize their dreams: an innovative, collaborative mentoring program. Acad Med. 2002;77:377-84.

6. **Waldman JD, Kelly F, Arora S, Smith HL.** The shocking cost of turnover in health care. Health Care Manage Rev. 2004;29:2-7.

7. **Bickel J, Wara D, Atkinson BF, Cohen LS, Dunn M, Hostler S, et al; Association of American Medical Colleges Project Implementation Committee.** Increasing women's leadership in academic medicine: report of the AAMC Project Implementation Committee. Acad Med. 2002;77:1043-61.

8. **Fox G, Schwartz A, Hart KM.** Work-family balance and academic advancement in medical schools. Acad Psychiatry. 2006;30:227-34.

9. **Carnes M.** Balancing family and career: advice from the trenches. Ann Intern Med. 1996;125:618-20.

10. **Humphrey H, ed.** Mentoring in Academic Medicine. Philadelphia: ACP Pr; 2010.

11. **Bland CJ, Schmitz CC, Stritter FT, Henry RC, Alusie JJ.** Successful Faculty in Academic Medicine: Essential Skills and How to Acquire Them. New York: Springer; 1990.

12. **Ullian JA, Stritter FT.** Types of faculty development programs. Fam Med. 1997;29:237-41.

13. **Wilkerson L, Irby DM.** Strategies for improving teaching practices: a comprehensive approach to faculty development. Acad Med. 1998;73:387-96.

14. **Kirkpatrick DL.** Evaluating Training Programs. San Francisco: Berrett-Koehler; 1994.

15. **Gjerde CL, Hla KM, Kokotailo PK, Anderson B.** Long-term outcomes of a primary care faculty development program at the University of Wisconsin. Fam Med. 2008;40:579-84.

16. **Brown AM, Morrow JD, Limbird LE, Byrne DW, Gabbe SG, Balser JR, et al.** Centralized oversight of physician-scientist faculty development at Vanderbilt: early outcomes. Acad Med. 2008;83:969-75.

17. **Morahan PS, Gold JS, Bickel J.** Status of faculty affairs and faculty development offices in U.S. medical schools. Acad Med. 2002;77:398-401.

18. **Kanter RM.** Men and Women of the Corporation. New York: Basic Books; 1993.

19. **Roche JP, Lamoureux E, Teehan T.** A partnership between nursing education and practice: using an empowerment model to retain new nurses. J Nurs Adm. 2004;34:26-32.

20. **Sarmiento TP, Laschinger HK, Iwasiw C.** Nurse educators' workplace empowerment, burnout, and job satisfaction: testing Kanter's theory. J Adv Nurs. 2004;46:134-43.

21. **Reynolds CF 3rd, Pilkonis PA, Kupfer DJ, Dunn L, Pincus HA.** Training future generations of mental health researchers: devising strategies for tough times. Acad Psychiatry. 2007;31:152-9.

22. **Sambunjak D, Straus SE, Marusic A.** Mentoring in academic medicine: a systematic review. JAMA. 2006;296:1103-15.

23. **Buckley PF.** Reflections on leadership as chair of a department of psychiatry. Acad Psychiatry. 2006;30:309-14.

24. **Boulware DW.** The subspecialty fellowship training program director: essentials and expectations. Am J Med. 2002;112:686-8.

25. **Steinert Y, Mann K, Centeno A, Dolmans D, Spencer J, Gelula M, et al.** A systematic review of faculty development initiatives designed to improve teaching effectiveness in medical education: BEME Guide No. 8. Med Teach. 2006;28:497-526.

26. **Armstrong EG, Doyle J, Bennett NL.** Transformative professional development of physicians as educators: assessment of a model. Acad Med. 2003;78:702-8.

27. **Kalet AL, Fletcher KE, Ferdman DJ, Bickell NA.** Defining, navigating, and negotiating success: the experiences of mid-career Robert Wood Johnson Clinical Scholar women. J Gen Intern Med. 2006;21:920-5.

28. **Dannels SA, Yamagata H, McDade SA, Chuang YC, Gleason KA, McLaughlin JM, et al.** Evaluating a leadership program: a comparative, longitudinal study to assess the impact of the Executive Leadership in Academic Medicine (ELAM) Program for Women. Acad Med. 2008;83:488-95.

6

What Do Leaders Need to Know About Curriculum Planning?

David E. Kern, MD, MPH, FACP

Patricia A. Thomas, MD, FACP

A cademic medical institutions have been entrusted by society to provide leadership in the health care of the public, the education of health professionals, and the advancement of medical knowledge through research. Leadership in health professional education requires the development and maintenance of educational programs that meet the needs of patients, health care practitioners, and society. Accreditation bodies for undergraduate, graduate, and continuing medical education in the United States have recognized this responsibility and require formal curricula that include goals, objectives, and explicitly articulated educational and evaluation strategies (1–3). There are increasing requirements, related to evaluation, to document the achievement of critical professional competencies by trainees (4).

To meet this public trust, those aspiring to be educational leaders at academic medical centers should develop their skills in curriculum development. As described in chapter 4 of this book, leaders (for example, deans or chairs) whose career path has not been in education, but who oversee educational leaders (for example, clerkship or program directors), should at least understand the principles of curriculum development so that they can choose, support, and counsel their educational leaders wisely.

KEY POINTS

- A systematic approach to curriculum development requires careful planning.
- Before a curriculum is developed, the definition of a successful outcome and ways in which that success will be documented should be established.
- This stepwise approach begins with determining your own program's needs and how these fit with any accreditation requirements.
- Teaching methods should match your learning objectives.
- Evaluation is an essential step of curriculum planning and includes several tasks.
- Collaborators and mentors are important components of the curriculum, as are resources and support.
- Curriculum planning can lead to dissemination and publication and can enable academic success and professional satisfaction.

❖ Planning a Curriculum

Definition of Curriculum

A curriculum can be defined as a planned educational experience. This definition encompasses a breadth of educational experiences, from one or more sessions on a specific subject to a year-long course, from a clinical rotation or clerkship to an entire training program. Certain underlying assumptions guide the approach to curricular planning for professional education (Box 6-1).

A Six-Step Approach to Curriculum Development

The approach to curriculum development discussed below derives from the generic approaches to curriculum development set forth by Taba (5), Tyler (6), Yura and Torres (7), and Sheets and colleagues (8), and from the work of McGaghie and coworkers (9) and Golden (10), who advocated the linking of curricula to health care needs. This six-step approach (Figure 6-1) is described in greater depth by Kern and colleagues (11).

Step 1: Problem Identification and General Needs Assessment
Most medical curricula address a health care need or other problem. Step 1 of curriculum development involves defining and critically analyzing that problem. It involves identifying whom the problem affects (patients, socie-

Box 6-1. Underlying Assumptions in Curricular Planning for Professional Education

- ► Educational programs have aims or goals, whether or not they are clearly articulated
- ► Medical educators have a professional and ethical obligation to meet the needs of their learners, patients, and society
- ► Medical educators should be held accountable for the outcomes of their interventions
- ► A logical, systematic approach to curriculum development will help achieve these ends

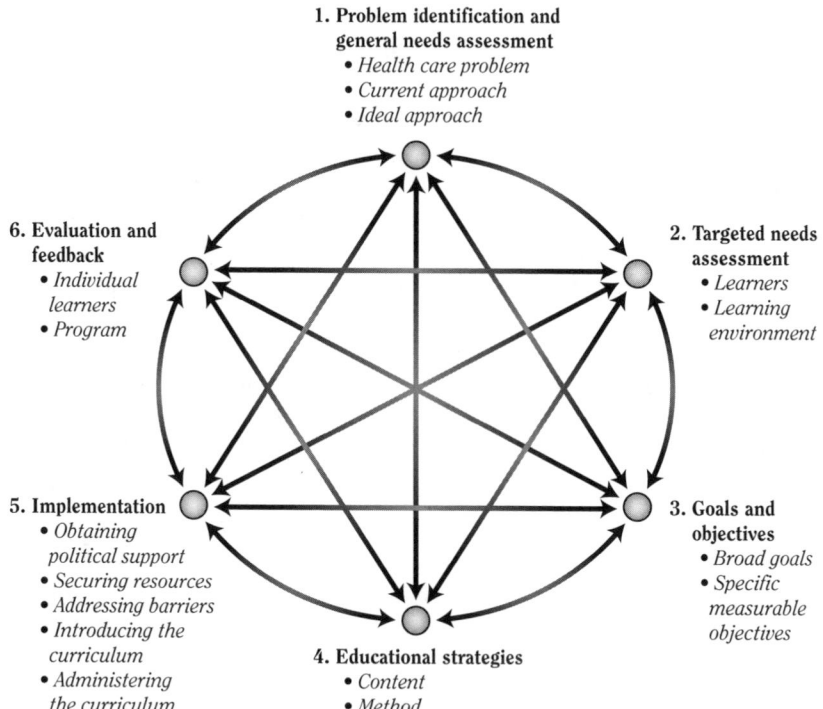

1. Problem identification and general needs assessment
- *Health care problem*
- *Current approach*
- *Ideal approach*

6. Evaluation and feedback
- *Individual learners*
- *Program*

2. Targeted needs assessment
- *Learners*
- *Learning environment*

5. Implementation
- *Obtaining political support*
- *Securing resources*
- *Addressing barriers*
- *Introducing the curriculum*
- *Administering the curriculum*

3. Goals and objectives
- *Broad goals*
- *Specific measurable objectives*

4. Educational strategies
- *Content*
- *Method*

Figure 6-1 A six-step approach to curriculum development. From Kern DE, Thomas PA, Hughes MT, eds. Curriculum Development for Medical Education: A Six-Step Approach. 2nd ed. Baltimore: Johns Hopkins Univ Pr; 2009. Reprinted with permission from the Johns Hopkins University Press.

ty, health care professionals, trainees) and how it affects them. The latter involves analyzing effects in areas such as clinical outcomes, quality of life, quality of health care, provision and use of health care and other resources, medical and nonmedical costs, patient and provider satisfaction, work and productivity, and societal function.

A complete problem identification also requires an analysis of the current approach of patients, practitioners, the medical education system, and society to addressing the health care need or problem. This is followed by identification of an ideal approach that describes how patients, practitioners, the medical education system, and society should be addressing the need. The difference between the ideal approach and the current approach represents a *general needs assessment*.

Adequate problem identification and general needs assessment always require the collection of relevant available information through an appropriate literature review. It also entails a search of other electronically available resources, such as educational clearinghouses and reports, guidelines, and requirements of professional and government organizations (12). When the available information about a problem is inadequate, the curriculum planners may wish to collect original data.

Problem identification and general needs assessment build a strong foundation for focusing a curriculum's goals and objectives, which in turn help to focus the curriculum's educational strategies and evaluation. It grounds the curriculum in the true needs of learners, patients, and society. It justifies dissemination of a successful curriculum by supporting its generalizability, and it provides a strong rationale that can help the curriculum planner obtain support for the curriculum (see step 5: Implementation).

Step 2: Targeted Needs Assessment
Because the needs of one's targeted learners and their own medical institution/learning environment may be different from the needs of learners and medical institutions in general, a *targeted needs assessment* is required.

Relevant information about one's targeted learners includes previous training and experience; already planned training and experience; existing knowledge, attitude, and skill; current performance or behaviors in practice; perceived deficiencies and learning needs; and learner preferences.

Relevant information about the targeted learning environment includes related existing curricula; characteristics of the hidden and informal curricula (13); specific enabling and reinforcing factors and barriers; resources; stakeholders in the curricular process; institutional politics; and factors related to institutional administration, policy, and procedure.

As with step 1, a targeted needs assessment requires the collection of relevant available information. Methods commonly used include an inventory of existing training experiences; informal discussions with stakeholders, such as learners, faculty, leaders of related curricula, and educational and other administrators; formal interviews; focus groups; questionnaires; observation of learners, learning environments, and existing curricula; review of existing test results or new testing; audits; and strategic planning sessions.

An appropriately performed targeted needs assessment refines step 1 by identifying the specific needs and preferences of targeted learners and other stakeholders and assessing the environment (including the hidden and informal curriculum) that will probably influence behavioral/performance outcomes. It permits tailoring one's educational intervention to specific needs. It increases efficiency and prevents duplication. Importantly, it builds relationships with key stakeholders. In conducting the targeted needs assessment, the curriculum planner is likely to identify potential and probable resources for the curricular effort, which will help to define the scope of the curriculum and shape strategies for step 5 (implementation).

By conducting thorough problem identifications and general and targeted needs assessments, curriculum planners build strong arguments for their curricula and ground them in true societal needs. Moreover, they build a foundation for prioritizing educational objectives and educational and evaluation strategies. In addition, they gain understanding of the particular needs of their targeted learners and institutions. A thorough identification of problems and needs assessment also may direct curriculum planners to potential resources and sources of institutional support. This same process sets the stage for the generalizability and dissemination of their curricula. If curriculum planners intend to publish their work, they will already have elements for the introduction and discussion for a manuscript. They will have become experts in their topic areas at their institution and beyond. The following shows how the first two steps are enacted:

Example: Curriculum planners for a musculoskeletal rotation for internal medicine residents at one institution developed the following arguments for their curriculum (14).

Problem Identification and General Needs Assessment: Musculoskeletal disorders are a common and major cause of disability. They account for 10% to 15% of all visits to primary care physicians. Patients desire quick access for assessment and management of these disorders. Although 90% of common nonsurgical orthopedic problems are thought to be manageable in the primary care setting, the musculoskeletal examination and procedures are often inadequately performed by primary care physicians at all levels of training. When primary care physicians are provided additional training in musculoskeletal conditions, their confidence in managing these conditions is increased and referrals are reduced. The Accreditation Council for Graduate Medical Education (ACGME), the Federated Council for Internal Medicine Task Force on the Internal Medicine Residency Curriculum, and the Council of Graduate Medical Education have recommended training in physical examination, diagnosis, and management of common musculoskeletal disorders (including joint aspiration and injection, when appropriate). The ACGME emphasized that education on musculoskeletal and sports injuries should occur in "settings representative of the environment in which graduates will eventually practice."

Targeted Needs Assessment: In exit interviews, focus group discussions, and a specially designed survey, residents identified musculoskeletal medicine as a gap in their internal medicine training. They reported barriers to training in musculoskeletal medicine, including a lack of a concentrated musculoskeletal clinic experience and a lack of exposure to general internal medicine preceptors with sufficient skills in musculoskeletal procedures. Training experiences in ambulatory rheumatology and orthopedics clinics did not provide the appropriate case mix. There was strong interest in a musculoskeletal curriculum that included supervised clinical practice and the appropriate mix of common musculoskeletal disorders.

Curriculum planners used this information to gain support for 1) establishing a musculoskeletal clinic staffed by residents and internal medicine preceptors with a special interest in musculoskeletal medicine, to which other primary care practitioners referred patients for diagnosis and injection, and 2) faculty development for the preceptors to gain additional expertise in dealing with and teaching about these disorders. The curriculum's clinical experience was supplemented by workshops and syllabi on common musculoskeletal disorders, such back, shoulder and knee pain.

Step 3: Goals and Objectives
A goal or objective is defined as an end toward which an effort is directed. In curriculum development, the term "goal" usually refers to a comprehen-

sive, expansive end that provides direction but is not specific enough to be measurable. By contrast, an objective is specific and measurable. A goal may encompass several specific, measurable objectives.

> *Example:* A goal of a gynecology curriculum for internal medicine residents might be that internal medicine residents develop the knowledge, attitudes, and skills necessary to diagnose, manage, and appropriately refer women who present to primary care settings with gynecologic needs or symptoms. A specific, measurable objective of the curriculum might be that by the end of the gynecology curriculum, each internal medicine resident will have demonstrated, at least once, the appropriate technique, as defined on a check sheet, for obtaining a Papanicolaou (Pap) smear and cervical cultures.

Objectives are important because they help to prioritize and direct the content for a curriculum, suggest what learning methods are appropriate, enable and direct evaluation, and permit clear communication to learners, faculty, and other stakeholders. They are also required by accrediting bodies such as the Liaison Committee on Medical Education (1), the ACGME (2), and the Accreditation Council for Continuing Medical Education (3).

Objectives can be classified as learner objectives, process objectives, or patient or health care outcome objectives. *Learner objectives* are divided into cognitive, affective, and psychomotor objectives. *Cognitive* objectives are further subdivided into lower-order cognitive or knowledge objectives, such as factual knowledge, and higher-order cognitive objectives, which include analysis and problem-solving. *Affective* objectives include attitudes, values, and role expectations; they are commonly called "attitudinal" objectives. *Psychomotor* objectives include both "skill" or "competence" objectives (the ability to perform a task) and "behavioral" or "performance" objectives (the incorporation of that skill into ongoing practice). *Process objectives* refer to objectives related to curricular implementation—for example, "Each resident will be observed once yearly in the medical housestaff practice doing a pelvic and Pap examination." *Patient or health care outcome objectives* refer to effects of a curricular intervention that extend beyond those delineated in learner and process objectives, such as patient outcomes or career choice. The term "outcome objective" is not consistently used, and learner cognitive, affective, and psychomotor objectives are sometimes called outcomes (knowledge, attitudinal, or skill outcomes). To avoid confusion, it is best to describe outcome objectives using precise language that includes the specific type of outcome that will be measured, such as a career or health outcome objective.

Writing objectives in specific, measurable terms that are clear and unambiguous to others is an acquired talent. A helpful guide is to include the following five elements in each objective: Who will do how much/how well of what by when. Applying these guidelines to the preceding example, we can see how that objective meets these criteria:

Example: By the end of the gynecology curriculum (by when), each internal medicine resident (who) will have demonstrated (will do), at least once (how much), the appropriate technique, as defined on a check sheet (how well), for obtaining a Pap smear and cervical cultures (what).

Content generally flows from the nouns in one's objectives, in this case the appropriate techniques for a Pap smear and cervical cultures. Educational methods are generally driven by the verbs in one's objectives. In this case, the verb indicates a skill or competence objective, the ability to obtain a Pap smear and cervical cultures using appropriate technique. When writing objectives, it is recommended that one use verbs that are open to fewer rather than more interpretations, such as "list", "define," or "describe" rather than "know"; "rate as valuable" rather than "appreciate"; "demonstrate" rather than "know how"; "incorporate into practice" rather than "internalize."

Because an important function of objectives is communication, curricular objectives need to be written in language that is clear and unambiguous to the intended reader; different versions of objectives may be required for different readers. For example, evaluators may require more detail in the objectives than learners, who may require more detail than overall program directors or funding agencies. An important step in developing clear objectives that achieve the right balance between specificity and readability is to have individuals naive to the curricular planning process read them and provide feedback until the objectives are understood in the manner intended.

Another challenge is limiting the number of curricular objectives. Usually, only a limited number are achievable within available resources. Even if one has bountiful resources, an exhaustive list of objectives can be overwhelming for learners and teachers alike. The problem identification and needs assessment can be used to prioritize the content and efficiently allocate available resources. Another tactic to keep the number of objectives manageable is to write the highest level of objective expected for the curriculum (for example, a behavioral objective), and not each of the "enabling" objectives (such as the knowledge, attitudinal, and skill objectives that enable accomplishment of the behavioral objective). For large, complex curricula that have many objectives, it is helpful to group objectives by major objectives, each of which may have several sub-objectives.

It is also important to remember that most educational experiences encompass more than a list of preconceived objectives. For example, on clinical rotations, much learning derives from unanticipated experiences with individual patients. In many situations, the most useful learning comes from learning needs identified and pursued by individual learners and their mentors. In such situations the curriculum planner will want to preserve space for and encourage such learning. A process objective may be helpful in this regard.

> *Example:* A broad goal for a training program might be that residents develop as self-directed learners. A specific, measurable process objective for a clinical rotation might be that each week each resident identify a question relevant to the care of one patient, and briefly report during rounds the following day the answer to the question, the sources used, and the search time required.

In summary, goals provide desired overall direction for a curriculum, against which the appropriateness of the curriculum's objectives and experiences can be assessed. An important and difficult task in curriculum development is to develop a manageable number of clearly articulated, specific, measurable objectives that interpret the goals and focus and prioritize curricular components that are critical to the realization of the goals.

Step 4: Educational Strategies

Educational strategies involve both content and methods. They are determined by the curriculum's objectives, which in turn are shaped by the problem identification and needs assessments. They are the educational intervention, the means by which a curriculum's objectives are achieved. As mentioned in the previous section, the nouns in a curriculum's learner objectives determine the curriculum's content (the specific material to be included in the curriculum). The verbs determine the education methods.

As described in chapter 2 of *Methods for Teaching Medicine*, also part of the *Teaching Medicine* series (15), it is important to choose educational methods that are *congruent* with a curriculum's learner objectives. For example, for lower-order cognitive objectives, appropriate learning methods might be lecture, readings, Web-based interactive learning modules, or testing with feedback and discussion of answers. For higher-order cognitive objectives, such as clinical decision-making, learning methods that involve the application and synthesis of knowledge are required, such as case discussions, problem-based learning, or team-based learning (16–19). Affective learning generally requires a combination of methods, such as exposure to knowledge, experiences (such as trigger tapes), or the views of respected others that contradict undesired and confirm desired attitudes (20); facilitation techniques with individuals or groups that promote safety, reflection, and the sharing of attitudes; successful experiences that reinforce desired attitudes; and role-modeling of desired attitudes and behaviors (21–23). It is important to realize that the achievement of skill or competence objectives (the ability to perform a task) requires different learning methods than behavioral or performance objectives (the incorporation of that skill into ongoing practice). Supervised practice and feedback that can be provided through simulations, supervised clinical experiences, and the audio or visual review of skills are appropriate methods for learning skills. Methods that promote the incorporation of learned skills into practice, on the other hand, include providing resources that enable and facilitate performance, providing reinforcements for performance, and removing barriers to performance.

> *Example:* In the preceding example, the statement "By the end of the gynecology curriculum, each internal medicine resident will have demonstrated, at least once, the appropriate technique, as defined on a check sheet, for obtaining a Pap smear and cervical cultures" is a skill objective. Appropriate educational methods would include lecture/demonstration of the proper communication and procedural skills to teach the requisite knowledge, practice with a genitourinary teaching associate, and observation and feedback of pelvic exams in resident clinic using a checklist to teach the skills.
>
> The following objective is a behavioral objective: "By the third year of residency, each internal medicine resident will offer and provide cervical cancer and sexually transmitted disease (STD) screening for their patients according to practice guidelines." Appropriate educational methods for this objective might include lecture/readings on the guidelines; discussion of the internist's role in providing cervical cancer and STD screening; skill training as described above; clinic reminder of preventive care guidelines; readily accessible Pap/STD examination trays and trained medical assistants in clinic; and the provision of audit feedback to residents on the number of the patients they have seen eligible for Pap/culture, the number of these who have received the tests, and the location of testing.

Both of these objectives are at the higher end of the hierarchy of educational objectives. The first skill objective encompasses a knowledge objective; the second behavioral objective encompasses knowledge, attitudinal (role expectation), and skill objectives.

As illustrated in the preceding examples, educational objectives are best achieved by the use of multiple educational methods. The use of different educational methods helps to maintain learner interest and reinforces learning. It is particularly relevant for curricula extending over longer time periods. As illustrated above, curricula attempting to achieve higher-order or complex objectives span several domains and, therefore, require several educational methods. Finally, individuals have different preferences for learning, sometimes called learning styles (24). Ideally, a curriculum would use methods that work best for individual learners. However, few curricula can be that malleable; often many learners must be accommodated in a short period. The use of different educational methods helps to overcome the problem of different learning styles.

In developing learning strategies for medical trainees, it is important for the curriculum planner to be aware of some principles and issues related to learning, and to adult learning in particular (23, 25–29) (see also chapter 1 of *Theory and Practice of Teaching Medicine*, another book in the *Teaching Medicine* series [30]). Adult learners tend to be goal-oriented and motivated to learn what is necessary to accomplish desired tasks or solve relevant problems. They are more likely to take responsibility for, direct, and evaluate their own learning (self-directed learning), especially if they are provided the requisite resources. They bring a wealth of different experiences and cultures to the learning situation that shape their interpretation of reality and their approach to learning, and that should be used to facilitate learning. Reflection on previous experiences, or new experiences built into a curriculum, is a key component of experiential learning. Because trainees may be at different stages of learning, it is desirable that a curriculum's learning methods be as learner-centered as feasible: Relate what is being learned to relevant tasks and problems; consider the cognitive, affective, and skill/behavioral achievements of its learners; build on learner experiences; adjust to learner preferences; and provide resources and motivation for independent learning.

Transformative learning, an important part of professional training, occurs when the learners change in meaningful ways. It usually involves experiences that promote the questioning of beliefs and values, and the consideration of multiple points of view. Such change tends to be resisted. It is promoted by skillful facilitation, and a safe and supportive learning environment. Being mindful of these principles should help the curriculum planner combine educational objectives with congruent, creative educational strate-gies to stimulate meaningful, profound, and enduring learning.

Step 5: Implementation

Implementation is an important but underappreciated step in curriculum development that converts a good plan into an accomplishment. It does not really follow step 4 or precede step 6, but is an ongoing process that con-tinuously interacts with each of the other steps.

A review of successful curricular changes in medical school identified characteristics that leaders should keep in mind when initiating or sup-porting change (31). The characteristics were organized around context, curriculum, and process. Under context were the compatibility of the cur-ricular change with the institution's mission and philosophy, a history of successful change in the institution, and the politics of obtaining support. Under curriculum, successful curricular changes were preceded by an articulated need that promoted consensus. The extent of change required a balance between being significant enough to be worth additional effort and not being so large as to be overwhelming. Attention to process was the last category that characterized successful curricular change. This includ-ed development of a cooperative climate, recruitment of participation by a broad representation, effective communication, human resource develop-ment, a reward structure, planned program evaluation, and effective lead-ership behaviors, as described throughout this book.

Implementation of a curriculum in our model (11) incorporates many of the preceding principles. It involves establishing the need and a place for the curriculum (helped by steps 1 and 2), engaging and generating political sup-port from stakeholders, securing resources for the curriculum while simul-taneously modifying the curriculum to match available resources, develop-ing administrative mechanisms to support the curriculum, anticipating and addressing barriers, and deciding on how to introduce the curriculum.

Obtaining political support for a curriculum within one's institution involves recognizing who the stakeholders are, then fostering their involvement and support early on (part of step 2) and throughout curricu-lum development and implementation. Securing external funding or help-ing one's institution meet external requirements, such as accreditation standards, can also garner support from within one's institution.

Resources include personnel, time, facilities, and funding. *Personnel* consists of curriculum directors, faculty, support staff, evaluators, statisti-cians, and standardized and real patients that provide the desired case mix. These personnel provide *time* to lead, coordinate, administer, teach, and evaluate the curriculum; time must be estimated and secured. Learners require time not only to attend scheduled learning activities but to read, reflect, do independent learning, and apply what they have learned. As part of the step 2, the targeted needs assessment, curriculum planners should become familiar with the learners' schedule and understand what barriers exist for participation in the curriculum. For instance, postgraduate medical trainees may have to meet expectations on regulatory work hour limits. Time for the curriculum usually has to be negotiated with academic leaders.

Facilities include space and equipment. Examples might be medical travel kits or black bags for a home visit curriculum, pelvic exam trays and appropriate examining rooms for a gynecology curriculum, space and appropriate equipment for a simulation curriculum in laparoscopic surgery, and a testing facility for objective structured clinical examinations (OSCEs) (32). Curriculum planners need to recognize the financial costs of implementing a curriculum. Each of the above resources requires *funding*. Sometimes curricula can be implemented by redeploying existing resources, but, even in this case, one should ask what is being given up in the process (that is, what is the opportunity or hidden cost of the curriculum). When additional funding is requested, it is necessary to develop and justify a budget. Obtaining external funding for one's curricular work can help secure internal political support for one's curricular project, increase the quality of the educational intervention, enhance the quality of related evaluation and research (33), and add to the academic portfolio of the curriculum planner.

When formal funding is not available, informal networking may reveal local resources, such as quality improvement personnel who would welcome teaming with trainees to accomplish projects; biostatisticians willing to assist in curricular evaluations; existing summative assessments in the form of subject, specialty board, and in-service training examinations that include measures relevant to a curriculum; or existing audits or OSCEs to which desired measures can be added. External networking may reveal curricular materials or validated assessment instruments that reduce development costs.

A curriculum does not operate by itself. It requires an administrative structure that clarifies leadership and decision-making roles and that assigns responsibilities for task completion. Lines of communication to and from stakeholders need to be open. The rationale, goals, and objectives of the curriculum, and changes in the curriculum, need to be communicated to stakeholders. Schedules and curricular and evaluation materials must be prepared and distributed. Web sites need to be maintained. Evaluation data must be collected, collated, and analyzed and reports distributed. And all have to be done in a timely manner.

Before initiating a new curriculum or making changes in an old curriculum, it is helpful to anticipate and address any potential barriers to their accomplishment. Barriers can relate to finances, other resources, or people. For example, there may be competing demands for resources; nonsupportive attitudes; and issues of job or role security, credit, turf, or political power. Curricular development projects sometimes require ongoing cooperation across specialties.

> *Example:* As part of a major revision in the overall medical school curriculum at Johns Hopkins, supported by the dean's office and based on a needs assessment of clerkship directors, multidisciplinary teams were assembled to create two new curricula: 1) a 4-week "Transition to the Wards" curriculum that would prepare students in the procedures and skills required in most clinical clerkships, for their emerging roles as professionals and team members, and for the transition from disease and organ system thinking to clinical problem-based reasoning; and 2) a 1- to 2-week curriculum to precede each major clerkship that would prepare students in clerkship-specific knowledge and skills, promote understanding and valuing of a multidisciplinary approach to the care of patients, and build upon the professional development started in "Transition to the Wards." Multidisciplinary teams of faculty were brought together to develop these curricula in the context of a longitudinal program in curriculum development. They developed structured mechanisms to engage other faculty from different departments, who could not participate in the faculty development program.

Once the curricular planning process has progressed sufficiently, curriculum planners should think about the best way to introduce the curriculum. Whenever possible, it is important to pilot critical segments of a new curriculum on friendly or convenient audiences before formally introducing it. Critical segments might include specific educational methods and evaluation instruments. Piloting enables curriculum planners to receive critical feedback and to make important revisions that increase the likelihood of successful implementation. Phasing in a complex curriculum one part at a time, or the entire curriculum, on a segment of the targeted learners permits a focusing of initial efforts as faculty and staff learn new procedures. When the curriculum represents a cultural shift in an institution or requires attitudinal changes in the stakeholders, introducing the curriculum one step at a time, rather than all at once, or on a group of interested learners, can lessen resistance and increase acceptance. Like piloting, phasing in affords the opportunity to have a cycle of experience, feedback, evaluation, and response before full implementation. Sometimes the demand for a full curriculum for all learners is so pressing, or a curriculum is so limited in scope, that immediate full implementation is preferable. In this case, the first cycle of the curriculum can be considered as a "pilot" cycle. Evaluation data on educational outcomes and processes from the initial cycles of a curriculum can then be used to refine the implementation of subsequent cycles.

Step 6: Evaluation and Feedback
Evaluation is an important step in curriculum development for many reasons (see chapter 7). It enables curriculum planners to determine whether curricular goals and objectives have been met, to assess individual learner achievements, to maintain and garner support for a curriculum, and to document the accomplishments of curriculum planners. It provides information for ongoing improvement of learners and the curriculum. It can satisfy external requirements, such as those of accrediting bodies (1–3). It can serve as a basis for related presentations and publications.

As summarized in Box 6-2, curriculum evaluation encompasses several tasks (34):

Identification of users and needs. In planning the evaluation for a curriculum, it is helpful to identify the users of the evaluation and their needs. Users generally include learners, faculty, and curriculum planners, but may also include program directors, administrative leaders, and external bodies that provide funding and resources for the curriculum, accrediting bodies, and other educators, particularly when the curriculum is innovative. Needs may include information that can be feedback to individual learners and

---

Box 6-2. Eight Tasks for Evaluating a Curriculum

1. Identification of users and needs
2. Clarification and prioritization of evaluation questions
3. Choice of evaluation designs
4. Selection of evaluation methods and instruments
5. Addressing ethical concerns
6. Collecting data
7. Analyzing data
8. Reporting results

curriculum planners that can be used to improve learner and curriculum performance (formative evaluation), certification of learner competence and documentation of program success and the efficacy of educational strategies (summative evaluation), justification for resource allocation, satisfaction of external requirements, data for dissemination, and evidence of a curriculum planner's scholarly accomplishment.

Clarification and prioritization of evaluation questions. Because resources are limited, needs, which translate into goals for an evaluation effort, must be prioritized. These goals can be written as evaluation questions. Some evaluation questions should relate to the achievement of a curriculum's educational objectives, which can provide information for the assessment of individual learners and, in aggregate, for evaluation of program effectiveness. For formative purposes, most curriculum planners also include evaluation questions that relate to the perceived effectiveness of specific curricular components or faculty and that elicit, in an open-ended manner, qualitative responses about a curriculum's strengths and areas for improvement. The phrasing of evaluation questions in turn directs evaluation designs and methods.

Choice of evaluation designs. Once the evaluation questions have been identified and prioritized, the curriculum planner should consider which evaluation designs are most appropriate to answer the evaluation questions and are most feasible in terms of resources. The evaluation designs most often used in educational evaluations are post-test only, pre- and post-test, and controlled (with or without randomization). Most evaluation designs assess short-term rather than longer-term impact, although the latter is usually more desirable. The choice of evaluation design affects both the internal validity of an evaluation (the degree to which it accurately assesses the effect of a specific intervention on specific subjects in a specific setting) and its external validity (the degree to which the findings are generalizable to other populations and other settings). Evaluations of multi-institutional curricula are more likely to be generalizable than those of single-institution curricula, but a multi-institutional evaluation with poor internal validity cannot possess high external validity. More advanced evaluations designs, such as randomized, controlled designs, are more likely to achieve internal validity and control for undesired biases (such as accounting for concomitant interventions or selection bias) but are also more resource intensive.

Selection of evaluation methods and instruments. Measurement methods commonly used to evaluate individuals (see chapter 8 of this book) and programs (chapter 7) include rating forms, self-assessment forms, essays, written or computer-interactive tests, oral examinations, questionnaires, individual interviews, group interviews/discussions, direct observation (such as OSCEs), and performance audits. It is desirable to choose measurement methods that have optimal accuracy (reliability and validity), credibility, and importance. Generally speaking, patient and health care outcomes are considered most important, followed by behaviors/performance, skills/competence, knowledge or attitudes, and satisfaction or perceptions, in that order. Objective measurements are preferred to subjective ratings. Curricular evaluations that incorporate measurement methods at the higher end of this hierarchy are more likely to be disseminated or published. As with evaluation designs, however, the use of more reliable, valid, and desirable measurement instruments generally requires more resources. Sometimes, measurement instruments with already established reliability and validity can be used. However, it is more important that what is measured be congruent with the program or learning objectives and the evaluation questions than use the "highest" level of measurement instrument. Questionnaires, interviews, and informal observations and discussions are often sufficient for the formative program evaluation, which guides subsequent improvement in a curriculum.

Obviously, curricular evaluation can be challenging. The following example illustrates achieving congruence and balancing rigor versus resource limitations in designing a curriculum evaluation.

> *Example:* Curriculum planners who wished to rigorously evaluate the effect of an innovative resident curriculum to improve sign-outs and transitions in care debated between three evaluation questions: "Do residents' sign-outs improve following training?" versus "Are the sign-outs of trained residents superior to those of untrained residents?" versus "Do trained residents' sign-outs improve more post-training than those of untrained residents over the same time period?" A congruent evaluation design for the first evaluation question would be a pre- and post-test design (two observations per resident); for the second, a randomized, controlled post-test–only design (one observation per resident); and the third, a randomized, controlled pre- and post-test design (two observations per resident). The planners chose the second design as being methodologically more desirable and less resource intensive in terms of observations, although more challenging in terms of scheduling, than the first design. They did not feel they had the resources for the third design. They initially decided on observations of sign-outs, using a check list for their measurement method, but a mentor pointed out that their evaluation questions were designed to assess behaviors in actual practice rather than

residents' ability to do good sign-outs under observation. She also pointed out that the number of observations required would be resource intensive. Instead, they decided to review a sample of each resident's electronic sign-out notes using a rating form that could be evaluated for inter- and intra-rater reliability and content validity and that would assess actual practice behaviors. They determined that doubling the number of rated electronic sign-outs would not be particularly burdensome if they used trained medical students interested in the project.

In fact, they decided to include an additional round of electronic note assessments 2 months after the immediate post-evaluations to assess sustainability of any improvement. Their evaluation design became a randomized, controlled pre- and post-test design. They addressed institutional review board concerns by providing the same training to control group residents after the evaluation ended. A few other evaluation questions were added for formative program evaluation: "How do residents rate the curriculum and its various components?" "What are its strengths?" "How can it be improved?" These questions were assessed by questionnaire using a post-test only design.

Additional components that are important for curriculum evaluation include:

Addressing ethical concerns. Most concerns relate to issues of confidentiality and uses of the evaluation, particularly when feasibility considerations have resulted in measurement methods of limited reliability and validity and when those using the assessments must understand these limitations. Who will have access to the evaluations? To what degree should subjects be informed about the potential users and uses of the evaluations, where the evaluations will be stored, and methods used to ensure confidentiality? Another ethical (and political) concern related to controlled evaluation designs is the denial of a curriculum to the control group. This can often be addressed by staggering the curricular intervention over time so that control group members can receive the curriculum later in the evaluation design or after the evaluation is complete. In other situations, the curriculum planner may have to settle for historical controls. Another ethical concern relates to the allocation of resources. For example, allocation of curricular resources to an evaluation effort that is important for a faculty member's academic advancement, but that diverts needed resources from learners or other faculty, is ethically problematic.

When dissemination is anticipated, evaluation becomes educational research. Although federal regulations governing research in the United States categorize many educational research projects as exempt from the regulations if the research involves the study of normal educational practices or records information about learners in such a way that they cannot be identified, some institutional review boards may differ in their interpretation of what is exempt under the regulations or want to ensure additional safeguards for learners than what the regulations require. Therefore, curriculum planners should consult their institutional review board in the planning stages of the evaluation, before data are collected.

Collecting data. Measurement instruments must be distributed and collected in a timely manner. They must then be safely stored. Failure to collect important evaluation data or low response rates can seriously compromise the value of an evaluation. Response rates can be boosted and the need for follow-up reduced when data collection is built into scheduled learner and faculty activities. Sometimes evaluation methods can be designed to serve simultaneously as educational methods, if reflection and feedback are included. While different individuals may distribute or administer measurement instruments within scheduled sessions, it is usually wise to delegate overall responsibility for data collection to one person.

Analyzing data. After the data have been collected, they need to be analyzed. In general, data analysis should be planned at the same time that the evaluation questions are being identified and measurement instruments developed, and all adjusted to the resources available for evaluation. For example, before embarking upon a study of whether a particular educational intervention is effective, it is appropriate to conduct a power analysis to determine whether there are sufficient subjects to answer the question with the desired level of statistical certainty. The nature of evaluation questions will determine, in part, the type of statistical approach required to answer them. For example, "What percentage of learners improve or achieve proficiency in skill X by the end of the curriculum?" requires only descriptive statistics. "Does the curriculum result in a statistically significant improvement in learners' proficiency in skill X?" or "Does training improve proficiency in learners compared to controls?" requires use of more sophisticated tests of statistical significance. When the evaluation questions require the use of sophisticated statistical analyses to assess efficacy or control for factors that could affect outcomes other than the curricular intervention, and when the curriculum planner does not possess that level of expertise, collaboration with a statistician or simplification of the evaluation question may be necessary. Finally, in interpreting a statistical analysis, curriculum planners should be able to distinguish between changes that are statistically significant versus those that are educationally meaningful and apply measures of the magnitude of change, such as effect size (see chapter 7).

Reporting results. Evaluation is without value unless the results are assembled into reports that meet the needs of its users. The timeliness of reports is critical. Individual learners benefit from the immediate feedback of formative assessment results. Evaluation results are helpful to faculty and curriculum planners when they are received in time to prepare for the next curricular cycle. Important decisions, such as the allocation of educational resources for the coming year, may be influenced by the timely reporting of evaluation results. The format of reports should match the needs of their users in content, language, and length. Individual learners, faculty members, and curriculum planners may want detailed evaluation reports pertaining to their particular (or the curriculum's) performance. Administrators, deans, and department chairs may prefer executive summaries that provide background information on the curriculum and that synthesize the evaluation information relevant to their respective needs. Results can be succinctly and persuasively displayed through the use of tables, graphs, or figures. The time and resources necessary to prepare such reports should be included in one's evaluation plan.

Interaction and Congruence Among the Steps

Although the six steps have been presented in sequence, from 1 to 6, in practice curriculum development is a dynamic, interactive process. Progress on two or more steps often occurs simultaneously, and progress on one step influences progress on another. In addition, one complete cycle of curriculum development informs the next. This is why Figure 6-1 is drawn as a circle, and why there are bidirectional arrows between all steps. For example, resource limitations (step 5) may require a rethinking of the curricular objectives (step 3), educational strategies (step 4), and evaluation (step 6). Considerations related to the evaluation (step 6) may require a rewording of the educational objectives. Evaluation (step 6) may be designed to provide information that contributes to the needs assessment of targeted learners (step 2). The bidirectional arrows between steps 3, 4, and 6 are particularly important because the curriculum planner should ensure that a curriculum's objectives, educational strategies, evaluation questions, evaluation designs, and evaluation methods speak to and are congruent with one another.

❖ Curriculum Cycles: Maintenance, Enhancement, and Transitions

Curricula are continually developing, or at least they should be. A curriculum that becomes static, even if initially successful, gradually declines and dies. The evaluation of one cycle of a curriculum informs the next. Subsequent cycles must respond not only to evaluation results but also to changes in knowledge, resources (including faculty), targeted learners, and institutional and societal values and needs.

To appropriately nurture a curriculum and manage change, one must understand the curriculum and appreciate its complexity. This includes not only the written curriculum but also its learners, its faculty, its support staff, the processes by which it is administered and evaluated, and the setting in which it takes place. Program evaluation (discussed in chapter 7) provides objective and representative subjective feedback on some of these areas. Methods that promote informal information exchange (such as internal and external reviews; observation of curricular components; and individual or group meetings with learners, faculty, and support staff) can enrich one's understanding of a curriculum. They can also build relationships that help to maintain and further develop a curriculum. Electronic curriculum management systems are being increasingly used to provide coordinated information for understanding and managing both subject-focused curricula as well as complex educational programs, such as an entire medical school curriculum.

Most curricula require midcourse and end-of-cycle or end-of-year changes. Changes may be prompted by informal feedback; evaluation results; accreditation standards; the evolving needs of learners, faculty, institutions, or society; or changes in available resources. Minor operational changes that are necessary for the smooth functioning of a curriculum are generally made at the level of the curriculum coordinator or core group responsible for managing the curriculum. More complicated needs that require in-depth analysis and thoughtful planning for change may best be assigned to a carefully selected task group. Before implementing major curricular changes, it is often wise to ensure broad, representative support. It can also be helpful to pilot major or complex changes before implementing them fully.

Curriculum maintenance requires sustenance of the curriculum team, which includes not only faculty but also the support staff. It is, therefore, important to attend to processes that motivate, develop, and support the team. These processes include ongoing communication of curricular changes and evaluation results, involvement of faculty in the change process, faculty development and team activities, recognition of accomplishments, and periodic celebrations.

An educational leader is looking not only for ways to sustain curricular excellence but for related activities that enhance or complement a curriculum. As noted earlier, one of the most important resources for a curriculum is its faculty, who may benefit from faculty development that is targeted at the needs of the curriculum. This is especially true for a curriculum that introduces new educational methods with which the faculty are unfamiliar, such as team-based learning (19). Institution-wide, regional, or national programs that train faculty in specific content areas or in time management, teaching, curriculum development, management, or research skills may also benefit a curriculum (12).

Changes in the environment in which a curriculum takes place or changes in its resources can create new opportunities or challenges for a curriculum. For example, practice development activities often affect clinical curricula.

Example: The development of a women's health program by an associated institution provided the opportunity to enhance clinical training for internal medicine residents in a curriculum on gynecology and women's health. The program was able to provide supervised training in birth control counseling and management, breast and cervical cancer screening, and osteoporosis prevention, all foci of the curriculum.

Example: The development of quality improvement teams as part of a hospitalist service created opportunities for student, resident, and fellow training in systems-based practice and multidisciplinary teamwork.

New institutional or extrainstitutional resources can be used to benefit curricular development.

Example: The development of a database that tracked residents' clinical experiences created the opportunity for assessment of and reflection on the residents' experiences, and for interventions when appropriate.

Example: The Schools of Nursing, Medicine, and Public Health jointly funded an office to coordinate volunteer opportunities. This facilitated the development of community service and cross-disciplinary curricula for students in the schools.

Networking and associated scholarly activity can strengthen a curriculum. Networking with colleagues from other institutions at professional meetings, for example, by presenting one's work or joining interest groups, can increase conceptual clarity and understanding of one's curriculum, new ideas for improvement, and multi-institutional curricular or research efforts that can directly or indirectly enhance a curriculum. Scholarly activity related to certain aspects of a curriculum, such as the needs assessment or evaluation, will probably enhance the quality of that and related components of the curriculum. Research by faculty in the content area of a curriculum will probably improve the depth of their knowledge of the topic area, and thereby benefit their learners. Scholarly activity can also invigorate a curriculum's faculty and create opportunities for mentored projects by learners.

> *Example:* The Medical Consultation Interest Group of the Society of General Internal Medicine has provided the opportunity for faculty from different institutions to meet yearly, discuss issues electronically, update medical knowledge, share curricula and teaching approaches, and engage in collaborative writing and research (35).

> *Example:* The American Academy on Communication in Healthcare (36) sponsors courses, meetings, and interest groups for teachers of interviewing skills and the psychosocial domain of medical practice that provide opportunities for faculty development, the sharing of curricula and teaching approaches, collaborative work relevant to curricula, and collaborative research.

In addition to the aforementioned transitions in a curriculum in terms of content and environmental and resource changes above, a transition that is particularly important to plan for is changes in faculty, particularly faculty leadership. Faculty interests or responsibilities may evolve over time. Faculty may move. For these reasons, it is important, whenever possible, to approach curriculum development and maintenance as a team activity with interchangeable roles, and to develop more than one faculty member as leaders for a curriculum, particularly when the curriculum is key to the overall educational program.

❖ Developing the Skill Set for Curriculum Development

Those aspiring to be educational leaders should develop their skills in curriculum development. Leaders whose career path has not been in education but who oversee educational leaders should understand the preceding principles so that they can choose, support, and counsel their educational leaders wisely. As in developing research skills, the best approach to developing the skill set for curriculum development is to engage in mentored projects. Often, mentors are available locally. Longitudinal programs and workshops in curriculum development can substitute for or supplement local mentorship (12). Degree programs in education usually incorporate training in the steps of curriculum development (12). A concise but much more detailed and referenced discussion of each of the preceding steps of curriculum development is available in book form (11).

❖ Curriculum Development as Scholarship: Making It Count Twice

The methodical approach to curricular planning discussed above includes most of the components of scholarship: clear goals and aims, adequate preparation, appropriate methods, significant results, and reflective critique (37, 38). Effective dissemination is the remaining component and can provide (as described in chapter 5 of this book) an opportunity for the curriculum planners to "make it count twice."

The time to start thinking about dissemination is in the planning stage of a curriculum. One should think about the targeted audience for dissemination, and what part of their curricular work will be disseminated (such as a needs assessment, an innovative educational strategy, or evaluation results). Obtaining external funding for curricular work is challenging, but if dissemination is a goal, curriculum planners may want to explore external sources, such as departmental or institutional funding, private foundations, professional organizations, or federal agencies (12). When dissemination is anticipated, the relevant institutional review board should be consulted early. Intellectual property and copyright issues may need to be addressed as well if curricular material is to be distributed. Knowing the criteria by which material is peer reviewed can also be helpful in the planning process (39).

Dissemination can be achieved through presentations at local, regional, national, and international professional meetings; the electronic media; or print publications. Educational clearinghouses, such as the Association of American Medical College's MedEdPORTAL (see chapter 5 in *Theory and Practice of Teaching Medicine* [30]), are available through professional organizations (40). Promotion committees are increasingly recognizing the acceptance of one's work in peer-reviewed electronic media as a measure of accomplishment (see also chapter 5 of this book). When publication of a peer-reviewed article is a goal, curriculum planners should be aware of the educational journals and journals in their area of professional focus that are most likely to publish education articles (39). Finally, the identification of collaborators not only enhances the curriculum development but also the dissemination process by bringing to one's work a variety of perspectives and skills, enhancing reflective critique, and sharing the workload. For junior faculty who have not developed curricula before, disseminated curriculum-related work, or successfully obtained external funding, the identification of a mentor can be invaluable.

While dissemination of curriculum related work adds to the workload of curriculum planners, it is an efficient way to establish a track record of scholarship, which is often required for academic advancement. Moreover, a focus on the scholarly aspects of curriculum development usually results in an improved product, rewarding collaborations, benefitting others, and increasing professional satisfaction. A systematic approach to curriculum development, as discussed earlier, provides a sound foundation for dissemination efforts.

REFERENCES

1. **Liaison Committee on Medical Education.** Functions and structure of a medical school. 2008. Accessed at www.lcme.org.
2. **Accreditation Council for Graduate Medical Education.** Common program requirements. 2009. Accessed at www.acgme.org/acWebsite/dutyHours/dh_dutyhoursCommon PR07012007.pdf.
3. **Accreditation Council for Continuing Medical Education.** Accreditation requirements. 2009. Accessed at www.accme.org/index.cfm/fa/home.popular/popular_id/a38e8127-34a6-4062-86a3-382b9d34e74e.cfm.
4. **Accreditation Council for Graduate Medical Education.** Outcomes project. 2009. Accessed at www.acgme.org/Outcome.
5. **Taba H.** Curriculum Development Theory and Practice. New York: Harcourt, Brace & World; 1962.
6. **Tyler R.** Basic Principles of Curriculum and Instruction. Chicago: Univ of Chicago Pr; 1969.
7. **Yura H, Torres GE.** Faculty Curriculum Development: Curriculum Design by Nursing Faculty. New York: National League for Nursing; 1986.
8. **Sheets KJ, Anderson WA, Alguire PC.** Curriculum development and evaluation in medical education. J Gen Intern Med. 1992;7:538-43.
9. **McGaghie WC, Miller GE, Sajid AW, Telder TV.** Competency Based Curriculum Development in Medical Education: An Introduction. Geneva: World Health Organization; 1978.
10. **Golden AS.** A model for curriculum development linking curriculum with health needs. In: Golden AS, Carlson DG, Hogan JL, eds. The Art of Teaching Primary Care. New York: Springer; 1982:9-25.
11. **Kern DE, Thomas PA, Hughes MT, eds.** Curriculum Development in Medical Education: A Six-Step Approach. 2nd ed. Baltimore: Johns Hopkins Univ Pr; 2009:244.

12. **Thomas PA, Kern DE.** Curricular, faculty development and funding resources. In: Kern DE, Thomas PA, Hughes MT, eds. Curriculum Development in Medical Education: A Six-Step Approach. Baltimore: Johns Hopkins Univ Pr; 2009:231-44.
13. **Hundert EM, Hafferty F, Christakis D.** Characteristics of the informal curriculum and trainees' ethical choices. Acad Med. 1996;71:624-42.
14. **Houston TK, Connors RL, Cutler N, Nidiry MA.** A primary care musculoskeletal clinic for residents: success and sustainability. J Gen Intern Med. 2004;19:524-9.
15. **Skeff KM, Stratos GA, eds.** Methods for Teaching Medicine. Philadelphia: ACP Pr; 2010.
16. **Distlehorst LH, Dawson E, Robbs RS, Barrows HS.** Problem-based learning outcomes: the glass half-full. Acad Med. 2005;80:294-9.
17. **Mamede S, Schmidt HG, Norman GR.** Innovations in problem-based learning: what can we learn from recent studies? Adv Health Sci Educ Theory Pract. 2006;11:403-22.
18. **Dolmans DH, De Grave W, Wolfhagen IH, van der Vleuten CP.** Problem-based learning: future challenges for educational practice and research. Med Educ. 2005;39:732-41.
19. **Michaelsen L, Knight AB, Fink LD.** Team-Based Learning: A Transformative Use of Small Groups in College Teaching. Sterling, VA: Stylus; 2004.
20. **Dick W, Carey L, Carey JO.** The Systematic Design of Instruction. 6th ed. Boston: Pearson, Allyn & Bacon; 2005:205-6, 210-1.
21. **Bentley TJ.** Facilitation: Providing Opportunities for Learning. Berkshire, England: McGraw-Hill; 1994:25-60.
22. **Brookfield SD.** Understanding and Facilitating Adult Learning. San Francisco: Jossey-Bass; 1987:123-6.
23. **Rogers CR.** Significant learning in therapy and education. In: Rogers CR, ed. On Becoming a Person: A Therapist's View of Psychotherapy. Boston: Houghton Mifflin; 1961:279-296.
24. **Price GE.** Diagnosing learning styles. In: Smith RM: Helping Adults Learn How to Learn. San Francisco: Jossey-Bass; 1983:49-55.
25. **Brookfield S.** Adult Learning: An Overview. International Encyclopedia of Education. Oxford: Pergamon Pr; 1995.
26. **Knowles M.** Andragogy in Action. San Francisco: Jossey-Bass; 1984.
27. **Mezirow J.** Transformative Dimensions of Adult Learning. San Francisco: Jossey-Bass; 1991.
28. **Schon D.** Educating the Reflective Practitioner. San Francisco: Jossey-Bass; 1990.
29. **Cross KP.** Adults as Learners: Increasing Participation and Facilitating Learning. San Francisco: Jossey-Bass; 1981.
30. **Ende J, ed.** Theory and Practice of Teaching Medicine. Philadelphia: ACP Pr; 2010.
31. **Bland CJ, Starnaman S, Wersal L, Moorehead-Rosenberg L, Zonia S, Henry R.** Curricular change in medical schools: how to succeed. Acad Med. 2000;75:575-94.
32. **Newble D.** Techniques for measuring clinical competence: objective structured clinical examinations. Med Educ. 2004;38:199-203.
33. **Reed DA, Cook DA, Beckman TJ, Levine RB, Kern DE, Wright SM.** Association between funding and quality of published medical education research. JAMA. 2007;298:1002-9.
34. **Lipsett PA, Kern DE.** Evaluation and feedback. In: Kern DE, Thomas PA, Hughes MT, eds. Curriculum Development in Medical Education: A Six-Step Approach. Baltimore: Johns Hopkins Univ Pr; 2009:100-144.
35. **Society of General Internal Medicine.** Interest groups. Accessed at www.sgim.org/index.cfm?pageId=380.

36. **American   Academy   on   Communication   in   Healthcare.** Accessed   at
    www.aachonline.org.
37. **Glassick CE.** Boyer's expanded definitions of scholarship, the standards for assessing schol-
    arship, and the elusiveness of the scholarship of teaching. Acad Med. 2000;75:877-80.
38. **Simpson D, Fincher RM, Hafler JP, Irby DM, Richards BF, Rosenfeld GC, Viggiano
    TR.** Advancing Educators and Education: Defining the Components and Evidence of
    Educational Scholarship. Washington, DC: Association of American Medical Colleges;
    2007:9.
39. **Kern DE, Bass EB.** Dissemination. In: Kern DE, Thomas PA, Hughes MT, eds.
    Curriculum Development in Medical Education: A Six-Step Approach. Baltimore: Johns
    Hopkins Univ Pr; 2009:161-79.
40. **MedEdPORTAL.** Accessed at http://services.aamc.org/30/mededportal.

7

Evaluating Educational Programs

Steven J. Durning, MD, FACP
Col Paul A. Hemmer, USAF, MC, MD, MPH, FACP

E valuating individual trainees is a familiar process for those involved in undergraduate and graduate medical education and should be considered a core skill for all who teach. Evaluating educational programs, or program evaluation, however, is primarily the responsibility of education leaders (course, clerkship, and program directors). Definitions of program evaluation vary. The Accreditation Council for Graduate Medical Education (ACGME) defines it as the "systematic collection and analysis of information related to the design, implementation, and outcomes of a program, for the purpose of monitoring and improving the quality and effectiveness of the program" (1). Thus, program evaluation is more than the sum of individual trainee data. It also determines whether an educational program is "successful" by critically examining components in a new or existing program in order to understand how a program is working and what is contributing to success or lack of success. Essentially, program evaluation is practice-based learning and improvement for academic managers.

There are several excellent and comprehensive references about program evaluation (2–9). This chapter provides a distillate of practical guidance and recommendations for understanding not only the structure of program evaluation but also the elements required for program evaluation. Examples of limitations, pitfalls, and success are given. The approach in this chapter applies to an entire educational

---

KEY POINTS

- Program evaluation is more than the sum of the assessments of individual trainees in the program.
- A "before, during, after" framework for data collection allows understanding of what actually happened by relating outcomes to both processes and inputs.
- Program evaluation shows the overall efficacy of curriculum but also improves understanding of strengths and weaknesses, addresses the interests of stakeholders, and justifies use of resources.
- Within departments, evaluating educational programs is primarily the work of course, clerkship, and program directors, but this process requires both departmental and institutional support.
- In addition to summative program evaluation, academic managers should implement a system of formative evaluation, including assessments that may be prompted by "yellow" or "red" flags.
- Academic managers take the lead in analyzing results, but having an education committee can greatly assist with the process by allocating work and pacing the process.

---

program (for example, all of medical school, an entire residency program), a component of a program (for example, a course or clerkship in medical school or a year in a residency program), or even an element of a program (for example, a new lecture series or a new required curricular component).

❖ Why Perform Program Evaluation?

In one sense, the answer to this question is obvious: It is required. At the graduate medical education level, the ACGME Outcome Project requires program directors to understand how elements of the program are helping to achieve outcomes (10, 11). Program directors must use information from within the training program and now also use external measures of success, such as demonstrating links from training to patient care. At the undergraduate medical education level, the Liaison Committee on Medical Education (LCME) also prescribes program evaluation (12). According to Educational Directive 46, "A medical school must collect and use a variety of outcome data, including national norms of accomplishment, to demonstrate the extent to which its educational program objectives are being met."

Other reasons for performing program evaluation are just as important. Beyond the growing interest in outcomes (3, 13), program evaluation improves understanding of the strengths and weaknesses in a program. This knowledge can help address the interests of a variety of stakeholders and, importantly, justify resources needed to run the program. Furthermore, unexpected outcomes occur, and understanding how this happens requires a close examination of the program. Finally, society expects that as a profession, we will closely examine our programs to ensure that we are providing the best possible education and oversight in order to graduate trainees who are ready to advance to the next level.

❖ Key Definitions and Distinctions

An understanding of definitions and distinctions can assist with the planning, execution, and refinement of program evaluation efforts. We define measurements as quantitative (numeric) or qualitative (using words) instruments that capture performance of individual trainees or the program. This discussion refers to *assessment* as the method of measurement (an assay) one chooses to examine the area of interest. *Evaluation* involves the analysis of those measurements (assessments) and the subsequent interpretation of the findings within the context of the individual program.

❖ Essential Versus Desirable

For both goals and assessments, it is important to distinguish between what is essential (must be collected) from what is desirable (can or should be collected). In some cases, the difference is obvious, such as requirements from accreditation organizations. Defining these measurements (essential and desirable) at the outset can help ensure that program evaluation efforts are possible as well as assist with obtaining additional resources. The latter point is particularly important when resources are needed to ensure the feasibility for essential or desirable tasks. For example, the response rate on end-of-clerkship or end-of-month residency evaluation forms considers not only the number of forms collected but the time needed (for example, orientation to faculty on how to use the forms, time to complete), cost (such as printing forms or using an online system), and human resources (for example, clerkship or residency administrator) needed to obtain the evaluations.

We believe that the vetting of essential and desirable measures with other educators and stakeholders (such as trainees, department chairs, and supervisors) in the program is an important step. Group vetting may highlight a broader range of possible measurements and outcomes, and help identify unnecessary measurements (those neither essential nor desirable). Shifting collection of such unnecessary data to collection of essential and desirable measurements helps to free up limited resources. It is important to keep in mind, however, that unexpected outcomes come to light in the process of program evaluation. Therefore, some caution should be used when dropping currently collected measures, especially if one is not convinced of the limited utility of the measurement or if one is considering significantly changing the current curriculum.

❖ Reliability and Validity

Determining the reliability and validity of measurements is crucial for the success of program evaluation; educators should understand some basics of the terminology. *Reliability* refers to the reproducibility of a specific measurement (14). If a measurement were perfectly reliable, the same result would be achieved with repeated administrations. Stated differently, reliability concerns understanding a signal-to-noise ratio—how much of what is being measured is due to what you are trying to assess (such as individual's knowledge with an examination) and how much is due to other factors (such as problems with the examination). Another common example might be the extent to which two teachers agree (signal) when they view and rate the performance of a trainee on the same task at the same point in time (with sources of noise being the teachers, the trainee, and the rating form). Common statistical measures of reliability include the Cronbach α (which, for example, measures the inter-item agreement or consistency on a rating form) and the intraclass correlation coefficient (if consistency of scores from different teachers is being examined). In general, the higher the stakes of the decision (such as board certification), the more reliable the measurement needs to be (for example, 80% or 0.8 is generally believed to be sufficient for high-stakes decisions, such as licensing or graduation).

Validity is the confidence that the inferences drawn from the data are true (15). Validity refers to measuring what one hopes to measure. Many terms for validity are used in the program evaluation literature: *content* (what is the assessment "testing"?); *construct* (what is the underlying explanation, concept, or common factor[s] at work to explain what is being seen?); *criterion* (how well does one variable predict an outcome?); and *consequential* (what happens as a result of the assessment?); the notion of "face validity" (does it look right?) has been dismissed (16).

Essentially, the most straightforward way to improve reliability is to increase the number of measurements (17). For example, to assess knowledge, a 100-item examination that samples several domains is likely to be a more reliable (and valid) assessment of a trainee's knowledge than a 30-item examination. Similarly, 10 observations of a resident by a faculty member are probably more reliable that two observations. However, increasing sampling frequency comes at a cost—it is more time-intensive, may use more resources, and may thus reduce feasibility (costs of sampling). Therefore, essential and desirable measurements should be sampled frequently enough to ensure reliable and valid results without compromising the feasibility of the approach.

In gathering evidence in support of reliability and validity, it is important to understand that "statistical significance" does not mean the finding is functionally or educationally meaningful, and that smaller P values are not "more significant." Methods that try to characterize the "size" of the statistical finding include analysis of variance; regression analyses (logistic for a dichotomous outcome; linear for a continuous outcome), which can look at how much of the outcome is explained by independent variables; and effect size, such as standardized mean differences (18, 19).

Finally, one must not assume that the reliability and validity of any assessment are fixed—they should be checked periodically (14, 15, 17, 20).

❖ Stakeholders

Stakeholders are all interested individuals involved—trainees, teachers, academic managers, administrators, patients, and future employers. As many stakeholders as are feasible can (and should) collect data for program evaluation. Involving the different stakeholders in the program can expand resources and improve the feasibility of the program evaluation efforts. Different stakeholders have unique viewpoints to inform the system of evaluation (Table 7-1).

Academic managers should have the lead in analyzing and interpreting results, but establishing a committee can help define stakeholder tasks for program evaluation and serve as a pacing method. Furthermore, consultants may be necessary for program evaluation; these could be internal (individuals within your institution, such as statistical consultants or administration officials) or external (individuals outside of your program). External evaluators can help with this process by sharing their own successes and shortcomings with program evaluation. For example, a team of

Table 7-1. Examples of Stakeholders in a Medical Education Program and Viewpoints Expressed for Incorporation Into Program Evaluation

Stakeholder	Viewpoints
Faculty	Program resources, limitations
	Overall trainee strengths and weaknesses
	Time/enjoyment with teaching
Patients	Real or standardized
Peers, nurses	Resident problems/progress
	Interpersonal and communication skills
	Professionalism
	Team-based care
Chief resident	Resident problems/progress
	Resident recruiting
Clerkship director	Site resources and limitations
	Faculty and resident morale, teaching
	Faculty development
Oversight committees	Academic actions
	Due process
Employers	Performance ratings
	Awards
	Adverse actions

academicians from an institution may visit another institution as a mock review for Residency Review Committee or LCME accreditation. The success of voluntary external evaluators has been documented for residency training programs (21).

❖ Unit of Analysis

The *unit of analysis* explains the context and the outcomes of interest. Several units of analysis can be defined in conducting a program evaluation. Examples include a group of trainees (such as a postgraduate year or a medical school course, clerkship, or class), time (such as an academic year or a rotation), or a location (such as comparing performance between two or more geographic sites). Examples of units of analysis are illustrated in examples later in the text.

❖ Existing Versus New Programs

The approach to program evaluation of *existing* versus *new programs* deserves comment. Generally speaking, the approach to program evaluation is similar for both (described below), but the pace is faster for new programs. One should study innovations of sufficient magnitude that are likely to have an effect (good or bad), such as making a residency program 50% ambulatory or shortening a clerkship program, starting clerkships earlier in medical school, or reducing standard lecture time to self-paced Web instruction. The increased frequency of measurement collection and analysis, the importance of qualitative measurements, attention to unexpected outcomes, and use of a control group are all factors to consider with new programs.

❖ Frameworks for Program Evaluation

Program evaluation success can be defined as obtaining information that can relate inputs to outcomes. This reflective approach allows understanding of potential sources of success or shortcomings so that the program can be improved.

It is helpful to begin with stating goals for program evaluation at the outset. At a minimum, the goal should be sufficiently precise to allow at least a dichotomous determination (success or no success) by analyzing quantitative or qualitative data; degrees of success may also be reasonable and desirable for program evaluation. Program evaluation goals are not sufficiently described by such phrases as "strong medical knowledge" or "good clinical skills." If uncertain about how to define one's goals, consider answering the following question: "I would be happy about my program if I knew that…" (2). For instance, the sentence could be completed by phrases such as "…my graduating residents are proficient at engaging patients in informed consent for procedures" or "…all of my students are successful on their first attempt on U.S. Medical Licensing Examination step 2: Clinical Skills."

Three selected *frameworks* are reviewed from the program evaluation literature, with brief discussions of potential strengths and shortcomings of each approach.

Goal and Measure Framework

The *goal and measure* framework for conducting program evaluation begins with defining one or more goals for a program (22). The more specific or concrete the goal (or vision of success), the better. For example, in an internal medicine residency training program, a goal of "knowledge of

U.S. Preventive Services Task Force health screening recommended guidelines for adults" is preferable to "knowledge of prevention principles." The next step involves listing one or more measures that could capture achievement of the goal. In this example, the measures could include chart review and an in-house multiple-choice test on screening guidelines. The final step is being certain that the measures are collected with sufficient frequency and that trainee improvement over time meets the expectations of academic managers. In our example, the assessment frequency might involve biannual chart review and an annual in-house test, and acceptable performance would be compliance with established standards for chart review and passing the end of postgraduate year 3 examination on this topic.

This framework is both feasible and easy to follow. Drawbacks include the inability to explain the reasons for meeting or not meeting a goal, no accounting for resources needed to conduct program evaluation, and no baseline (control) measures to account for trainee performance before entering the program.

Input, Process, Product Framework

This framework is derived from the quality literature (23). *Input* refers to needed resources, such as funding or human resources. In medical education, *process* measurements are collected while trainees are going through the program, and they reflect curriculum content. For example, in a core internal medicine clerkship, process measurements could include logbooks of numbers and types of patients seen, a procedure log, and teacher evaluations at the midpoint of the rotation. *Product* measurements are outcomes of training and reflect how learners change. For example, product measurements after a clerkship could include subinternship performance in internal medicine or U.S. Medical Licensing Examination step 2 scores. Product measurements are usually obtained after training in the program has concluded, although these measurements can also be obtained at the end of training. For example, an end-of-clerkship examination could be considered a product measurement for the core internal medicine clerkship.

By incorporating needed resources as well as process measurements, this framework, and a related framework known as CIPP (context, input, process, product) (7), provides additional clarity and detail not reflected in the goal and measure approach. An important limitation, however, is the absence of baseline measurements to put product or outcome measurements into perspective. For example, is the passing rate or mean score on the core internal medicine clerkship examination a sign of success for the program or a potential problem? Knowing how the trainees performed before entering the program (baseline measurements such as grade point average, class rank, or performance on a pretest [24]) is an essential source of data for knowing how to interpret this outcome (examination performance).

Before, During, After Framework

This three-phase framework is desirable for program evaluation purposes (2). The main benefit of this approach over the input, process, product framework is the explicit incorporation of baseline measurements so that an analysis of outcomes can attempt to explain why outcomes were achieved or not. Examples of using this framework can be found elsewhere (2, 24, 25).

This framework helps establish relationships before (baseline), during (process), and after (product or outcome measurements). Table 7-2 shows examples of these measurements. Consider also tracking whether the assessment is currently done well and its priority, to highlight the importance of feasibility, sampling, and distinguishing essential, desirable, and unnecessary measurements.

The table includes both quantitative and qualitative measurements in each of the three phases. It is critical to include measures expressed numerically and by using words at each phase. Qualitative measurements are essential for hypothesis generation and for illuminating the reasons that variance was explained or not explained in the outcomes of interest. We recommend collecting at least three, if not five or more, measurements in each of the three phases.

Additional benefits of this approach include promoting collaboration across phases in medical education (baselines for graduate medical education are outcomes for undergraduate medical education), promoting the use of commonly collected measurements, the ability to use this framework for both new or existing programs, and the ability to choose the duration of each of the three phases. This approach could be used to evaluate an entire internal medicine residency training program, a postgraduate-year class, an individual monthly rotation, or a component of a specific rotation, such as a weeklong electrocardiogram seminar. Table 7-3 shows an exercise on program evaluation using the before, during, after approach. This step-by-step approach is meant to help the reader perform program evaluation, and sections in this exercise are discussed throughout this chapter.

Table 7-2. Sample of Measurements for Program Evaluation: Before, During, After

Before	During	After
Undergraduate medical education		
Qualitative		
Medical school application essays	Portfolio	Portfolio
Letters of recommendation	Reflective writing assignments	Graduate survey
Volunteering experience	Clerkship narratives	Employer survey
Leadership experience	Teaching evaluations	Teaching evaluations
Quantitative		
MCAT scores	USMLE scores	ITE scores
SAT or ACT score	NBME scores	In-house exam scores
College GPA	Medical school GPA	OSCE scores
Class rank	Class rank	Class rank
School rating	OSCE scores	Mini-CEX scores
Highest degree received	Attendance rates	360° evaluation
Graduate medical education		
Qualitative		
Portfolio	Portfolio	Leadership
Application essay	Comments from teacher critiques	Professional society advancement
Medical school grade narratives	Comments from student critiques	
Dean or other letters	Faculty meetings	
Interview comments	360° evaluation	
Volunteer activities		
Leadership activities		

continued

Quantitative		
Exams (USMLE, NBME)	ACGME toolbox measures	Exams (certifying)
Clinical skills (OSCE)	Procedure/patient logs	Graduate survey
Grades	Hours worked	Employer survey
GPA		Papers published
Class rank		Grants awarded
AOA membership		Journals on which serving as reviewer
		Editorial board memberships

Continuing medical education

Qualitative		
Portfolio	Portfolio	Portfolio
Reflective writings	Self-assessment	Self-assessment
Graduate survey	Patient praise/complaints	Patient praise/complaints
Employer ratings	Employer ratings	Employer ratings
Teaching evaluations	Teaching evaluations	Teaching evaluations

Quantitative		
ABIM exam performance	PIM performance	MOC results
OSCE scores	Grants, papers, book, chapters	Grants, papers, book, chapters
Mini-CEX scores	Professional society participation/advancement	Professional society participation/advancement
360° evaluations	360° evaluations	360° evaluations
Chart-stimulated recall	Chart reviews	Chart review
Leadership roles	Pursuit of additional degree/training	Pursuit of additional degree/training
	Leadership roles	Leadership roles

ABIM = American Board of Internal Medicine; ACGME = Accreditation Council for Graduate Medical Education; AOA = Alpha Omega Alpha Honor Society; GPA = grade point average; ITE = In-Training Examination; MCAT = Medical College Admission Test; Mini-CEX = Mini-Clinical Examination; MOC = maintenance of certification; NBME = National Board of Medical Examiners; OSCE = objective structured clinical examination; PIM = Performance Improvement Module; SAT = Scholastic Aptitude Test; USMLE = U.S. Medical Licensing Examination.

Table 7-3. Exercise in Program Evaluation

Consider one specific challenge that you're facing with your training program—something is not going as well as you'd like, or you don't really know how things are going.

Step 1. Goal statement related to this challenge. Finish one of these sentences: "I would feel really good about my program if I knew that..." or "I need to know whether...."

Step 2. What "outcome" or "after" measures (immediate and longer-term) will help you determine "success" in answering your question? List as many as you think might help (add an asterisk next to those you feel are essential).

Step 3. What measurements (assessments) will you make/gather *during* the program? These measures should be in line with the outcome you're interested in.

• Consider feasibility (can you do it), reliability, and validity of assessment methods.

• Are these process or product; quantitative or qualitative; essential or desirable?

Step 4. What baseline or "before" measures are needed? These should be identified to compare intervention and control groups, correct for baseline differences in performance, and understand what is a result of the program.

• Are these process or product; quantitative or qualitative; essential or desirable?

Step 5. Identify yellow and red flags for this evaluation (the "medical monitor" of clinical research). What will make you lose sleep if you find it is occurring? Try to list measures that are quantifiable (numeric), qualitative (words), process (content), and product measures. Yellow flags = things you should be concerned about if you find them; red flags = things that should prompt immediate action if you find them.

Step 6. Go back to steps 3 to 5. Is there any additional information that you will need to gather ("what to evaluate"; "before, during, after" measurements) on the basis of your red and yellow flags?

Step 7. Go back to steps 3 to 6 and write down resources needed (consider time, human resources, and funding) and potential barriers for each step.

Step 8. What are possible unexpected outcomes with this intervention, and how might you detect these outcomes?

❖ Types of Outcome Measures

In any framework for program evaluation, it can be difficult to decide on the outcomes (products; "after" measures) to examine; the easiest outcomes might not be the most important. Kirkpatrick (26) provides one model that can be helpful when thinking about defining "success" (Box 7-1).

Box 7-1. Kirkpatrick's Levels of Defining Success

Level 1: *Reaction*—did the learners like or dislike the program and why?

Level 2: *Learning*—did the learners learn, improve their knowledge, over baseline measures?

Level 3: *Behavior*—did the learners *do* something differently (desirable or undesirable changes) after the program?

Level 4: *Results*—what was the return on investment, such as the benefit to patient care?

A similar way to look at outcome measures (or any measures in the framework for that matter) has been described by Miller (27). This describes levels of accomplishment as knows, knows how, shows how, and does. Essentially, this views measures of assessment in moving from developing the necessary knowledge to implementing and integrating knowledge with skills and attitudes in the progressive development of expertise. Table 7-4 shows both the Kirkpatrick and the Miller levels, along with suggestions of measures that accompany each level.

As one progresses through Kirkpatrick's (and Miller's) levels, one can see that qualitative and quantitative measures are integral at each level. In addition, the outcomes become more meaningful and more difficult to measure. For example, while learner reaction is important (for example, one would modify a program if it were unacceptable to participants) and knowledge gain is often relatively easy to assess (for example, examination scores before and after interventions or time periods), they remain at the basic levels. Accrediting organizations are asking academic managers to look at Kirkpatrick levels 3 and 4 (Miller level 4). There are growing repositories of assessments that academic managers can use and share to help with assessing trainee performance, such as the ACGME Toolbox (www.acgme.org/outcome/assess/toolbox.asp). Although this may help in terms of limiting the effort to recreate assessments, it is important to realize that the validity and reliability of the instruments may be unknown. This may fall to the user to determine.

Table 7–4. Kirkpatrick's and Miller's Descriptions of Outcome Measures as Applied to Program Evaluation

Kirkpatrick	Miller	Examples	Comments
Reaction		Surveys, Likert scales, focus groups, descriptive comments from participants	Easy to gather, assess Helps guide changes to program Is it meaningful if this is the only level assessed?
Knowledge change	Knows, knows how	Standardized examinations, pre- and post-tests, skills lab, simulations	Costs are higher Easier for knowledge and skills assessment Use a control group when possible
Behavior change	Shows how, does	Direct observation of competence, objective structured clinical examinations, unannounced simulated patients, chart review, 360° evaluations	Rater training needed Clear criteria for assessment Resource-intensive Need to know baseline behavior (control) Assessed weeks to months after intervention
Results	Does (the "doing" at this level is beyond performance of a task and involves examining the impact of one's practice on patients, such as in practice-based learning and improvement program)	Quality of care measures, surveys of graduates and subsequent training program directors, unannounced standardized patients, chart review/audits	Difficult to do Organizational support required Resource-intensive

Data obtained from 1) van der Vleuten CP, Schuwirth LW. Assessing professional competence: from methods to programmes. Med Educ. 2005;39:309-17; 2) Kirkpatrick DL. Evaluation of training. In: Bittel LR, ed. Training and Development Handbook. New York: McGraw-Hill; 1967:87-112; and 3) Miller GE. The assessment of clinical skills/competence/performance. Acad Med. 1990;65:S63-7.

Essential Elements of the "Before, During, After" Framework

Assessments

A variety of measures exist to help educators evaluate their programs. Using the three-phase approach (before, during, after), consider short-term as well as longer-term "after" measurements and decide on both essential and desirable measurements. Next, consider "during" measures (or process measurements). Finally, consider "before" or baseline measures.

For instance, a program director in internal medicine selects the following goal: "I would feel happy about my program if I knew that my graduates passed the American Board of Internal Medicine (ABIM) certifying exam on their first attempt." An "after" measure of interest is clear in this example—a passing score on the ABIM certifying exam. An additional "after" measurement might include administering a survey before the exam that would reflect the trainees' study habits, time devoted, and confidence in the upcoming examination. This survey could contain both numeric and descriptive questions, with the latter serving as a qualitative measurement. A third "after" measurement in this example could be a survey given to faculty rating knowledge and study habits of each trainee. "During" measures might include performance on the Internal Medicine In-Training Examination (28); ABIM monthly evaluation form knowledge ratings; and 360° evaluation ratings from peers, students, and consultants regarding knowledge, with both numeric and free-text items (the latter serving as qualitative measurements). "Before" measures could include U.S. Medical Licensing Examination Step 2 performance, scores on core clerkship examinations, knowledge ratings on medical school evaluation forms, and free-text comments during the acting internship rotation.

In this example, the qualitative measures could provide particularly important information if residents do poorly on the examination and have a high failure rate. The qualitative measurements might reflect poor study habits or test-taking skills as a potential reason for not achieving the outcome of a 100% pass rate.

The goal statements will drive the "before," "during," and "after" measurements collected. Stated another way, the assessments used within the framework should be congruent with the goals (17). For example, if you implemented a component of a program to teach residents to improve their ability to obtain informed consent from patients and wanted to know whether the resident's behavior changed (Kirkpatrick level 3), a multiple-choice examination would be a poor assessment of this ability. However, an unannounced standardized patient, direct observation by trained faculty, or video review of performance on an objective structured clinical examination station might all be appropriate ways to determine whether the residents could show how they would achieve, and then achieve, the expected change in behavior (27).

By carefully choosing tools that reflect different aspects of performance in an area, triangulation can be achieved—confidence that trainee knowledge has been measured would be increased if multiple measures (triangulation) reflect strong performance in this domain, such as ABIM certifying examination scores and knowledge ratings from teachers and peers.

The importance of faculty or rater training with using evaluation measurements has been discussed elsewhere (29). Indeed, many educators argue that we do not need more or "better" assessment tools to improve the reliability and validity of data obtained; rather, we need to invest efforts to train our teachers on how to use the tools.

Many training programs already gather a significant amount of information about trainees and the program, but the utility and importance of collecting information should be questioned if the information will not be analyzed. In other words, spend time deciding what is necessary, not simply convenient. Certainly, electronic systems used in the evaluation process make the dissemination, collection, and organization of rating forms, critiques, and other data much easier for those who run programs. However, if these data are not reviewed and analyzed systematically, unexpected results, or warning signs, may be overlooked. If assessments are made and information collected, a mechanism should be in place to review, analyze, and, if necessary, disseminate the results to stakeholders.

As an example, trainees are typically asked to critique clerkship rotations and faculty, all of which may include written comments. How should this information be handled? One approach could be to conduct a formal qualitative analysis, determine themes, and categorize comments. Another might be to review all critiques with relevant stakeholders (such as the site director, chief of medical residents, program director, and chief of medicine), with return of the critique to the individual teacher and to the program director (for residents) as part of a 360° evaluation process. Such a review process involves stakeholders, can detect problems quickly, and provides feedback, even without a formal qualitative analysis of comments.

Resources
Evident throughout the discussion thus far is that resources—human capital, time, and funding—are needed to conduct program evaluation.

Human Resources. There needs to be a core group of people within the program (see chapter 4 of this book) who are invested in program evaluation and who have the necessary skills, or access to those with skills, for the evaluation process. Those who lead program evaluation should be familiar with database creation, database maintenance, basic statistical methods, and basic study design, although these skills need not all reside in a single individual. There may also be a need to develop assessment methods. In some institutions, offices or departments can help with this (30), but if those are not present, additional training or classes to develop the skills may be needed.

To conduct program evaluation, one may need people who have expertise in standardized patients, objective structured clinical examinations, qualitative analysis, or other qualities. Different skills sets, training, and backgrounds of individuals within a group can bring an important perspective to addressing program evaluation, and can foster collaboration. In addition, working as a member of a group not only helps to build skills across individuals but also sets up an expectation of work to be accomplished. It is very motivating to have others expect something of you (such as a product, an update, an analysis, or background research).

Time. Other than having the human resources available, time is undoubtedly the biggest barrier to effective program evaluation. People are affected by the time needed for all elements of program evaluation, including researching, planning, developing, implementing, monitoring, analyzing, discussing, and even disseminating the findings. Such demands are balanced against all the other competing demands of leaders in academic programs, such as patient care, teaching, research, committee work, and community service.

While residency program directors are required to have half of their time protected to administer the training program (including program evaluation), such "protected time" is often consumed by other duties. The situation is worse for clerkship and course directors, who have no established requirement (only recommendations) for "protected time" (31). There are no easy solutions to the need to devote time to program evaluation, but the following are some suggestions.

First, capitalize on what you are already doing. The current processes used to collect information about individuals and programs may already be done well and are probably yielding a wealth of information that should be used for program evaluation. Second, as much as possible, collect and enter data prospectively. Accomplishing the work of program evaluation in "real time" may add time in the present but will make the ultimate analysis seem less burdensome. Third, don't go it alone—find people with whom to collaborate, or others willing or able to help with data entry. Fourth, as described in previous chapters of this book, "make it count twice." The effort put into program evaluation can yield important findings that may interest the larger medical education community through workshops, abstracts, or papers. Finally, meet with your leadership to negotiate for the time it takes to do program evaluation, making sure that, at a minimum, you receive the time that accreditation organizations require. But reach an agreement about what is expected of you in return.

Funding. One must determine what is realistic to accomplish with the time, people, and money available. Funding for routine program evaluation may come from the institutional level (such as support for a common evaluation and data collection system across clerkship or residency programs) or may have department-specific requirements (such as software programs and personnel). For curricular innovations, one should factor in the cost to accomplish program evaluation in order to know whether the change has led to benefit or harm; intramural funds might be available to support this. Sources and methods of funding should be explicitly considered for program evaluation.

❖ Monitoring Programs

The frequency of routine, summative program evaluation is often determined by the natural educational cycle—for example, annually within a residency program or clerkship program or quarterly or semiannually for recurring courses in preclinical courses. However, some level of formative program evaluation should be ongoing, to monitor the pulse of the program. Furthermore, curricular innovations (see chapter 6 of this book), or new educational programs, may deserve more frequent, formal analysis of results, akin to a "medical monitor" for clinical trials, to ensure that any harm or benefit is understood early in the process. The necessary frequency of program evaluation introduces the concept of warning flags that academic leaders need to follow.

"Red flags" are information from the program evaluation that require immediate attention and action. "Yellow flags" should be followed more closely than usual and may require intervention. Both sets of flags can help to set priorities on what to expend resources on in the evaluation process. For instance, if a group of students were repetitively absent from mandatory teaching conferences on a rotation, the clerkship director should not wait until the annual review to intervene. Similarly, if a resident reported working 100 hours in a given week while on the wards, the residency program director would need to act immediately. A "yellow flag" for a program director might be a resident who worked 78 hours a week for several consecutive weeks; for a clerkship director, it might be a teacher who received negative comments on a critique from a student. Further examples of red and yellow flags in undergraduate and graduate medical education are available (2). Because every program is unique in some respects, this categorization of red and yellow flags somewhat depends on the educational program.

❖ Additional Practicalities and Getting Started

See Box 7-2 for tips on getting started and on staying committed to program evaluation. A few of those points are emphasized here. First, as mentioned earlier, don't go it alone. A program evaluation will improve performance and the quality of the work by setting expectations, pacing, and incorporating alternative views into potential goals, measurements, and the interpretation of findings. It can also create a scholarship team.

As a corollary, be willing to seek help. This could be a consultant who can help with study design, data collection methods, or data analysis. Similarly, consider creating interdepartmental mock (or real) reviews or external reviews with external evaluators.

Start with what you must do, but play to your strengths. Some elements of program evaluation are not negotiable and must be done. But to expand the view of evaluating your program, find what you do well, or areas in which you have a specific interest, and use that as the spark.

In addition, accrediting organizations such as the ACGME and the LCME offer a variety of materials, including lists of common program citations that can serve as a starting point for constructing red and yellow flags.

Finally, get involved in regional and national medical education conferences, such as the Research in Medical Education Conference, Academic Internal Medicine Week (sponsored by the Alliance for Academic Internal Medicine), and the Society of General Internal Medicine. These meetings are excellent places to share best practices and experiences and to learn from others.

❖ Conclusion

Program evaluation is the process by which medical educators and leaders determine whether their programs are successful, by examining outcomes and determining what is contributing to the outcomes. The before, during, after framework helps visualize the continuum of program evaluation and can be used to embed assessments (measures) that will help achieve the goal of meaningful results.

Box 7-2. Tips for Getting Started and Staying Committed to Program Evaluation

► Make it routine—program evaluation is part of running any educational training program.

► Don't go it alone. Start a core group of stakeholders with whom to work and develop expectations. Having others expect something from you is a powerful motivator.

► Seek collaboration. Find those with skills you may not have (such as sophisticated statistical analysis).

► Decide in advance what you want to evaluate and how you want to evaluate it.

► Plan what information you need for a before, during, after analysis.

► Know what is essential (required for accreditation) and what is desirable.

► Collect and enter data prospectively. Waiting to enter data at some later time can be demoralizing as the amount and time needed for data entry become daunting.

► Develop basic skills for data analysis, including creating databases, data entry, and descriptive data analysis. If you need to, take a class to learn how to do this.

► "Make it count twice": much of the work will yield information that is scholarly, so disseminate it to colleagues (i.e., make it scholarship).

► Understand local policy about what is considered quality assurance and what may require institutional review board approval.

► Measure the reliability and validity of assessments.

Disclaimer: The views expressed are those of the authors and do not reflect the official policy or position of the Uniformed Services University of the Health Sciences, the Department of Defense, or the U.S. Government.

REFERENCES

1. **Accreditation Council for Graduate Medical Education.** Glossary of Terms. 2009. Accessed at www.acgme.org/acWebsite/about/ab_ACGMEglossary.pdf.
2. **Durning SJ, Hemmer PA, Pangaro LN.** The structure of program evaluation: an approach for evaluating a course, clerkship, or components of a residency or fellowship training program. Teach Learn Med. 2007;19:308-18.
3. **Goldie J.** AMEE Education Guide no. 29: evaluating educational programmes. Med Teach. 2006;28:210-24.
4. **Green ML.** Identifying, appraising, and implementing medical education curricula: a guide for medical educators. Ann Intern Med. 2001;135:889-96.
5. **Musick DW.** A conceptual model for program evaluation in graduate medical education. Acad Med. 2006;81:759-65.
6. **Stufflebeam DL.** CIPP Evaluation Model Checklist: a tool for applying the fifth installment of the CIPP Model to assess long-term enterprises. Accessed at www.wmich.edu/evalctr/checklists/cippchecklist.pdf.
7. **Stufflebeam DL.** The CIPP model for evaluation. In: Stufflebeam DL, Madaus GF, Kellaghan T, eds. Evaluation Models. 2nd ed. Boston: Kluwer; 2000.
8. **Woodard CA.** Program evaluation. In: Norman GR, van der Vleueten CP, Newble DI, eds. International Handbook of Research in Medical Education. Boston: Kluwer; 2002.
9. **Hawkins RE, Holmboe ES.** Constructing an evaluation system for an educational program. In: Holmboe ES, Hawkins RE, eds. Practical Guide to the Evaluation of Clinical Competence. Philadelphia: Mosby Elsevier; 2008:216-38.
10. **Accreditation Council for Graduate Medical Education.** ACGME Outcome Project: Enhancing Residency Education Through Outcomes Assessment. Accessed at www.acgme.org/outcome.
11. **Goroll AH, Sirio C, Duffy FD, LeBlond RF, Alguire P, Blackwell TA, et al; Residency Review Committee for Internal Medicine.** A new model for accreditation of residency programs in internal medicine. Ann Intern Med. 2004;140:902-9.
12. **Liaison Committee on Medical Education.** Functions and structure of a medical school. Standards for accreditation of medical education programs leading to the MD Degree. 2008. Accessed at www.lcme.org/standard.htm.
13. **Asch DA, Epstein A, Nicholson S.** Evaluating medical training programs by the quality of care delivered by their alumni. JAMA. 2007;298:1049-51.
14. **Downing SM.** Reliability: on the reproducibility of assessment data. Med Educ. 2004;38:1006-12.
15. **Downing SM.** Validity: on meaningful interpretation of assessment data. Med Educ. 2003;37:830-7.
16. **Downing SM.** Face validity of assessments: faith-based interpretations or evidence-based science? Med Educ. 2006;40:7-8.
17. **van der Vleuten CP, Schuwirth LW.** Assessing professional competence: from methods to programmes. Med Educ. 2005;39:309-17.
18. **Colliver JA.** Call for greater emphasis on effect-size measures in published articles in Teaching and Learning in Medicine [Editorial]. Teach Learn Med. 2002;14:206-10.
19. **Colliver JA, Markwell SJ.** ANCOVA, selection bias, statistical equating, and effect size: recommendations for publication [Editorial]. Teach Learn Med. 2006;18:284-6.
20. **Downing SM, Haladyna TM.** Validity threats: overcoming interference with proposed interpretations of assessment data. Med Educ. 2004;38:327-33.

21. **Pugno PA, Kahn NB Jr.** The residency assistance program: 1,000+ opportunities and 30 years of experience promoting excellence in family medicine education. Fam Med. 2005;37:253-8.
22. **Kassebaum DG.** The measurement of outcomes in the assessment of educational program effectiveness. Acad Med. 1990;65:293-6.
23. **Holzemer WL.** A protocol for program evaluation. J Med Educ. 1976;51:101-8.
24. **Denton GD, Durning SJ, Wimmer AP, Pangaro LN, Hemmer PA.** Is a faculty developed pretest equivalent to pre-third year GPA or USMLE step 1 as a predictor of third-year internal medicine clerkship outcomes? Teach Learn Med. 2004;16:329-32.
25. **Durning SJ, Pangaro LN, Denton GD, Hemmer PA, Wimmer A, Grau T, et al.** Intersite consistency as a measurement of programmatic evaluation in a medicine clerkship with multiple, geographically separated sites. Acad Med. 2003;78:S36-8.
26. **Kirkpatrick DL.** Evaluation of training. In: Bittel LR, ed. Training and Development Handbook. New York: McGraw-Hill; 1967:87-112.
27. **Miller GE.** The assessment of clinical skills/competence/performance. Acad Med. 1990;65:S63-7.
28. **Babbott SF, Beasley BW, Hinchey KT, Blotzer JW, Holmboe ES.** The predictive validity of the internal medicine in-training examination. Am J Med. 2007;120:735-40.
29. **Pangaro LN, Holmboe ES.** Evaluation forms and global rating scales. In: Holmboe ES, Hawkins RE, eds. Practical Guide to the Evaluation of Clinical Competence. Philadelphia: Mosby Elsevier; 2008:24-41.
30. **Gruppen L.** Creating and sustaining centres for medical education research and development. Med Educ. 2008;42:121-3.
31. **Pangaro L, Bachicha J, Brodkey A, Chumley-Jones H, Fincher RM, Gelb D, et al; Alliance for Clinical Education.** Expectations of and for clerkship directors: a collaborative statement from the Alliance for Clinical Education. Teach Learn Med. 2003;15:217-22.

8

Developing a System for Evaluation of Learners

Daniel J. Klass, MD, FRCPC, FACP

You have just accepted an invitation from the chair of the department of medicine to become the new program director for the internal medicine residency. Your chair advises you to focus on an upcoming accreditation review by the Residency Review Committee in 2 years. A key criticism from the last review was that the program needed a more systematic process for evaluating the residents—more specifically, whether each of them had met expectations and were ready for independent practice.

This chapter will help you to organize your thoughts and steer your activity for the task of evaluating your learners, be they residents in your house staff program or students in your course or clerkship. The chapter addresses 1) the organizing principles and underlying assumptions of evaluation of learners, including the legacy of past evaluation systems and the culture of evaluation; 2) evaluation across the spectrum of medical education; and 3) principles and concrete examples for selecting tools for evaluation, such as developing a blueprint that supports a multimethod assessment for all of the dimensions of competence. In addition to practical suggestions on creating blueprints for evaluation of learners, the chapter will provide perspective on your new task as a manager of your assessment systems, and prepare you to identify and assemble the necessary resources.

KEY POINTS

- Create a blueprint to match your assessment methods with goals for your learners.
- Use several methods for each goal; for efficiency, try to cover several competencies with each method.
- Form a committee of stakeholders to help you understand and shape the assessment culture of your program
- In defining standards for trainees, make sure that any implicit expectations become explicit for level of training.
- Ground the evaluation system in the real world of medical practice, relying on the best possible tools, including those used for quality management.

Because the chapter is written for clerkship and course directors in undergraduate medical education, program directors in graduate medical education, and leaders of programs for continuing medical education, it is not intended to be prescriptive for any particular group of academic managers. In addition, it does not contain a detailed formula for setting up and managing the available multiple-choice tests, for example, or patient simulations. For that, refer to comprehensive, book-length resources aimed at these tasks for undergraduate (1) and graduate (2) medical education. The goal of this chapter is to help any of the aforementioned directors, including those who may be just starting out in their position of responsibility for an academic program, with an overview of the activities needed for the effective evaluation of medical trainees.

It is important for clinical educators to understand—and not be frustrated by—the fact that available tools for evaluating clinical trainees lack the precision of the diagnostic tests used in clinical medicine. Teachers' direct observations do not approach the accuracy of the history and physical examination of a patient, and supplementary tests (such as standardized patients or computer case management simulations) are very different from measures of serum chemistries and magnetic resonance imaging. A common trap for beginning clinical evaluators is to press the analogy between diagnosing disease and measuring competency. The uncertainties of assessment methods for individual human performance reflect the complexity of competence itself, and this necessitate an overall strategy that uses multiple methods.

❖ Linking the Culture of Evaluation and Quality Improvement

The world of clinical evaluation is in flux. Typically, evaluation of learners focused on end-of-course or end-of-program "capstone" summative decisions rather than ongoing formative processes for feedback. These assessments have been high-stakes events, with momentous, make-or-break implications for trainees. In turn, this has made the process difficult for faculty and intimidating for trainees. In general, once these assessment hurdles have been cleared, the resultant benefit is viewed as "good for life." This concept has been described as part of the "ballistic model" of evaluating medical competence (3). But this model is yielding to a more contemporary expectation that practitioners continually show competence and maintenance of certification. Standards are important, but they can serve as targets and milestones of training, not solely as cut-offs.

Thus, a first injunction is to commit resources to ensure that the department values a culture of assessment with regular evaluation and feedback (that is, quality improvement), and not just end-of-clerkship or end-of-program testing. Assessment should be viewed as the critical evaluative component within a system of clinical quality improvement, rather than as the sharp edge of a summative academic exercise. The major purposes of assessment must be educational (formative), not just judgmental (summative). Medical students and residents have been carefully selected. Nearly all are capable of succeeding, and do so. No doubt an occasional "bad apple" must be excluded, but this should not be at the expense of devaluing effective, improvement-oriented assessment. This positive attitude should serve as the framework for your own organizational efforts and should be pervasive throughout the development and outcome of the evaluation system.

The second injunction is this: Don't just tinker at the edges; be bold! Leadership means more than just following the conventional path. Be prepared to thoroughly revise the evaluation system currently used in your clerkship or residency, and approach your task with an appropriate sense of urgency. In the context of the impending Residency Review Committee accreditation visit, the short time frame can be your friend if innovation is your target.

❖ The Initial Questions

At the outset, your work in developing a system for evaluating your learners should be guided by the following questions:

    1. What are the goals and objectives of the evaluation system?

2. Which assessment tools match the goals and objectives needed to fulfill the educational mission?
3. What resources and organizational effort, especially faculty development, are needed to implement the new program?
4. How can program evaluation be built into the process so that you will easily know whether the program is successful? (See chapter 7 of this book for further details.)

❖ Getting Help

In a typical program, evaluation of trainees is too large a task for a single person. Your hospital or medical school may already have crafted a general evaluation strategy. The hope is that you will find experienced educators to help you with specific assessment tools (such as standardized patients) and to ensure alignment between your own and institutional evaluation schemes. You may find colleagues in other departments who are in the same boat as you.

An early task is to build a representative committee that will help you develop the directions and details of your program. Each committee member should be encouraged to "specialize" in one (or more) of the major dimensions of the task (such as expertise in use of simulation) and to take ownership of the implementation of that component. Deep engagement of faculty colleagues, and their eventual support in the evolving process, is a critical requirement of any new assessment scheme. Unless faculty "buy-in" can be obtained, your best efforts could be wasted. Look up and down; keep the chair of your department in touch with the project and involve the trainees as well—they are key stakeholders and will be advocates for positive change.

Assistance in defining goals and objectives comes from the education organizations, such as the Accreditation Council for Graduate Medical Education (ACGME), Liaison Committee on Medical Education, and American Board of Internal Medicine (ABIM), which have clear statements about the overall purpose and objectives for evaluation strategies. Your own success will depend on achieving some alignment with these overriding directions. Be sure to understand the specific parts of the accreditation process that relate to assessment to be certain the system for evaluation of learners that you design will pass muster with the organizations (2).

Finally, don't ignore your institution's previous or current evaluation systems. Every school has a tradition of evaluation that shapes important elements of its curriculum. There is also cross-fertilization of assessment culture from undergraduate medical education through postgraduate education, along with maintenance of competence programs, that can positively or negatively affect both student expectation and faculty practice.

❖ Traditional Approaches to Evaluation of Clinical Competence

Traditionally, the continuum of medical training included getting into medical school, graduating from school and entering graduate education, and completing residency and beginning practice. There might be some continuing medical education requirements for hospital credentialing, but by and large this was not of great consequence. Indeed, once physicians were in practice, they would encounter no further high-stakes assessments of their skills or competence. Thus, assessments at the end of undergraduate and graduate medical education were tools to weed out the incapable. This objective justified a certain "hawkish" stance in the minds of some faculty and grade inflation—or avoidance of evaluation—in others. In a world of "once in, good for life," what was needed above all was assurance of key attributes of competence. Despite this view, the standards of achievement were rarely made explicit; rather, it was assumed that these standards were incorporated into the judgment of the faculty and, therefore, applied fairly and consistently. This lack of transparency continues to haunt the direct observation component of clinical assessment, and the validation of the overall standards has only recently been undertaken.

From the content perspective, two key dimensions for determining clinical competence existed: *knowledge* and *case-related professional behaviors*. The knowledge domain, whose boundaries in the field of internal medicine were mainly defined in the pages of *Cecil and Loeb's* or *Harrison's* textbooks of medicine, could be assessed by written exams. Originally these exams consisted of written essays, but in the 1960s and 1970s, multiple-choice questions that could be machine-scored were increasingly used. These new test formats provided reliable results and allowed the efficient surveying of large amounts of clinical information. Case-related behaviors were further categorized into such processes as history-taking, performing physical examination, making the diagnosis, and outlining management steps.

The clinical content of the capstone examination mirrored the "content" that happened to be on the wards of teaching hospitals. However, it rarely bore a formal relationship to the patient population or disease mix that would ultimately be served in practice. Standards for case-related behaviors depended on the intuition-based judgments of individual examining physicians. Even after Elstein and colleagues (4) pointed out that physician competence was specific for, and limited to, individual patient cases, generalizations about the capability of candidates were still based on their performances in small numbers of random cases. This latter form of assessment by "oral" case-based exams and clinical competency examinations continues to be considered an authentic test of clinical ability, even though systematic study (5) led to its discontinuation in the certification process.

Thus, until a quarter of a century ago, if you were responsible for evaluating residents or students, your task would have been clerical: recruiting and scheduling the examining physicians for the observational clinical tests and finding enough valid questions to mount a credible multiple-choice test of knowledge.

❖ The Rise of Psychometrics

The origin of the sea change in clinical evaluation is attributable to the maturation of psychometrics (the science of educational and psychological measurement), particularly the invention of everyday tools to measure the reliability of assessments—that is, their consistency across raters and tests (3). Reliability studies by the National Board of Medical Examiners (6), for example, performed around 1965, revealed that clinical faculty who observed individual students performing clinical examinations showed about the same reliability as a coin toss.

Deficiencies of the common evaluation formats, related to both reliability and validity issues, had become sufficiently concerning by the mid-1980s that testing organizations, professional societies, and educators began to address the need for change. The classic clinical oral examination (known as the CEX, or clinical examination)—in which a single, unknown patient is interviewed, examined, and counseled by the candidate under direct observation of a examiner—began to lose credibility because of its resource demands, its psychometric deficiencies (poor reliability, lack of evidence of validity, and a tendency to bias), and its lack of transparency (7). The multiple-choice format of questioning, despite its comprehensive nature and technical reliability, has, with a few notable exceptions (4), somewhat lacked "authenticity." How does a particular score on a 180-item multiple-choice test predict a candidate's ability to actually practice medicine? Or, more technically, what proportion of the variance in a valid measure of patient care can be explained by results of a multiple-choice test of knowledge? Howard Barrows, who pioneered the use of standardized patients in performance assessments, used to ask, "Would you trust pilots to fly you anywhere if their chief credential was based upon passing a multiple choice exam?" This question of validity remains unsettled to this day, largely because of the difficulty of making the kind of systematic observations needed to address the important issue of the meaning of these tests (7). Fortunately, enthusiasm for new frameworks of assessment, the innovative redeployment of old tools, and the introduction of new tools into the field has risen; all of these address this issue of validity, or meaning, of assessments.

❖ Do You Evaluate Performance or Competence?

It is important to distinguish between two differing constructs of evaluation of learners: competence and performance. In Miller's terminology (8), competence evaluation answers the question of whether the trainee "can do" the tasks of patient care; performance evaluation answers whether the trainee "does do" (or "has done") the tasks. Attention is focused on a learner engaged in a series of situations, and evidence is gathered to infer the learner's capability (or lack thereof) of performing future similar tasks in a competent fashion. The construct of the test is the logic that links the tested performance to the future performances. The typical motor vehicle drivers test is the best example of a competence assessment. It consists of several parts designed to simulate the full "construct" of driving, including knowledge of the law, ability to parallel-park, tests of vision, and, in some cases, an actual sample of driving. Performance assessment, on the other hand, focuses on the quality of "a whole act" and concerns all the elements of a situation, including the actors.

But what does this mean for clinical evaluation of learners? The increasing use of performance assessments for accountability purposes in clinical practice situations drives change in clinical evaluation of trainees.

❖ Contemporary Approaches to Clinical Evaluation

As tools for evaluation have become more varied and sophisticated, assessment has moved from a focus on "achievement" before practice to far more nuanced approaches, most of which apply to testing practitioners as well as trainees. These new approaches, from a technical perspective, have strengthened the armamentarium of the assessment processes (9, 10). For example, in addition to using written tests and the direct observation of trainees with patients, performance can be assessed by the use of clinical outcomes (such as readmissions after surgical procedures or frequency of particular complications); documented compliance with clinical processes (such as "found in notation" in charts); observation in direct peer-based performance reviews; achievement of levels of "approval or appreciation" by coworkers or patients and their families (11); or participation in particular processes in continuing professional development, such as log books, diaries, or organized portfolios (12). Some of these methods will be discussed in more detail later in this chapter. We now have many more tools that can actually examine the working process of physicians and, likewise, physicians in training. This is contributing to the development of a strong performance orientation across the spectrum of assessment, including that of trainees before practice.

From Competence to Performance
The use of performance-oriented tools changes the framework of assessment from "competence" to "performance." The traditional competence-oriented framework of assessment has better reflected the tools that were available; now a performance-oriented assessment is possible. We had tested what we *could*; now we can test what we *should*. And because in a competence-based framework evaluators assume that competence is the sum of an individual's knowledge and their observable and discrete clinical skills, the key assessment decisions had been to choose the tools that best measured these dimensions. The fundamental problem with this approach, apart from the weakness of the methods themselves, is that the measures of competence have become ends in themselves. They have not been formally linked to a contextualized concept of competence, or to performance-related outcome variables that reflected actual medical practice. The core of the new performance-based paradigm of clinical evaluation is the linking of assessment content to evidence of measurable clinical processes and outcomes in patient care.

This last point is especially relevant to the revised definitions of competence and the evaluation targets of the ACGME and similar organizations, such as the goals of Educating Future Physicians of Ontario and the CanMEDS roles (Box 8-1). Each of these formulations represents an attempt to define the competent physician as one who integrates many roles or attributes, not just one who possesses certain disconnected qualities (Figure 8-1).

Assessment in a Quality Improvement Framework
The availability of new testing methods and the public's demand for professional accountability for clinical outcomes have driven dramatic developments in clinical medicine and evaluation and, in particular, a new focus on the outcomes of practice. For example, your focus as program director tasked with evaluating the competence of your trainees should include the performance of your graduates in their subsequent settings, and you

Box 8-1. Frameworks for Assessment of Competence

Clinical Competence Elements Defined by ACGME (33)

- ▶ Patient care (including medical interviewing, physical examination, and procedural skills)
- ▶ Medical knowledge
- ▶ Practice-based learning and improvement
- ▶ Interpersonal and communication skills
- ▶ Professionalism
- ▶ Systems-based practice

Canadian Medical Education Directives for Specialists (CanMEDS Roles) (34)

- ▶ Medical expert
- ▶ Communicator
- ▶ Collaborator
- ▶ Manager
- ▶ Health advocate
- ▶ Scholar
- ▶ Professional

should use those data to improve your own curriculum (5). Until now, our test methods have concentrated on the concept of competence in the sense of "being ready" for practice. The alternative paradigm of assessment, much more aligned with quality improvement, examines physician trainees' action in context; it judges competence (6) on the basis of completion of real-life performances in the workplace or in highly authentic simulations.

A driving force for many of the new assessment methods of the past 25 years has been the opportunity, afforded by health care institutional data banks, to witness the connection between the acts (processes) of medical encounters and patient care outcomes. As a result, important links can be forged between the traditionally separate processes of academic clinical evaluation and quality improvement. These assessment activities should now be seen as part of an educational process within a system of health care delivery, and are captured in the ACGME competency of "practice-based learning and improvement." Ultimately, this synthesis of quality improve-

"He looks very promising—but let's see how he does on the written test."

Figure 8-1 The competent physician is one who integrates many roles or attributes, not just certain disconnected qualities. From Sidney Harris/Condé Nast Publications Inc. courtesy of The Cartoon Bank, ©2000.

ment and performance assessment in an educational framework will add value to academic medicine—for example, through answers to long-standing questions such as, "Does this assessment predict an individual's high-quality performance in practice?" or "Does this particular process contribute to a positive health outcome?"

The practical challenge is to find ways to systematically link the critical tasks of the discipline to the realities of practice in real-world settings. Table 8-1, based on the ideas of Laduca and colleagues (13, 14), assembles the task dimension in the context of characteristic clinical encounters in

Table 8-1. Proposed Framework (Blueprint) of Assessment Based on Scopes (or Models) of Practice*

Model of Practice	Clinical Settings	Typical Clinical Encounter Types	Typical Spectra of Disease†	Typical Diagnostic Skill Sets to Be Assessed‡	Typical Technical Skills	Patient/Team Management Skills
Solo or group specialty practice in rural or suburban settings	Private office, ambulatory clinic, home visits, general hospital wards, inpatient consultation services, long-term care facilities	Stable follow-up and exacerbations of chronic, *known* illnesses and behavioral/emotional, grave, non-remitting disease with relatively few active treatment options; acute, *first-time* presentations of common illnesses; frequent referrals and handoffs	Demographic-dependent; spectrum of chronic illness predominant: diabetes, chronic CVD disorders and their prevention; chronic gastrointestinal symptoms; genitourinary infections; chronic lung, liver, and joint disease; acute infections; AIDS, anemias; tumors	Focused physical examination; diagnostic interviewing; efficient test ordering; effective drug use for, prevention of, and management of chronic illness	Procedural skills related to common chronic illness (e.g., thoracentesis, joint/bone marrow aspiration, liver biopsy)	Counseling, family counseling, coordination of care, interprofessional collaboration, education for medication self-adjustment

continued

Table 8-1. Proposed Framework (Blueprint) of Assessment Based on Scopes (or Models) of Practice* (continued)

Model of Practice	Clinical Settings	Typical Clinical Encounter Types	Typical Spectra of Disease†	Typical Diagnostic Skill Sets to Be Assessed‡	Typical Technical Skills	Patient/Team Management Skills
Group specialty practice in large urban/teaching hospitals	Acute treatment/ inpatient ward, consultation services, continuity practices for management of chronic illness	New presentations of acute conditions, complex chronic cases, interactions of multiple systems, readmissions, failure of prior treatment regimens	Demographically adjusted spectrum of chronic disease: CVD, COPD, joint disease, chemotherapy	Specialty-specific physical examination, specific diagnostic protocols	Central line placement, thoracentesis, specific joint injection, paracentesis	Informed consent for procedures and treatment protocols
Practices that are largely procedural or invasive in nature	Procedure room, emergency department, operating room, intensive care unit	Newly diagnosed patients with acute presentations of life-threatening illnesses	Preoperative clearance, cardiac risk factors, neutropenic crises	Stress testing, interpretation of complex studies	Pacemaker implantation, bone marrow biopsy	Informed consent, giving bad news

COPD = chronic obstructive pulmonary disease; CVD = cardiovascular disease.

*This table is largely theoretical and is presented for explanatory purposes. Each program needs to determine its own final objectives in terms of the kinds of scopes of practice for which its successful trainees are suited. Although not all trainees follow these same objectives, the training of the group must fulfill the main objectives. Similarly, the breakdown of cases in each setting, as well as the preponderant encounter types, must be worked out empirically. To complete this task, access to hospital or practice system data is required to compete each department's understanding of the "epidemiology" of practice within the relevant institutions. These data should include demographic profiles of patients within the system, admission data to each unit, discharge diagnoses, and hospital- or clinic-based procedural records. The overall objective is to build an empirical "model" of internal medicine practice on which both teaching efforts and assessments can be rationally distributed.

†Based on a regionally valid list of "top 20" diseases.

‡Diagnostic and technical skill sets are compatible with the Accreditation Council for Graduate Medical Education competencies.

typical settings. This hierarchy facilitates the construction of a competence test that is linked to clinical reality.

❖ Tool Selection and Use

Once the general framework (for example, ACGME competencies, CanMEDS roles, or an institution-specific version of these) for assessment has been determined, detailed work needs to begin on the exact shape of the assessment process. You should 1) establish the strategy to build the test content (typically using a blueprint [see Table 8-1]); 2) flesh out the details of the specific assessment tools and tests (Tables 8-2, 8-3, and 8-4); and 3) plan how frequently you will sample your trainees' abilities and how you will collect, store, and analyze data on the tests.

In choosing the tools to be used, it is important that the tools fit with the dimensions of assessment defined by the regulatory bodies. If ACGME says they want "practice-based learning and improvement" to be assessed, then you must have a tool with this capability.

Methods of assessment, or tools, should be selected for each dimension of competence in the framework. Since the late 1980s, a variety of innovative testing formats has become available.

Almost all these assessment tools target "performance" in context (that is, actual practice of medicine). They include peer assessment tools to evaluate individual performance in practice (15); objective structured clinical examinations (16); standardized patients to test clinical skills (17, 18); more accurate targeting of knowledge-based tests (14, 19); tools that test "judgment" or application of knowledge through chart-based recall methods and improved simulations of clinical scenarios, whether by computer (20) or in newly developed high-technology simulation methods (21); testing for practice that occurs within a system (11, 22); and improved tools for self assessment (23). In addition, administrative data (for instance, compliance with practice guidelines) obtained during health care delivery can be used to advantage as indicators of good medical performance. Many of these tools can be expensive or human resource intensive, and some not yet well understood by the profession. Remember, you cannot use all the available tests, and you need a process or model of selecting those that will tell you what you want to know, and do so efficiently. Basing your selection on an explicit model and blueprint can be very helpful in this regard.

Table 8-2. Matching the "Test Methods" With the Competencies or Roles to Be Assessed*

ACGME Competencies	CanMED Roles	Multiple-Choice Tests, Written Examinations	Computer Case Simulations	Ongoing Clinical Observation Across Supervisors	Standardized Patients and OSCEs	Mini-CEX, Other Direct Formal Observation Protocols	Feedback From External Personnel (360° and Peer Assessment)	Portfolio and External Data-Gathering†
Medical knowledge	Medical expert, scholar	XXX	XX	XX	X	XX	XX	X
Interpersonal and communication skills	Communicator, collaborator	X	X	XX	XXX	XX	XXX	X
Professionalism	Professional, collaborator, health advocate	X	X	XXX	X	X	XX	XX
Patient care	Manager, health advocate, medical expert	XX	XX	XXX	XX	XXX	XX	XXX
System-based Practice	Manager, health advocate, collaborator	X	X	XX	X	X	XXX	X

continued

Table 8-2. Matching the "Test Methods" With the Competencies or Roles to Be Assessed* (continued)

ACGME Competencies	CanMED Roles	Multiple-Choice Tests, Written Examinations	Computer Case Simulations	Ongoing Clinical Observation Across Supervisors	Standardized Patients and OSCEs	Mini-CEX, Other Direct Formal Observation Protocols	Feedback From External Personnel (360° and Peer Assessment)	Portfolio and External Data-Gathering†
Practice-based learning and improvement	Medical expert, scholar	x	x	x	x	x	x	xxx

ACGME = Accreditation Council for Graduate Medical Education; Mini-CEX = mini-clinical examination; OSCE = objective structured clinical examination.

*Table presents a sample matrix for a program director's assessment planning for internal medicine residents or a clerkship director's planning for students, yielding a multimethod assessment of multiple dimensions. Key to sources of evidence of competence in learning settings: x = marginal contribution to evidence; xx = significant contribution but not large or efficient; xxx = large and efficient contribution, not always sufficient for decision-making; xxxx = substantial contribution, independently sufficient for decision-making; not used in this table because no current method of assessment is always sufficienct in itself.

†This category includes methods under development (see text), including use of learning portfolios as well as the gathering of outcome and process data from internal or external data repositories.

Table 8-3. Example of Blueprint for Direct Observation, in Mini-CEX Format, of Resident Skills in Actual Practice*

Setting	Clinical Problems	Skill Sets			
		Diagnostic Interviewing	Focused Physical Examination	Counseling	Procedural Skills
Inpatient ward (all on one patient)†	Pneumonia	Acute problem (cough, fever, etc.)	Respiratory-related examination	Informed consent for thoracentesis	Thoracentesis
Inpatient ward (four different patients)‡	COPD/chemotherapy patient/CHF/hypotension	Readmission for COPD	Neutropenic fever	Education for medication self-adjustment	Central line placement
Outpatient clinic (all on one patient)†	Rotator cuff	Persistent shoulder pain	Shoulder examination	Informed consent	Joint injection
Outpatient clinic (four different patients)‡	Low back pain/thyrotoxicosis/diabetes/	Low back pain	Thyroid examination and related systemic findings	Therapy selection for glucose control	Paracentesis
Consultation service (all on one patient)†	Preoperative clearance	Cardiac risk factors	Cardiovascular	Atherosclerosis risk reduction	Exercise treadmill test
Consultation service (four different patients)‡	See under "Skill Sets"	Vertigo	Dizziness	Anticoagulation	Lumbar puncture

CHF = congestive heart failure; COPD = chronic obstructive pulmonary disease.

*Based on 15 *available* patients; assessment can be accomplished collectively by several faculty members over 6 to 12 months.

†This is a traditional "long case"; it allows the teacher to observe for coherence and focus across tasks in a single patient.

‡This allows the teacher to observe for consistency, and a minimal skill level across problems and patients.

Table 8-4. Sample Blueprint for a Six-Station Objective Structured Clinical Examination for Internal Medicine Subinterns or Interns*

Problem	Interviewing (3 Observations)	Physical Examination (4 Observations)	Counseling (2 Observations)	Procedures (2 Observations)
Asthma	History	Respiratory examination	Management of exacerbation	
Depression	History	Depression inventory		
Cardiac valvular disease		Cardiovascular examination†		Electrocardiogram interpretation
Geriatric	Dementia screening	Gait and mobility testing†		
Resuscitation				Manikin intubation or central line placement‡
Oncology, cancer recurrence			Breaking bad news	

*Clinical skills are sampled under test conditions by using standardized challenges. Simulations are used except as noted.

†Actual patients with findings are preferred.

‡As available.

❖ Models and Blueprints in the Assessment of Trainees

Models and blueprints for evaluation of learners are complementary. The *model* specifies the major domains to be tested. Written in the concrete language of physician tasks in specified clinical situations, the model should represent no less than a statement of the meaning of competence for your department. The *blueprint*, as the word implies, provides the specifics to execute the assessment plan, detailing which tools will be used for each of the assessed domains and what weight each component will have in the overall assessment.

The Model: Connecting the Clinical Roles to Scopes of Practice

Your system of assessment should begin by stating what competence entails; in other words, you must make explicit the expectations and scope of trainee competence. It is not enough to say that all graduates must be good communicators, or that they possess any other particular attribute. The starting point is to define the range of situations in which trainees are expected to be competent. This exercise requires creating an empirically based list of situations and the settings in which a trainee is eventually expected to work. This includes, of course, the typical kinds of patients and conditions the trainee can be expected to encounter in these settings, as in the following example:

- Settings: inpatient ward, outpatient clinic, consultation service
- Patient demographics: sex, age distribution, ethnicity/race, socioeconomic class
- Clinical task: prevention, diagnosis, procedural intervention, complex therapy
- Clinical skill: interview, focused physical examination, patient counseling, procedural skill
- Levels of acuity: acute life-threatening illness; acute minor illness; chronic, recurrent, or ill-defined disease
- Clinical problem: cardiovascular, endocrine, infectious, et cetera.

A model using this framework provides the program or clerkship director with an outline to guide planning an assessment system that encompasses both the big picture (type of practice, settings, and populations) and the details (assessment tools matched to general and specific competencies). This overall framework maps the different settings in which the resident may practice (Table 8-1) and embraces the range of problems to be tested by a given method (Table 8-2). Subsequently, there are blueprints for the assessment methods chosen, as illustrated for the Mini-CEX method of direct observation by faculty members (Table 8-3) and for an objective structured clinical examination to be set up by the program or clerkship director (Table 8-4).

This kind of organization provides a target for teachers and students alike (evaluation drives the curriculum and, it is hoped, what learners attain) and establishes explicit standards of performance for an empirical sample that constitutes the "core" curriculum. This explicit planning avoids a central defect of the "what comes in the door" approach to selecting patients for teaching and assessment that previously characterized both the curriculum and the process of evaluation. That older approach resulted in the arbitrary experience of trainees and the consequent difficulty for the program to set meaningful and consistent standards or to be held accountable for the competence of its trainees.

This form of assessment modeling also accelerates the shift from certification of the skills of trainees unanchored in a competency framework (the old competency model) to a model that assures the actual quality of performance within explicit domains and situations of clinical interest.

Developing the Blueprint

The model provides a framework for the content of the assessment, while the blueprint becomes the working document for the organization of the processes. In most cases it will consist of a matrix (Table 8-2) with test dimension (such as patient care) on one axis and test method (such as multiple-choice question testing) on the other. In the blueprint, you can expect overlap and gaps, but a significant benefit of this approach is that it ensures that there are no major omissions in the assessment and that each tool will focus on a specific testing area. For example, if a clinical observer is aware that the assigned task for a mini-CEX activity (Table 8-3) is to focus on the interaction between doctor and patient (patient care and communication skills), time and effort need not be extended to evaluate different domains, such as medical knowledge and systems-based practice. The blueprint assures trainees that their assessments have been comprehensive.

These major tasks of assessment planning (modeling and blueprinting) are not easy ones. These are recommended strategies (24), but in fact their validity has not yet been documented by any educational group in medicine (25). The overriding challenge is to establish the systematic links between the important high-level dimensions of competence (as defined, for example, by the ACGME competencies) and clinical practice, and then to drill even deeper—to define which, and in what measure, each of these roles or attributes must be portrayed, in what particular situations they should be demonstrated, and, finally, by what method they will be assessed to account for competent performance of the "practice of medicine." The work of Laduca and colleagues (13) has been groundbreaking in this area.

❖ Choosing Tools

Once the model and blueprint are in place, hard choices must be made. What methods and tools will be used as measures for each performance domain? In today's environment, it is reasonable to assume that any medical school or major teaching hospital has some infrastructure to support a system for evaluation of trainees. This includes mechanisms for recording direct observations by faculty, survey tools for use by other health professionals, a program to facilitate the use of standardized (or real) trained

---

Box 8-2. Tools for Assessment

- ► Direct observation by trained clinicians, using "long cases" (full history and physical examinations, along with patient discussions, including the observation of multiple skills within a single real patient [Table 8-3]), mainly for feedback purposes

- ► Mini-CEX exercises (focused, 10-minute observations of specific skills for more formal assessments [Table 8-3])

- ► Standardized patients and cases to assess the relational dimensions of competence (Table 8-4)

- ► Computer case simulations to assess exercise of judgment and application of knowledge in defined clinical scenarios (Table 8-2)

- ► Simulations and other laboratory exercises for particular technical and procedural requirements (Tables 8-2 and 8-4)

- ► Carefully selected multiple-choice questions to assure a broad and deep fund of knowledge (Table 8-2)

- ► 360° surveys to ensure that interactive and team behaviors are emphasized (Table 8-2)

- ► Portfolios designed to capture self-assessment and reflective abilities as well as to track learning experiences (Table 8-2)

- ► Administrative data for quality management

- ► Peer assessment

patients for assessments, a learning laboratory (or simulation center) that uses computers or other technical simulations to assess trainees, and, perhaps, expertise in the use of portfolios or other qualitative examination techniques. In addition, banks of validated multiple-choice questions are available from a variety of sources (albeit sometimes at considerable expense), although help from education departments will be needed with selecting appropriate items based on the department's test model and blueprint. Tools that can be used are shown in Box 8-2.

❖ Direct Observation by Trained Clinicians

In addition to the tools listed in Box 8-2, evaluation systems should maintain a high level of participation by clinical teaching faculty, who, after all, observe trainees (students, residents, and fellows) as part of their daily assignments. But while the lynch pin for the assessment should remain observation by trained and experienced clinicians, there should be stringent conditions for the effective use of this resource. This process can be resource intensive, including many hours of faculty development so that faculty "get it right."

Experienced clinicians should contribute to the evaluation process by making regular, perceptive comments about trainees, whether formally through testing or informally through simple observation and feedback. But the problem, historically, with this important measurement tool has been the difficulty in converting anecdotal observations into something sufficiently valid and reliable to support fair and defensible decisions about individual trainees (26). The principal measurement errors of direct observation by even experienced clinicians have been pinpointed (19, 26): rater bias or halo effect, attribution error, misplaced or restricted range of observation, and insufficient sampling. How can these errors be avoided?

The primary problem with direct observation is the intuitive misapprehension of most clinical assessors that a trainee's "competence" can be judged adequately by observing one or few cases. Underlying this is the parallel, mistaken notion that skills required to master one case can be transferred to another. Many studies of clinical competence, and most other kinds of competence, reveal the "case or situation specificity" of knowledge and skills; a clinician's "competence" largely depends on the nature of the case itself (27). This may seem counterintuitive to clinicians who may not realize that their competence depends on the problems at hand, rather than a more generic competency in their field. Thus, the principal challenge of any organizer of evaluation systems is to think about not only the sampling method but also the nature and number of cases that will test the candidates.

From a practical perspective, the most promising solution to this difficult problem is the use of multiple, short, clinical observations (such as the Mini-CEX, in which individual faculty members observe a resident focused on clinical tasks in any of several settings) (28) that impose a structure on the range of cases seen by candidates.

The second main problem of direct observation is the imprecision of observers' criteria for observation. This problem seems to persist even with significant training of the observers (5). Evidence suggests that a limited range of observation is the key problem (24). For the most part, it appears that observers' evaluations are dominated by two factors: 1) perceptions of candidates' "friendliness" and 2) the degree to which they seem to be "in the case." However, formal exercises to improve experienced clinicians' evaluation of trainee performance in clinical situations provide hope that more accurate observations may follow from appropriate faculty development and practice (23, 29).

Rating forms may help also. Attention should be paid to developing the appropriate forms for the observers, training observers to use the forms, and providing trainee and observer feedback. In addition, a data collection system for the form information needs to be assembled, as does a committee structure to review the forms and set standards. Finally, there needs to be a system for generating summative reports and for determining when a problem learner requires remediation.

Mini-CEX Format

Already alluded to, the Mini-CEX format is being used more frequently for direct observation by experienced clinical observers. It is popular because it provides reliable and valid information while fitting nicely into the work flow of teaching. A primary benefit of the Mini-CEX is that its brevity and simplicity promote a good sampling of cases, and it facilitates the use of short and focused observations to target case-related objectives. It makes little sense to attempt to fill out comprehensive forms for each brief observation. Survey forms that simply focus on the observations that are targeted in the test blueprint should be developed.

Standardized Patient Testing

Standardized patients allow for observation by an "expert" observer of a trainee in a clinical encounter with a patient (or others). In standardized patient assessments, the critical features that determine the success of the evaluation are 1) the characteristics of the "case" and the degree to which these characteristics fit into an appropriate sample of the blueprint and 2) the degree to which the observers (typically a clinical observer external to the encounter or the patients themselves) can focus on and record the critical interactions that occur between the patient and the candidate. What renders the standardized patient encounter "reliable" is the degree to which key features of the cases can be observed consistently. A standardized patient assessment exploits the luxury of advanced planning; consistent and valid observations can be made if the cases are properly identified within a blueprint (Table 8-4) and the assessment expectations for each case can be characterized.

It is important not to have too high an expectation of the breadth of each standardized patient assessment. Assessments from a given standardized patient should be limited to specific issues, such as communication, physical examination skills, or ethical issues. "Checklists" or rating scales filled out by the trained patients should be specific and relatively narrow in focus. Avoid the temptation to use this expensive resource to solve assessment gaps for which the tool is poorly fitted (for example, broad areas such as fund of knowledge).

Computerized Case Simulations

Recent developments support the use of complex "cold" simulations using technology (20), as opposed to the "warm" simulations of standardized patients. Many years of development work at the National Board of Medical Examiners has led to the creation of computerized case-based assessment. These cases, and others like them, allow a moderately realistic format for assessing the ability of candidates or trainees to make timely and effective clinical decisions. A disadvantage is the large investment in case development compared with the actual assessment value derived; anything but large-scale use of these cases is inefficient. Where these kinds of cases are available and where their content and focus fit a departmental or divisional assessment need, their use is recommended.

Technical Simulations

Beginning with the development of "Harvey," the cardiovascular manikin simulation, complex technical simulations for assessment and procedural testing have proliferated. As with the computerized case simulations, considerable investment is required to acquire and use these simulations. Where these simulators are available and specific testing is clearly needed, their use is encouraged. On the other hand, for the foreseeable future, these high-technology formats remain developmental, and it is only the fortunate department that has access to a range of simulators comparable to the scope of competencies required for clinical evaluation.

Multiple-Choice-Question Testing

Multiple-choice-question testing is the most efficient method to assess a trainee's fund of medical knowledge. It also has proven to be a flexible tool to assess more sophisticated levels of knowledge application in clinical situations. A science of the development and testing of multiple-choice questions exists; if you do not purchase subject examinations from the National Board of Medical Examiners or the In-Training Examination from the ABIM, soliciting advice on the appropriate way to deploy these questions is recommended. However, it is important to develop a bank of validated items that fit your blueprint matrix; once in place, they should be used regularly, particularly in quizzes that both test and provide feedback to trainees on their progress on the "knowledge" front. Most experts suggest that the items be the single-best-answer type and that they should focus on clinical scenarios that fit the range of cases that the trainees are expected to see in their daily work.

360° Surveys and Peer Assessment

Surveys of what might be called "casual" observers of clinical performances were originally developed by Ramsey and colleagues (22) and funded by the ABIM. This represents a major step forward in the area of peer assessments, or 360° surveys. Developed in the era of "competence" assessment, they may have been prematurely discounted as a feasible assessment tool for resident or physician competence—a large number of observations were required to reach the reliability deemed useful for a stand-alone test of competence. But their use has been revived in Canada (11), where a system of data collection from multiple sources, including peers and colleagues, is used in clinical settings to assess the ability of physicians to work effectively with other physicians, members of the health care team, and patients.

A related assessment tool that will also fit into the quality management framework and accelerate trainee involvement in the competencies of practice-based learning and improvement and systems-based practice is the structured peer assessment format. Peer assessment is almost unknown in the United States, but Canadian regulatory authorities have been using it for nearly 30 years. Ontario randomly assesses well over 1000 physicians per year, to great effect (15, 26). Especially because this method would be inserted into an assessment scheme that was already moving toward the framework of quality management, it would be valuable in its own right. It would also serve as a formative experience in the spheres of practice-based learning and improvement and systems-based practice.

Portfolios

Significant work has been done in clinical settings, particularly in Canada (23, 30), on the utility of physician self-assessment, self-reflection, and determination of learning priorities for establishing and maintaining competence. This technique shows the most promise of being useful in the domains of system-based and practice-based learning and improvement.

Administrative Data for Quality Management

Probably the most promising but least studied tool for performance evaluation of trainees is based on using outcomes of clinical care, similar to that used for quality management (31). Many systems of "accounting" for clinical success have been developed, some by insurance companies, some by provider groups, some by payers, and some by professional societies and other groups. A great advantage of the test model and blueprint system for assessment described earlier is the ability to focus on a sample of archetypal cases that all trainees will be expected to regularly manage and for which a "suite" of proxy process and outcome measures can be developed prospectively. Using these measures as part of the trainee evaluation system will have some immediate benefits. First, their use will familiarize the trainees with one of the most powerful tools of quality management. Second, if found to be useful, they can validate the effectiveness of care in the training system. Third, successful implementation of an assessment scheme based on quality improvement principles will be an exciting advance in bringing accountability to the training program by using mainstream clinical quality measurements.

❖ Additional Frontiers and Challenges

Existing models and tools hardly are complete, or even adequate, particularly for certain sectors of the clinical matrix, such as professionalism. Because many of the currently used tools have come to prominence only recently, it remains a matter of local experience and judgment to determine optimal use. It is also important to repeat the reminder that the existence of a measurement tool is not a sufficient justification for its use. A growing literature exists to guide your judgment; few systematic reviews have been done, however, and much research needs to be completed. This is an important and exciting opportunity for young faculty members looking for a research target as they prepare for a leadership role in assessment (see chapters 5 and 9 for more information). Furthermore, the ACGME is receptive to disciplined innovation if advance notice of intent and direction is provided.

Accountability is the watchword of medical professionalism in the 21st century. And assessment is the "tool" of accountability. Any educational program in medicine must have the outcome of its efforts clearly in its sights, and must be willing to be accountable for the competence of its graduates not just at their graduation but also in their subsequent practice careers. Medical education leaders must recognize that clinical assessments can no longer be limited to academic achievement and the accumulation of disaggregated competencies in individuals; rather, it needs to address the ability of individuals to perform competently in real-world situations (3).

To be accountable in this performance-based concept of competence, a system must define the scope of medical practice to be delivered within a projected population, and it should allow feedback to assure that the outcomes of health care delivery to that population validate the evaluation system.

The elements of trainee assessment might be seen as a prototype for a more elaborate plan that could be devised by a department of medicine to ensure that all its practitioners satisfy their accountability to the public they serve. Performance evaluation of the practicing profession is a hot topic as a means of maintaining financial and professional accountability (32). The availability of measures originally designed as performance measures for practicing physicians will, in turn, rapidly disseminate into training programs. In due course, some stability will again be achieved in the world of clinical evaluation. The resulting new tradition and culture will link the assessments of competencies in trainees to equivalent quality-related measures for practicing physicians. The hope is that the philosophy behind these latter assessments—that of quality improvement—will also become the ethos of assessments in the teaching arena. If that actually becomes the case, a large step forward in the field of clinical learner assessment will have been taken and will represent a major achievement for medical educators, who have been searching for positive frameworks of assessment for generations.

In conclusion, the "invitation" from your chair to create a better system of evaluation of the department's residents can be seen as more than just an offer of an assignment. It is an opportunity to make a difference that extends well beyond the residents you train.

REFERENCES

1. **Pangaro LN, McGaghie W.** Evaluation and grading of students. In: Fincher RM, ed. Guidebook for Clerkship Directors. 3rd ed. Omaha, NE: Alliance for Clinical Education; 2005.

2. **Holmboe ES, Hawkins RE.** Practical Guide to the Evaluation of Clinical Competence. Philadelphia: Mosby Elsevier; 2008.
3. **Klass D.** A performance-based conception of competence is changing the regulation of physicians' professional behavior. Acad Med. 2007;82:529-35.
4. **Elstein AS, Shulman LS, Sprafka SA.** Medical problem-solving. J Med Educ. 1981; 56:75-6.
5. **Noel GL, Herbers JE Jr, Caplow MP, Cooper GS, Pangaro LN, Harvey J.** How well do internal medicine faculty members evaluate the clinical skills of residents? Ann Intern Med. 1992;117:757-65.
6. **Hubbard J, Levit E.** The National Board of Medical Examiners: The First Seventy Years. Philadelphia: National Board of Medical Examiners; 1985.
7. **Tamblyn R, Abrahamowicz M, Dauphinee D, Wenghofer E, Jacques A, Klass D, et al.** Physician scores on a national clinical skills examination as predictors of complaints to medical regulatory authorities. JAMA. 2007;298:993-1001.
8. **Miller GE.** The assessment of clinical skills/competence/performance. Acad Med. 1990;65:S63-7.
9. **Klass D.** Assessing doctors at work—progress and challenges [Editorial]. N Engl J Med. 2007;356:414-5.
10. **Norcini JJ.** Current perspectives in assessment: the assessment of performance at work. Med Educ. 2005;39:880-9.
11. **Lockyer J.** Multisource feedback in the assessment of physician competencies. J Contin Educ Health Prof. 2003;23:4-12.
12. **Campbell M, Parboosingh J, Fox R, Gondocz T.** Use of a diary to record physician self-directed learning activities. J Contin Educ Health Prof. 1995;15:209-16.
13. **Hockberger RS, Laduca A, Orr NA, Reinhart MA, Sklar DP.** Creating the model of a clinical practice: the case of emergency medicine. Acad Emerg Med. 2003;10:161-8.
14. **Laduca A, Taylor DD, Hill IK.** The design of a new physician licensure examination. Eval Health Prof. 1984;7:115-40.
15. **Norton PG, Dunn EV, Beckett R, Faulkner D.** Long-term follow-up in the Peer Assessment Program for nonspecialist physicians in Ontario, Canada. Jt Comm J Qual Improv. 1998;24:334-41.
16. **Harden RM, Stevenson M, Downie WW, Wilson GM.** Assessment of clinical competence using objective structured examination. Br Med J. 1975;1:447-51.
17. **De Champlain AF, Klass DJ.** Assessing the factor structure of a nationally administered standardized patient examination. Acad Med. 1997;72:S88-90.
18. **Klass DJ, Hassard TH, Kopelow ML, Tamblyn RM, Barrows H, Williams R.** Portability of a multiple-station, performance-based assessment of clinical competence. The Third Ottawa International Conference Proceedings. Further Developments in Assessing Clinical Competence. 1987;434-42.
19. **Downing SM, Haladyna TM.** Handbook of Test Development. New York: Routledge; 2006.
20. **Dillon GF, Clyman SG, Clauser BE, Margolis MJ.** The introduction of computer-based case simulations into the United States medical licensing examination. Acad Med. 2002;77:S94-6.
21. **Boulet JR.** Summative assessment in medicine: the promise of simulation for high-stakes evaluation. Acad Emerg Med. 2008;15:1017-24.
22. **Ramsey PG, Wenrich MD, Carline JD, Inui TS, Larson EB, LoGerfo JP.** Use of peer ratings to evaluate physician performance. JAMA. 1993;269:1655-60.

23. **Pangaro LN, Holmboe ES.** Evaluation forms and formal rating scales. In: Holmboe ES, Hawkins RE, eds. Practical Guide to the Evaluation of Clinical Competence. Philadelphia: Elsevier Mosby; 2008:24-41.

24. **Hawkins RE, Holmboe ES.** Contructing an evaluation system for an educational program. In: Holmboe ES, Hawkins RE, eds. Practical Guide to the Evaluation of Clinical Competence. Philadelphia: Mosby Elsevier; 2008:216-236.

25. **Lurie SJ, Mooney CJ, Lyness JM.** Measurement of the general competencies of the accreditation council for graduate medical education: a systematic review. Acad Med. 2009;84:301-9.

26. **Hammond KR, Kern F.** Teaching Comprehensive Medical Care: A Psychological Study of a Change in Medical Education. Cambridge, MA: Commonwealth Fund, Harvard Univ Pr; 1959.

27. **Wenghofer EF, Williams AP, Klass DJ, Faulkner D.** Physician-patient encounters: the structure of performance in family and general office practice. J Contin Educ Health Prof. 2006;26:285-93.

28. **Norcini JJ, Blank LL, Arnold GK, Kimball HR.** The mini-CEX (clinical evaluation exercise): a preliminary investigation. Ann Intern Med. 1995;123:795-9.

29. **Margolis MJ, Clauser BE, Cuddy MM, Ciccone A, Mee J, Harik P, et al.** Use of the mini-clinical evaluation exercise to rate examinee performance on a multiple-station clinical skills examination: a validity study. Acad Med. 2006;81:S56-60.

30. **Wilkinson TJ, Challis M, Hobma SO, Newble DI, Parboosingh JT, Sibbald RG, et al.** The use of portfolios for assessment of the competence and performance of doctors in practice. Med Educ. 2002;36:918-24.

31. Outcomes Assessment: Jefferson Longitudinal Study of Medical Education. www.jefferson.edu/jmc/crmehc/medu/longitudinal.cfm

32. **Handfield-Jones RS, Mann KV, Challis ME, Hobma SO, Klass DJ, McManus IC, et al.** Linking assessment to learning: a new route to quality assurance in medical practice. Med Educ. 2002;36:949-58.

33. **Accreditation Council for Graduate Medical Education.** Common Program Requirements: General Competencies. Accessed at www.acgme.org/outcome/comp/GeneralCompetenciesStandards21307.pdf.

34. **Royal College of Physicians and Surgeons of Canada.** The CanMEDS Physician Competency Framework. Accessed at http://rcpsc.medical.org/canmeds/index.php.

9

Getting Started in Educational Research

Capt Eric S. Holmboe, USNR-Ret, MC, MD, FACP

M ajor shifts in health care delivery are pushing the medical
education system in new directions, analogous to the rapid
growth and importance in quality improvement and health
systems science research that began to make a strong impact in the
1980s. Educational research is now poised to contribute substantially
to improving training and patient care.

Most notable is the change in educational paradigm: from one that
focused on structure and process using broad curricular experiences
based on the duration of educational rotations to an outcome or competency-based system that emphasizes outcomes (where the educational
program must show that trainees have truly acquired the knowledge,
skills, and attitudes to move onto the next stage of their career). However, many medical educators and leaders are highly skeptical of the evolution to competency-based medical education, resulting in inertia for
transforming medical education to meet the needs of an aging population (1, 2). Despite strong emotional ties, the empirical evidence base for
the "traditional" time and curricular-based system is surprisingly weak.

For example, in a systematic review of hospital-based curricula in
internal medicine residencies, Di Francesco and colleagues (3) could
find only 14 articles published over a nearly 40-year period that performed any outcome measurement. Most of these outcomes only
involved learner satisfaction, and none involved trainee competence or

---

KEY POINTS

- Exciting innovations in educational methods and imminent changes in the health care system now make educational research an essential—and fruitful—area for scholarship in the coming decades.
- Faculty are encouraged to study curricular and assessment methods that are traditional, as well as those that are truly new.
- Educational effects are complex interactions. Even single-institution studies can be worthwhile when you try to clarify the mechanisms and theory that link process to outcomes, especially outcomes that show impact on patients themselves
- Education researchers should appreciate the importance of context, and use process evaluations that also help future investigators to replicate the interventions in different contexts.
- Many resources are available to help researchers choose methods of observation. When planning to study complex educational interventions, investigators will often need to use a combination of quantitative and qualitative methods.
- Resources are available for learning more about education research and for obtaining funding.

---

patient outcomes. Another common "assumption" that guides current training models is that the progressive independence of the learner is critical for effective professional development. This tradition is under intense scrutiny, with the Institute of Medicine's recent call for better supervision of trainees, especially in graduate medical education (4). While progressive independence may in fact be essential, no evidence supports this practice (5). Both examples provide compelling support for the need to robust educational research.

This "clash" of educational cultures and our incomplete understanding of what produces a highly competent physician signals the urgent need for meaningful research into what works and what doesn't in medical education. This isn't just about academic scholarship—a public that contributes billions of dollars a year to the medical education enterprise increasingly wants assurance that this system provides a meaningful return on their investment. Specifically, they desire competent physicians who provide safe, effective, efficient, timely, patient-centered, and equitable care (6). For this reason alone, medical education research should no longer be seen as a peripheral department activity or a "hobby" but rather a professional obligation that requires greater support from academic leaders.

This chapter has four primary goals: 1) to describe how educational research can support the changes that have already occurred and those that are coming; 2) to introduce key research strategies and methods; 3) to engage academic leaders to support educational research; and 4) to provide initial guidance for faculty, including course, clerkship, residency, and fellowship directors, who wish to become involved in educational research.

❖ Moving to an Outcomes-based System

A new principle in medical education is gradually being adopted: competency-based education and training (CBET). This new area could provide educational researchers, who must have the healthy sense of uncertainty and skepticism common to all successful researchers, with great opportunities for inquiry and scholarship. While this area is appealing in concept, very little is known about how and whether CBET will work in medicine. While the community has spent substantial effort in developing frameworks for competencies, most of these frameworks still lack the necessary details needed to operationalize a CBET system. We also need substantial research work in improving assessment; without robust assessment CBET cannot be successfully implemented. Finally, research should examine whether future medical education system should be a hybrid of the traditional and CBET models.

In support of those desiring to study such innovations, academic leaders such as deans and chairs have significant opportunities to help facilitate the research needed to answer these complex and complicated questions. The ultimate goal is to ensure that all trainees are truly prepared to practice and can adapt to a continually changing and evolving health care system and that patients in educational programs receive excellent care. Leaders need to perform several important tasks:

1. Acknowledge that medical education must evolve and change to meet the health care needs of the population. The messages and behaviors of leaders are a powerful part of the informal and hidden curricula (7). What you say and do is quickly picked up by your colleagues.
2. Publicly recognize the importance of educational research in your respective school, department, and sections. Challenge your educators to study any changes they make to curriculum and assessment, whether for students, residents, or fellows.

3. Support educational research as a viable career path in your department.
4. Encourage your educational researchers to reach out to like-minded individuals to perform multi-institution studies where applicable and feasible.
5. Include educational research as part of grand rounds and other departmental activities, such as a "research day."

Many believe that the medical education research enterprise is at a juncture similar to the quality improvement movement in the 1980s. Concerted efforts by key leaders in the quality movement led to substantial growth of important research in health services, patient safety, and systems science. A similar transformation is now possible in medical education, but educational leaders will need to step forward and make research in medical education a priority if we are to achieve similar gains.

❖ Deciding What to Study

For the medical education researcher, there is no lack of important questions to study. However, the ultimate goal of all educational research should be to determine what educational approaches and assessments assure that the trainee can truly provide high-quality patient care. With society's important and legitimate concerns for quality and safety, educational research must always keep the patient in mind. This is the professional responsibility of the medical education system. One framework that can be helpful to educational researchers studying interventions is Kirkpatrick's hierarchy (Figure 9-1).

Obviously, it is often not feasible or even appropriate to start with a project that specifically measures patient outcomes. However, educational investigators can consider how their project might ultimately affect patients as they explore new learning experiences or assessment methods. If we are truly to achieve a patient-centered health care system, then it follows that sustained, systematic educational research has to keep the patient in view as new projects are designed and implemented.

Determining what to study in medical education can be guided by several other considerations. Some beginning researchers start with a literature search to identify a gap in medical education, but this may not be the best approach. The project must have salience to the researcher and ideally should help to solve a "local problem." This creates a "win-win" situation, especially for the young investigator starting a career in educational research. If the research project doesn't help to solve a problem locally, it may be harder to obtain local buy-in or support for the project. Some of the

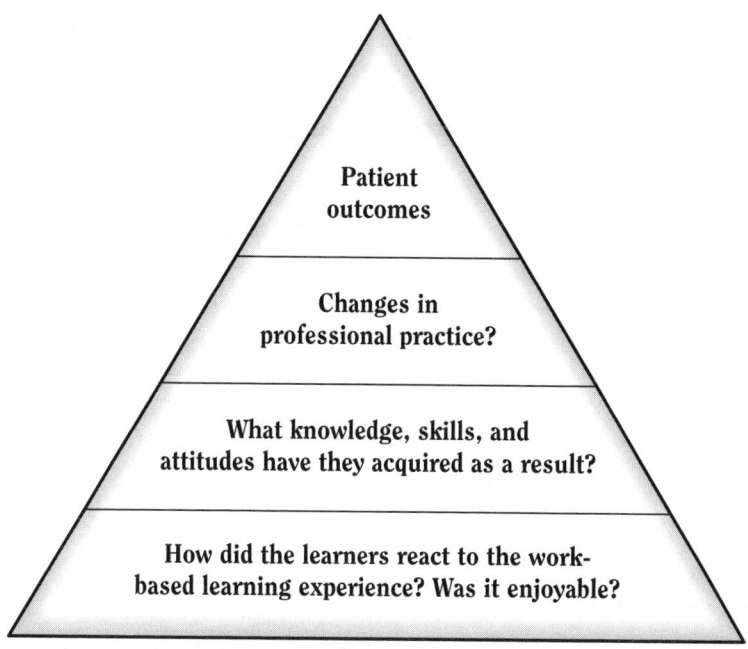

Figure 9-1 Kirkpatrick's hierarchy: application to work-based assessment. Reproduced from Kirkpatrick DL. Evaluation of training. In: Craig R, Mittel I, eds. Training and Development Handbook. New York: McGraw-Hill; 1967:87-112.

best research is the result of careful and thoughtful observation of things that do or not work well in one's own educational environment (8). More than likely, other institutions will also be struggling with the same issue. Even if someone else has reported results from a project that investigated the same or similar issue, early findings require further development or validation. Furthermore, single-institution studies can be useful in the early stages of investigation, a theme this chapter will return to a little later.

When investigators have identified the problem they wish to solve and formulated their own research issue, they are ready to search the literature. Several databases can be helpful (Box 9-1).

Regardless of the project, the investigator should reach out to local librarians. Some libraries will actually assist with literature searches, but at a minimum, medical library staff can help construct an effective and efficient search. Finally, the investigator should explore literature outside of the medical field. In designing a intervention for a new approach to faculty development in direct

Box 9-1. Helpful Databases

Primary Databases

► PubMed is the traditional database used by researchers. While it increasingly includes more educational journals, it still does not cover the entire educational landscape.

► Educational Resources Information Center (ERIC; www.eric.ed.gov) is another useful database that includes literature on medical education and, more important, educational literature outside of medicine. You should encourage your educational researchers to search for educational research outside medicine.

► PsychLit and CINAHL, targeting the psychological and nursing literature, can be helpful depending on the nature of the project. For example, CINAHL may be a good database for interdisciplinary projects.

Systematic Reviews

Systematic reviews can provide excellent synopsis of what has been done in specific areas. Useful databases for reviews include:

► Best Evidence Medical Education (BEME; www.bemecollaboration.org/beme/pages/index.html) contains systematic reviews on topics ranging from simulation to faculty development. You can also see what reviews are in progress, as well as course offerings in systematic reviews for medical education.

► The Cochrane Collaboration (www.cochrane.org/index.htm) also provides systematic reviews related to medical education. One example is a systematic review on continuing medical education.

► The Campbell Collaboration (www.campbellcollaboration.org/) focuses on systematic reviews of education, but mostly outside of medicine. Researchers in medical education should look at educational research in other disciplines.

observation, for example, extensive information about performance appraisal was gathered from the business and the psychology literature (9).

❖ Educational Research Methods

Studying curricula, assessments, or other types of interventions presents several challenges in the educational setting. First, changes to educational programs seldom target just a *single* change or intervention. Most educational interventions are best classified as a "complex intervention." A simple and useful definition for complex interventions comes from the Medical Research Council of the United Kingdom: "Complex interventions are built up from a number of components, which may act both independently and interdependently" (10).

Medical education researchers can learn from the mistakes made in much of the early health services research. Many of those studies attempted to study single interventions, such as guideline implementation, use of reminders, and audit and feedback, using controlled study designs from the outset, only to find disappointing or marginal outcomes. One reason for these unsatisfying results was the failure to recognize that apparently simple single interventions were in effect actually complex interventions. For example, in a randomized study of physician opinion leaders that found mixed results (11), the opinion leaders received training at the different sites (was the training equally effective at all sites?) and were also given a comprehensive quality toolkit (what components of the toolkit were used and why?). Thus, this "single" intervention actually had multiple components.

Let's look at a hypothetical example in medical education. With the release of the Institute of Medicine's 2008 report, "Retooling for an Aging America: Building the Health Workforce" (12), the Osler Medical School decides all its fourth-year students should become more knowledgeable and skilled in basic geriatric competencies before beginning residency. The school decides to adopt the geriatric medical school competencies developed by a multistakeholder group and published in *Academic Medicine* in May 2009 (13). With these "outcomes" in mind (26 basic competencies), the school appoints a task force to develop a curricular experience for the students with associated assessments to ensure the students have truly attained these competencies.

The curriculum task force ultimately decides on the following approach:

1. A series of interactive workshops through the first half of the fourth year that will bring all the students together for eight sessions to learn and work with the competencies.

2. Assignments to use the Portal of Online Geriatric education Web site to reinforce the lessons from the workshops (www.pogoe.org/front2).

3. A 2-week rotation in a geriatric setting (such as a geriatric assessment clinic or skilled-nursing facility). The students will have to be distributed across different setting because any one setting cannot accommodate all the students.

The faculty team decides to target the second level of Kirkpatrick's hierarchy (what knowledge, skill, and attitudes are acquired) by having all the students complete a geriatric-focused objective structured clinical examination (OSCE) in January and February of their fourth year. This exam will assess whether the student can demonstrate the competencies in a controlled setting.

As you can see, this new educational experience has multiple components, including some that will clearly interact. Given the resources required to initiate this new program, you will want to know whether this new curriculum actually makes a difference. Should you assess this by using a controlled trial, or is an observational pre–post approach a reasonable place to start? Will the quantitative results from the OSCE be sufficient to determine success or failure of the curriculum, or should qualitative research assessment be included? These are just a few of the common questions for educational investigators. However, before answering such questions and choosing what specific research method to use, investigators should first examine their research *strategy*.

❖ Research Strategy

Attention to research strategy for complex interventions requires the investigator to pay close attention to several aspects of the project. First, educational investigators should know what they believe is the theory of change underlying the intervention. In our example, the question for the investigators is, Why do they believe that this particular combination of experiences should lead to higher levels of knowledge, skills, and attitudes in the 26 geriatric competencies among students? Lack of reasonably formed theories will make it difficult for the investigator to interpret why an intervention (in this case a multifaceted curriculum) did or did not succeed. For example, one theory is that success will depend on the degree to which the experiential component allows the student to apply the knowledge and skills learned in the interactive workshops.

Second, investigators must understand the actual processes used to deliver the intervention, and by what mechanisms these processes produced their effect on the student. Returning to our example, one component of the new curriculum is an interactive workshop. Some process questions are: 1) What content will be covered in the workshops? and 2) How will the students engage the content, and what type of interactive exercise(s) will be used to help students assimilate and work with the new material? However, understanding the *mechanisms* by which the processes produce learning is what other educational investigators must know to replicate the intervention in other settings or institutions. Too often these mechanism questions are neglected in early phases of educational research.

Let's look at a contemporary example where understanding the mechanisms of an educational approach was critical to its success. Pangaro's RIME model of assessment (discussed elsewhere in this book), is a well-established competency framework. RIME, which stands for "reporter-interpreter-manager-educator," provides a synthetic, development approach to assessing a third-year medical student's performance on medicine clerkships (14). When grading students, faculty are asked to evaluate students on the basis of which of the four RIME levels they have achieved during the clerkship.

An important aspect of RIME was the developmental theory behind the levels and a set of processes to train faculty on how to observe and interact with students so as to recognize the characteristics with each level. However, what has made RIME successful as an evaluation framework is the deep understanding of its *mechanisms* in guiding evaluation. First, the RIME framework created shared mental models among faculty for each student level of performance. Second, Pangaro recognized the importance of formal evaluation sessions, introduced by Noel (15), to discuss each student. These sessions facilitated recalibration of faculty with real-time faculty development. Conversations with a trained clerkship director facilitated progressive understanding of the model. The *mechanisms* of RIME are the creation of shared mental models that directly influence how the faculty observe and assess the student.

❖ Context

Context includes such issues as the chaotic and hectic clinical environments, professional behaviors of faculty and other health care workers (the informal and hidden curriculum), and learning climate. Failure to recognize and understand the impact of context on educational interventions can sink even well-designed interventions. For example, if most students in the new geriatric curriculum spend their 2-week clinical experience in a health care setting that doesn't provide opportunities for skill practice under faculty observation or lacks faculty who value the geriatric competencies, the curriculum could ultimately fail. Thus, the researcher in this study may want to use some type of instrument that can measure the learning climate and culture.

Educational investigators should review two research strategy models designed for the study of complex interventions. The first, from the Medical Research Council of the United Kingdom, highlights the study of complex interventions as an iterative process (Figure 9-2). The design and methods of the research project will depend on where in the cycle the intervention or program is, but feasibility and pilot testing for new interventions and programs are especially important.

The other framework comes from sociology and is called "realist evaluation" (Figure 9-3). According to this concept, which underscores the importance of the environment, or context, "an action is causal only if its outcome is triggered by a mechanism acting in context" (16).

As you can see from both strategy frameworks, the first decision point is not what research method to choose. The specific research methods, whether a randomized, controlled trial with quantitative outcomes or a focus group qualitative study, depend entirely on the question being asked and the developmental stage of the intervention or project. The holy grail of biomedical research, the multi-institution randomized, controlled trial, clearly has its place in medical education research. Interventions whose processes and mechanisms are well understood in context are best suited to move to a larger randomized, controlled trial to validate the interven-

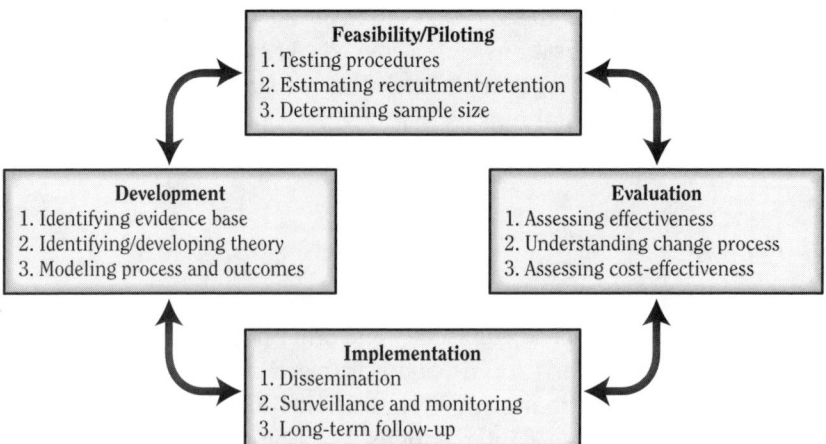

Figure 9-2 Framework for the evaluation of complex interventions.

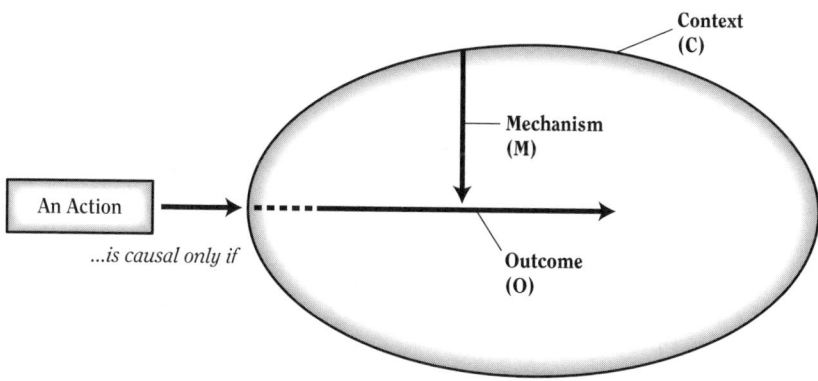

...its *Outcome is triggered by Mechanism acting in Context*

Figure 9-3 Realist evaluation.

tions and assess generalizability. The major problem is that the mechanisms and context of too many educational interventions are often ill-formed and poorly understood before the controlled trial is attempted. For example, qualitative interviews that target the primary mechanisms of an intervention can actually help to strengthen the link between the cause (intervention) and effect (desired outcome). The Medical Research Council framework specifically recommends that even controlled trials include a "process evaluation" that will also help future investigators to best know how to replicate the intervention in different contexts.

❖ Using Both Quantitative and Qualitative Methods

When planning to study complex educational interventions, investigators will most often need to use a combination of quantitative and qualitative methods, even for single-institution studies. One definition of qualitative research, from the United Kingdom's National Health Service (17), is "research that uses individual in-depth interviews, focus groups or questionnaires to collect, analyse and interpret data by observing what people do and say. It reports on the meanings, concepts, definitions, characteristics, metaphors, symbols and descriptions of things. It is more subjective than quantitative research and is often exploratory and open-ended. Small numbers of people are interviewed in-depth and/or a relatively small number of focus groups are conducted." Quantitative research, on the other hand, "uses statistical methods to count and measure outcomes from a study. The outcomes are usually objective and predetermined. A large number of participants are usually involved to ensure that the results are statistically significant."

Let's return to our geriatric curriculum example. The OSCE will certainly provide excellent quantitative data about whether students attained the desired knowledge, skills, and attitudes. However, even if the OSCE scores are high, will the investigator know what components of the intervention were most helpful? Did a subgroup of students do better because they spent time in a geriatric clinic compared with other students assigned to a skilled-nursing facility where they did not receive as much direct observation? These would be important questions for the investigator to answer. As a result, collecting experiential information from the students by using qualitative methods, whether through surveys, focus groups or interviews, would help the investigator to know what components of the intervention worked best, how they worked (the mechanisms), and how context affected the learning experience and acquisition of the competencies. The bottom line is to choose the research strategy and methods to answer the problem you are trying to solve, not the other way around.

❖ Other Forms of Scholarship

In addition to the "discovery" research of new programs and interventions, other forms of scholarly work can be equally valuable (see chapter 5 of this book). First, systematic reviews provide valuable information to the entire educational community about the state of the art for specific topics. The Best Evidence Medical Education Web site (www.bemecollaboration.org; see Box 9-1) is a good example of the power of systematic reviews. Given that much of the current medical education literature is grounded in single-institution studies, systematic reviews are one method to pull together what is known to guide the community on where future multi-institution research should be focused.

Another potentially important form of scholarly work is narratives and commentaries. Thoughtful, well-written narratives and commentaries can provide new insights into vexing problems, call attention to aspects of a problem being neglected, and help to guide future research. Let's look at a contemporary example. In many settings, the primary means of assessing quality of care is the use of performance measures, such as what proportion of patients had a hemoglobin A_{1c} test. However, several recent commentaries highlighted the importance of including clinical skills as part of the quality-of-care calculus and their contribution to safety and medical errors, especially diagnostic errors (18, 19).

❖ Single-Institution Studies

There is no question that too much of the current medical education literature is grounded in single-institution studies. However, as shown with the geriatric curriculum example, starting with a single-institution study to first test feasibility and understand the mechanisms and contextual factors is a very reasonable approach. The problem arises when investigators do not take the next step to test interventions and curricula in other settings and build on the lessons learned in the first, small-scale study. Ideally, educational researchers should not stop after single, one-shot studies but rather plan for a series of studies that can answer critical questions important to them and the larger educational community. Once your research has demonstrated the value of a specific educational approach or assessment, it is important for you to reach out to others to test the intervention in other settings, with strong consideration for including a comparative intervention and control group. Ultimately, moving to a multi-institution, controlled trial helps to move the science forward and develop best practices.

❖ Disseminating Your Findings

Publishing

Whenever possible, all investigators should include in their project planning a goal to publish in the peer-reviewed literature. You may ask why trying to publish most educational research projects would be important, especially if the project is focused only on a local problem. First, there are still substantial gaps in our understanding of how best to deliver effective medical education. When based on sound theory, projects focused on "local" problems are likely to have relevance beyond your own institution. Second, publishing allows for broad dissemination across the educational community and meaningful feedback. Publishing is a valuable form of public conversation with the educational community and peers. Third, the act of writing and preparing manuscripts helps to build greater and deeper knowledge among investigators in their area of interest. Fourth, publishing can spark additional studies of the same area. Finally, scholarly publications do help clinician-educators and other educational investigators get promoted, but you'll notice this reason is given last. Promotion *is* important, but if scholarly work is simply treated as a task and not a passion, it is not likely to be sustainable. (See chapter 5 in this book for more details on building a career.)

Presentations

What about other modes of dissemination? At the local level, grand rounds, research days, faculty meetings, and conferences focused on education are all potentially useful means to disseminate findings. It is important to build reporting of educational projects into the intellectual activities of a department or section. First, this reporting helps to increase the visibility and importance of the research. Second, it allows the medical educator investigator to benefit from the cross-pollination of colleagues from other research fields and traditions. Third, it can help others in your department to potentially improve their own teaching and assessment, even if neither activity is part of their primary job.

Presentations at regional and national meetings are also useful ways to disseminate research. First, the investigator can receive feedback from colleagues working in the same field, feedback that can be used to improve the project or manuscript. Second, regional and national meetings present good networking opportunities and can lead to meaningful collaborations over time.

❖ Resources and Funding

Research in medical education, in contrast to biomedical and health services research, does not have as robust a foundation for funding as other types of research. This is truly unfortunate, for reasons highlighted at the start of the chapter, but investigators do have some potential sources of external funding.

Many foundations focus on or are interested in medical education, and although most are relatively small, they do provide opportunities. Table 9-1 lists three examples of foundation funding.

In addition to foundation grants, three other important sources should be explored. First, many institutions have small local grant programs for educational research; the investigator should check with the medical school or department. It is helpful for institutional leaders to provide such in-house grants to foster research and provide seed money for pilot programs and preliminary data (see chapter 3 of this book for more details). Second, many specialty societies also have small grant programs; again, the educational investigator should consult the society for possible opportunities. Finally, although government agencies such as the National Institutes of Health or the Health Resources Service Administration focus on supporting individuals in training programs, they also provide funding for educational interventions. For example, the Agency for Healthcare Research and Quality is interested in studying educational interventions that target quality improvement and patient safety.

Table 9-1. Foundations That Fund Educational Research

Name	Funding Priorities*	Contact
Josiah Macy, Jr. Foundation	1. Projects to improve medical and health professional education in the context of the changing health care system 2. Projects that will increase diversity among health care professionals 3. Projects that demonstrate or encourage ways to increase teamwork between and among health care professionals 4. Educational strategies to increase care for underserved populations	www.josiahmacyfoundation.org/index.php?section=home
National Board of Medical Examiners: The Stemmler Medical Education Research Fund	"The goal of the Stemmler Fund is to provide support for research or development of innovative assessment approaches that will enhance the evaluation of those preparing to, or continuing to, practice medicine."	www.nbme.org/research/stemmler/index.html
Arnold P. Gold Foundation	"The Gold Foundation only provides financial support to programs and projects which encourage more compassionate and relationship-centered healthcare."	http://humanism-in-medicine.org/cgi-bin/htmlos.cgi/041343.2.057533374316566061/intros/index.html?srchString=Home

* Subject to change based on the foundation's strategic goals.

❖ Resources to Get Started

Many projects can often be started without grant funding. The geriatric project discussed earlier is a good example that could proceed without funding. However, several conditions are necessary to ensure that the project can reach completion without additional internal or external grants. First, departmental leaders must be willing to supply the "time" of the participants on the investigative team. Will extra time be required, or is this an issue of reprioritizing current projects? Second, are there available resources to help administer the project during implementation; when the data have been collected, does the project have access to analytic resources such as a statistician?

One way to ensure success is to distribute the work across a team of investigators. This often requires a change in culture for the institution because more than one individual will need to receive credit for the work. In the individualistic promotion culture of most medical schools, leaders must acknowledge that team-based projects are valuable and represent meaningful academic currency. Determining roles and responsibilities up front in a complex project can also help to avoid tension and friction later.

Finally, where applicable, think about seeking resources outside your own department or even discipline. Many times other groups, such as departments of policy, nursing, psychology, and sociology, may be interested in similar educational constructs and thus are willing to share resources with your investigator. There is tremendous interest in interdisciplinary education, team learning, team assessment, and care coordination. All these topics by definition involve interactions and work with other key health care disciplines. This type of work may also allow for support from the hospital itself; those administrators might view an intervention as helping to solve a "local problem" and therefore may be willing to provide resources for the project.

❖ Learning About Educational Research

The annual meetings of the Clerkship Directors in Internal Medicine, the Association of Program Directors in Internal Medicine, and the Association of American Medical Colleges typically have workshops that facilitate a basic understanding of medical education research and scholarship. Internationally, the Association of Medical Education in Europe (held annually) and the "Ottawa Conferences" on Assessment in the Health Sciences (held every 2 years) are additional venues for excellent workshops and sharing of medical education research. Box 9-2 provides a few additional resources.

❖ Concluding Thoughts

Perhaps never in the evolution of medical education has research into what works, for whom, and why been more important. The health care system, itself in transformation, urgently needs a physician workforce that can meet the needs of an aging population in the 21st century. Medical education research is poised to answer critical questions about optimal educational methods and assessments. Educational leaders are in an excellent position to promote and support meaningful educational research in their faculty, and upcoming investigators can have a rich career by thoughtfully and systematically pursuing studies that meet a high standard of rigor. The

---

Box 9-2. Additional Resources for Educational Research

Articles

▶ Bordage G, Caelleigh AS, Steinecke A, Bland CJ, Crandall SJ, McGaghie WC, et al; Joint Task Force of Academic Medicine and the GEA-RIME Committee. Review criteria for research manuscripts. Acad Med. 2001;76:897-978.

▶ Davidoff F, Batalden P, Stevens D, Ogrinc G, Mooney S; SQUIRE Development Group. Publication guidelines for quality improvement in health care: evolution of the SQUIRE project. Qual Saf Health Care. 2008;17 Suppl 1:i3-9.

Courses

▶ Medical Education Research Certificate (MERC) Program from the Association of American Medical Colleges: www.aamc.org/members/gea/merc/start.htm

Books

▶ Fraenkel JR, Wallen NE. How to Design and Evaluate Research in Education. 6th ed. New York: McGraw-Hill; 2006.

▶ Norman GR, van der Vleuten CP, Newble DI. International Handbook of Research in Medical Education. Dordrecht, the Netherlands: Kluwer Academic Publishers; 2002.

▶ Tashakkori A, Teddlie C. Mixed Methodology: Combining Qualitative and Quantitative Approaches. Thousand Oaks, CA: Sage Publications; 1998.

hope is that this chapter has stimulated interest among and provided guidance to academic faculty, program directors of all types, and their leaders regarding research methods and strategies in medical education.

Disclaimer: The views expressed are those of the author and do not reflect the official policy or position of the Department of Defense or the U.S. Government.

REFERENCES

1. **Grant J.** The incapacitating effects of competence: a critique. Adv Health Sci Educ Theory Pract. 1999;4:271-277.
2. **Medicare Payment Advisory Commission.** Medical education in the united states: supporting long-term delivery systems reform. In: Report to the Congress: Improving Incentives in the Medicare Program. June 2009. Accessed at www.medpac.gov.
3. **Di Francesco L, Pistoria MJ, Auerbach AD, Nardino RJ, Holmboe ES.** Internal medicine training in the inpatient setting. A review of published educational interventions. J Gen Intern Med. 2005;20:1173-80.
4. **Institute of Medicine.** Resident Duty Hours: Enhancing Sleep, Supervision, and Safety. Washington, DC: National Academies Pr; 2008.
5. **Kennedy TJ, Regehr G, Baker GR, Lingard LA.** Progressive independence in clinical training: a tradition worth defending? Acad Med. 2005;80:S106-11.
6. **Institute of Medicine.** Health Professions Education: A Bridge to Quality. Washington, DC: National Academy Pr; 2003.
7. **Hafferty FW, Franks R.** The hidden curriculum, ethics teaching, and the structure of medical education. Acad Med. 1994;69:861-71.
8. **Feinstein AR.** "Clinical Judgment" revisited: the distraction of quantitative models. Ann Intern Med. 1994;120:799-805.
9. **Holmboe ES, Hawkins RE, Huot SJ.** Effects of training in direct observation of medical residents' clinical competence: a randomized trial. Ann Intern Med. 2004;140:874-81.
10. **Campbell NC, Murray E, Darbyshire J, Emery J, Farmer A, Griffiths F, et al.** Designing and evaluating complex interventions to improve health care. BMJ. 2007;334:455-9.
11. **Soumerai SB, McLaughlin TJ, Gurwitz JH, Guadagnoli E, Hauptman PJ, Borbas C, et al.** Effect of local medical opinion leaders on quality of care for acute myocardial infarction: a randomized controlled trial. JAMA. 1998;279:1358-63.
12. **Institute of Medicine.** Retooling for an Aging America: Building the Health Care Workforce. Accessed at www.iom.edu/CMS/3809/40113/53452/54320.aspx.
13. **Leipzig RM, Granville L, Simpson D, Anderson MB, Sauvigné K, Soriano RP.** Keeping granny safe on July 1: a consensus on minimum geriatrics competencies for graduating medical students. Acad Med. 2009;84:604-10.
14. **Pangaro L.** A new vocabulary and other innovations for improving descriptive in-training evaluations. Acad Med. 1999;74:1203-7.
15. **Noel GL.** A system for evaluating and counseling marginal students during clinical clerkships. J Med Educ. 1987;62:353-5.
16. **Pawson R, Tilley N.** Realistic Evaluation. London: Sage Publications; 1997.
17. **National Health Services.** Glossary. Accessed at www.nhs.uk/news/Pages/Newsglossary.aspx.
18. **Berner ES, Graber ML.** Overconfidence as a cause of diagnostic error in medicine. Am J Med. 2008;121:S2-23.
19. **Holmboe ES, Lipner R, Greiner A.** Assessing quality of care: knowledge matters. JAMA. 2008;299:338-40.

Profiles
of Leaders
in Medical
Education

Profiles of Leaders in Medical Education

Louis Pangaro, MD, MACP

❖ Contents

This final section in this book provides examples of leadership careers in medical education. It is written for residents, chief residents, faculty, and others contemplating a career as medical educators. At the suggestion of the series editor, Dr. Jack Ende, I approached leaders who were trained in internal medicine and asked for their participation. In a sense we are using the case method to help readers learn more about what it is like to become a leader, and then to function as a leader in medical education. We have tried to provide a sufficient number of examples to show the breadth of careers available, and that will reassure junior faculty that there is no single pathway. The common prerequisite—as in the practice of medicine—is the ability to draw strength from taking care of others, in this case your students, residents and colleagues.

❖ The Method

The 15 profiles presented in this section constitute a series of observations, essentially a data set, on the subject of leadership careers in internal medicine, and it is important for readers to know the methods used. We began with a blueprint to select a cross-section of men and women who were internists and now are in different leadership roles, such as clerkship directors, program directors, chairs, and deans. They came from different academic and training backgrounds, such as clinical care, research, teaching, and educational research. The brief introduction I have written to each profile gives one or two key positions they have held, and the text of the interview will provide some more details about other roles they have held. There is no attempt to completely describe their entire careers; these are very successful, even eminent people, and it was not possible or indeed our intention to summarize their careers, to detail all the awards they have won, or to pay tribute to all they have accomplished.

The individuals were contacted by phone or e-mail and invited to do a 45-minute telephone interview, which would be taped and subsequently transcribed. Our "subjects" were provided in advance the questions that would be the basis of the discussion:

1. Can you summarize how you arrived at your current position?
2. What led you on a path that included leadership in medical education?
3. Were there any specific circumstances—or people—that significantly influenced your career path?
4. What are the traits of outstanding leaders that you value most?
5. When you look back, what accomplishments make you most proud?
6. In a career that may have included many difficult situations, what stands out as the most difficult?
7. What mistakes have you made? What has surprised you, or caught you off guard?
8. What are the major challenges facing medical education right now?
9. What advice would you most like to pass along to future leaders in medical education?

At the end of the conversation they were asked what else that would like to mention. They understood that I would allow them to review the final draft of the "profile" I had produced, so that they could revise their phrasing if they wished. There was no formal consent, and the project was not reviewed by an institutional review board because it was considered to be more in the nature of journalism than research.

❖ "Results"

Each interview typically yielded a text of at least 7500 words; these had to be condensed to no more than one third of the original length. Space requirements did not allow all answers to all questions to be included in each profile. In fact, there was overlap of viewpoints and agreement on key aspects of leadership, mentors, and challenges facing medical education (a few themes are summarized below). The choice of what to keep from each transcript and what to sacrifice for the sake of space was mine, not that of the subject of the profile. I beg readers not to infer that any given subject did not have something to say on an important question. Each of them were generous with their time, and later it became painful to leave out many wonderful comments in order to include a sufficient range of career examples. In other words, we chose to have 15 shorter profiles rather than seven or eight of greater length.

In reducing each interview by about two thirds, a guiding principle was simply to capture as much as possible each person speaking in his or her own voice. I tried not to be intrusive, and I have used direct quotation as much as possible. Occasionally, footnotes are used to help the reader, typically to identify a person spoken about. There is minimal paraphrase, and— I hope—no explicit editorial comment from me. The editors and I often had to decide on the punctuation, for instance whether a hesitation was a comma or a semi-colon, occasionally where comments needed to be adjusted to be more easily read, but this was always to achieve an acceptable flow for someone reading. Although I shortened some of the longer sentences, and occasionally combined clauses from different sentences, for the most part the comments are in the speaker's own words.

I sent each interviewee the final profile, not the original transcript because it was weeks to months afterward, they may not have remembered their answers to each of the questions in any case. Those profiled made very few changes or corrections to the draft of the profile that I sent them.

I remain grateful for the candor of these leaders, and their willingness to share their stories and insights. Their honesty and self-reflection of the group were inspiring, and may be what I myself take away from the series of interviews. If I have emphasized any difficulties and personal trials, it is only because I believe it is reassuring that wonderful careers in medical education, including the epitome of leadership, are often achieved after apparent detours and by being open to opportunities when they came along.

❖ Themes and Discussion

There were some commonalities that are worth pointing out to junior faculty who aspire to leadership positions. Our subjects had mentors and influential teachers, but not many had the path cleared for them. Many, at first, did not know the path they would finally take. Many spoke of the role of chance and luck in their careers—being at the right place at the right time. During the interview I did not second-guess them, but it was also clear that there were often mentors and leaders in the background who were on the alert for talented people with a passion for medicine and medical education. Some in our series trained with or worked with others in the series; but some were not well connected and became successful when their talent and energy became clear. It was clear that a deep love of their work is often what carried all of them through difficult times and the importance of family in making career decisions was often present.

One common concern among all of these leaders is how medical education had been seriously affected, even compromised, by the health care environment, by how medicine is now practiced in society, and by how financial considerations are deeply affecting academic institutions. There is also a concern that the strong force of program accreditation and external regulation might be having unintended, negative consequences. At the same time our interviews documented the emergence of medical education as a career track within schools and hospitals; those interviewed consider it to be a legitimate discipline for academic productivity and advancement.

Paramount among out group was a sense of gratitude to their own mentors, and finding fulfillment in taking on this role for others. The tradition of one generation helping the next—not just to learn medicine, but to learn to teach and to lead—emerged in every story. I particularly loved hearing about their discovery that the "big names" and powerful figures they encountered were more than approachable, and typically grateful to be able to help.

❖ Conclusion

There are many lessons here for faculty to reflect on. The honesty and humility of these very successful leaders are worth noting. Their commitment to students and residents and to their colleagues is inspiring, and talking with them has been a highlight of my own career. There are many, many other leaders from our specialty whose stories might have been included in these profiles, but I hope that those included here are heard as encouraging voices speaking from one generation to the next.

❖ Daniel Federman

"A medical student's life should be intellectually dazzling, emotionally rewarding, and morally transcendent." While this remark is from a lecture in honor of Dr. Jordan Cohen,[1] and not from our interview, it did encapsulate ideas running through Dr. Federman's remarks for this profile, through his career, and, in fact, through all the interviews in this series of profiles. Dr. Daniel Federman is Carl W. Walter Distinguished Professor of Medicine at Harvard Medical School. He has served as Associate Chair of Medicine and Director of the Medical Residency at the Massachusetts General Hospital, Chair of Medicine at Stanford, and Dean for Students and Alumni and Dean for Medical Education at Harvard Medical School.

Choosing Education Rather Than Investigation

After medical school at Harvard and residency at the Massachusetts General Hospital (MGH), Dr. Federman trained in endocrinology and thought of that as his career. Yet, he moved more and more toward education. "I actually think it goes back to the first talk I ever gave, which was in the physiology course. I enjoyed thinking about who was going to be listening, and why they should care about the topic. I enjoyed making it clear, rather than excessively detailed. It was such a thrill that I always wanted teaching to be part of my life."

The next big moment was "an accident" when he was asked, though just a fellow, to give grand rounds on Klinefelter syndrome. "It was August, and the person they wanted was on vacation. So they turned to me as a fellow and asked me to talk about it. It was an exciting topic. There was no chance for formal in-depth library research. You had 36 hours' notice, and putting it together quickly was a thrill. So I began to think of teaching, but even more I started to think about education."

The Critical Role of the Chair

Finishing his fellowship, he found himself in a fabulous department under the chair of medicine, Walter Bauer.[2] "Walter had picked a string of chief residents to be division chiefs. He would send them away for a year or two, and they'd come back ready to hold their own clinically and to apply research to that discipline. And I was the lucky one. I hadn't been chief resident, I hadn't been trained in research, but Walter Bauer respected this emphasis on teaching and clinical medicine. And it somehow endured. I never thought it would. My wife and I both thought it was a temporary experience, but from that it grew.

"I was an anomaly in the setting. It's best captured by someone who came up to my wife at an MGH party and said, 'You know, your husband is probably smart enough, why doesn't he do research?' And that question, which was so unsettling at the time, perfectly captured the career I wanted to have. I didn't want, or wasn't creative enough, to be a productive researcher." Dr. Federman became the first one at Harvard given tenure on the basis of being a clinician and teacher, opening the path for others.

Moving to Stanford

He described the big moment in his career as an invitation from Stanford to be chair of the Department of Medicine. "I've always known it wasn't really a personal invitation. It was an institutional hope that they had. Stanford was an outstanding school in research and in laboratory education, and what they wanted in me was excellence in clinical teaching, in patient care, in student and resident education. At Stanford, you are a senior figure within a great university, and you are responsible for the education of medical students from the day they come to the school, through their introduction to clinical medicine and clinical clerkships and, finally, residency training. It was in that setting that I became an educator."

Dr. Federman distinguished being a professional "educator" (with knowledge of the theory of education) from being a "teacher," and feels that he lacked formal training in education. "I am a natural teacher, comfortable with audiences because I relate to them quickly and easily and informally and not really didactically. I'm still an amateur, and yet I've enjoyed it. I've been given many forums in which to express it, and been lucky to work with terrific trainees in multiple settings so that I pass as an educator, although I never formally became one. Being chairman of the department gives you certain openings, and I was quickly active in the American Board of Internal Medicine.[3] I was also active in the American College of Physicians,[4] which from its 1915 establishment emphasized the role of education in the excellence of medicine."

A Key Characteristic of Leadership

Dr. Federman began articulating his thoughts about leadership by speaking again of Walter Bauer. "He called me into his office once in October of my internship year. Quaking and wondering what it was about, I went in and he said, 'You know, I'm going away tomorrow to South America for 10 days, but you look down to me, and I can't go away without asking you what's wrong and giving me a chance to do something about it.' Can you imagine?

That was emblematic of Bauer's approach—a deep personal interest in each person under him."

Like others in these profiles, Dr. Federman described some of the key events in his own career as "accidents," but for him, too, there was a person rather than a situation that was critical. "The real recognition is leaders motivated towards their house staff, and towards the people under them. [It's] caring about how they developed, and wanting to give scope to what those trainees wanted to do. That was Bauer's genius."

Pride in Recognitions, Students, and Residents

Of the many awards he has received, three symbolize to him the growing importance of a generalist educational specialty within academic medicine. First was receiving the Outstanding Teacher Award from the American College of Physicians. "The ACP at that time was very much a generalist organization. It now has a subspecialty richness and it works with the subspecialty boards; but at that time … the teaching award from ACP, like the presidency, reflected general internal medicine. I was a general internist first. I did primary care. I taught the first-year course in introduction to physical diagnosis. I taught the second, third, and fourth years at different levels. I made house calls when I started out in primary care and can remember the patients now that I saw at home."

The second recognition was from the Endocrine Society, which had created an award for a clinical educator in endocrinology. "Even if you're not doing research in a subspecialty, you should keep up with the science that's going on in that field and be able to draw on it in your own thinking and your own teaching."

The third symbolic recognition was the Flexner Award of the Association of American Medical Colleges. "At first I couldn't see myself in the company of the pantheon of people who had won that award, but the citation that went with it talks about contributions to medical education, things outside research excellence, and I allowed myself the illusion that I deserved it."

Centering on Patients and Learners

Dr. Federman feels lucky to have had outstanding trainees. Some became deans; many, chairs of departments (not just of medicine). Four Nobel laureates were his interns and residents. Most important to him, his role allowed him to help when they needed it in their training. "They need just to learn how to get comfortable writing a set of orders, or how to talk to somebody about his illness at night, or how to get a patient to level with you about what she really wants in chemotherapy. They needed those very beginning things, and for me it was a privilege because of the dedication of the people that I was lucky to work with."

These are examples of helping trainees to be patient-centered; his own regrets as a teacher were when he forgot to be learner-centered. (He didn't use that jargon, but it was clearly central to his approach to everything.) "Most of the things I regret were teaching moments where I failed to perceive what the learner or learners needed at that time [and] ... to analyze it carefully enough to remember what [I was] teaching. Is it third year? Is it fourth year? Is it endocrine fellows about to take the boards? Is it CME [continuing medical education] for people who are falling behind in science?"

"Stick to Basics, Think Out Loud, Be Kind"

Dr. Federman has a basic mantra of advice for teachers reflecting an awareness of others that is always there. "It's very simple. Eight words. And I have found that is terrific in guiding residents toward student education and intern education.

"To *stick to basics* is important. Third-year students need basics. Endocrine fellows still need the basics in any field except the one they're very strong in. To *think out loud* is very powerful. For one thing, it slows you down and you don't go as fast. You stay closer to your audience, and your own brain gets a separate input about what it is putting out. And *be kind* because in the hurlyburly of the teaching hospital there is never enough positive feedback or kindness to beginning students and interns."

External and Internal Challenges to Medical Education

Dr. Federman feels that our biggest challenge at the moment is external to medical education. His thoughts were similar to those of other physicians profiled here, and he states it very strongly. "I believe education and health care are taking place in an immoral universe because there isn't universal access, because there's so much profit going to relatively few people who don't do medicine themselves, and because medical schools have not been in the vanguard in insisting on broadened access.

"Within medical education, I would say that our biggest challenges are the rate of change and advances in science that are relevant to what we do. [It's also a challenge] to preserve a focus on trainees in a world that puts patient care and research ahead of teaching. I don't want to be misunderstood on this point—patient care is intimately connected with teaching—but I meant the income from patient care and the pressure to take care of everybody push aside the time needed for education. Education takes a second place to research and the pressures of patient care. We need a rebalancing within education that just now might occur in the light of a rebalancing of health care."

What Should Educators Be Studying?

"What I say might surprise you, but I think medical educators should be conscious, aware, and excited by what's happening in neuroscience and neurobiology. So much is happening in the area of how the brain functions and how learning takes place that I would like to imagine educators keeping close to the neuroscience. [This would let] our teaching take on a form which reflects the neuroscience of learning, and we gradually emphasize approaches that accord with how the brain functions."

Another whole area of education that needs work is what he calls "translational education" to reflect the current emergence of translational research. "It's a long way from the bench to the bedside. There's a lot that has to be done to keep close to the emerging science, and to its translation to clinical activity for house staff and students. There's a need to learn to keep new literature next to your pen when you're writing a prescription. You have to help the students think about how they draw on what they know to work up a patient or to write a prescription or make a decision."

Thoughts for Developing a Career

Dr. Federman has precise, well-organized advice for educators' career development, even those in the dean's office. It begins with close ties with a clinical department. "I've seen nobody thrive as an educator without being welcome in a clinical department and championed for promotion by that department. You have to remain active as a clinician. Most clerkship directors I've known have been too smart to want to be the dean, but if no clinical department will recognize you, mentor you, and ultimately write the promotion papers, you'll never get anywhere.

"Secondly, I don't think you can flourish as a medical educator unless you're a good doctor, care about patients, teach well with patients, and convey the respect for the profession and its values that show up best in a clinical context. It's important to be close to the science that's emerging and to use it in your teaching so that you're not saying the same things 4 years later.

"Third, I think that the person who wants to be an educator should expect to publish, not at the volume that you can when you have fellows in a big lab, but at a respectable volume that reflects your thinking, your maturing, and your recognition of the educational responsibility.

"Fourth, I think you should find an area of educational research, and there's plenty that's emerging. But I certainly think that it should be clear that you have to write and publish, and you can't get away with what my own career was like, which did so little of that."

Getting Young People Excited About Education

To Dr. Federman, educational innovation is a key to the future, and we need to attract more students and residents. "Medical schools attract fantastic students, and the model that's been put out for them, implicitly, has been research and outstanding clinical work. But schools should tilt towards recognition of their educators, their professional development, and, in time, their academic development, so that some of the best people who come through see medical education as a career.

"I have found this a fabulously privileged life, to be associated with a recurring stream of terrific young people and to feel a real responsibility for what they learn and what happens to them. What I like about this ACP project is that it has a chance to put needed weight in this area, and I would want everybody to know that at least this person thinks it's an incredible way to spend your only lifetime."

[1]Daniel Federman, November 5, 2007, the Jordan J. Cohen Lecture at the Association of American Medical Colleges.

[2]Walter Bauer, MD (1898–1963), was chief of medical services at Massachusetts General Hospital and Jackson Professor of Clinical Medicine at Harvard Medical School.

[3]He later became chair of the American Board of Internal Medicine.

[4]He later became president of the American College of Physicians.

❖ Kelley Skeff

"There was a huge gap between the field of education and the field of medicine that I might play a role in helping to cross." Kelley M. Skeff, MD, PhD, has been program director in internal medicine at Stanford for 20 years. With Georgette Stratos, PhD, he directs the Stanford Faculty Development Center, which has been a transforming innovation in American medical education. "Many told me, don't do this. There's no career in this. But it just seemed like the thing to do. Teaching was so important, and helping people was so much fun, that I just did it. But there was a difficult time there when I think my family was crucial in getting me over the hump."

We began with how he became program director. "It intersects dramatically with the Faculty Development Program[5] because in 1989, I was the director of the Inpatient Service at the Palo Alto VA Hospital. We had weekly meetings with the program director at Stanford and with the chair. We had a new chair at Stanford by the name of Ted Harris,[6] and I said to him, 'You might want to take this course that we're offering. I know you're probably a great teacher already, but you might find it useful.'"

Dr. Harris agreed and attended a seminar that gave practice to those new to teaching the course. "He realized that what I was doing was coming into a new place. As a result of that experience, he knew what I was thinking about, and then asked me, literally that week, to be the program director."

Being program director would add a lot of responsibility while the program was growing, but he didn't hesitate. "It just made sense. It was a reasonable follow-up administrative role because I had been the director of the outpatient clinic, the clerkship, and then the wards at the VA. More importantly, it was a reasonable laboratory in which to implement the types of processes and goals that I had had as education within the program."

Deciding on a Career in Education

Dr. Skeff described how his education and training led him to a career in education and eventually to starting the Faculty Development Center. "That story goes back to 1975, when I was fortunate to come to Stanford as a third-year resident. I had gone to medical school at the University of Colorado. I actually did my residency in three separate places. I was an intern in Los Angeles, at Harbor-UCLA. Then I got drafted into the Navy. Then I went back to Colorado as a second-year resident. I had a wonderful time and, meaningfully, met my wife. Stanford had a third-year position open, and I already knew the importance that the chair at Stanford, Dan Federman,[7] was placing on education."

He was chosen for the open slot at Stanford. "And then the serendipity all begins to unfold. I came in July. In the fall of that year, Dan Federman and Bob Glaser[8] from the Kaiser Family Foundation began the first fellowship in general internal medicine with two fellows at Stanford, and six others at three other sites around the country. I was very fortunate to be here when that was started, and to be given one of the fellowship positions.

"It was at that time that I met Hal Sox,[9] Dan Federman, and Bob Glaser. Impressive to me was the dedication of the mentors in that fellowship to the fulfillment of whatever it was that the individual wanted to do. It was recognized, probably within the first 6 months of the fellowship, that I was spending most of my time teaching. Dan Federman and Hal Sox, in particular, both recognized that inherent desire, and they were the ones who suggested that I get an advanced degree in education."

A Trip Around the Country

"Then Dan Federman suggested that I go around the country, meet other people in the field, and then decide if I wanted to enter the field in a serious way. It was remarkable. On that 2-week trip, I met and exchanged ideas with a wonderful man by the name of Norm Kagan[10] at Michigan State University, who had been using videotapes in his work. Then I went to Washington, DC, where I met Hilly Jason,[11] who was at that time working at the Association of American Medical Colleges. His staff introduced me to David Irby,[12] who was still at the University of Washington. Then I went to North Carolina and met Frank Stritter.[13] I ended up at the Center for Educational Development at the University of Illinois in Chicago and met a wonderful group of educators there."

This was in 1977. The trip convinced him that there was a lot that educational theory and innovation could do for the teaching of medicine, and that he himself could contribute to closing the gap. He also met a group of PhDs whom he respected and wanted to be like.

"David Irby suggested that I walk across the street to the Stanford Education School and meet Nathan Gage,[14] who then invited me to start taking classes with him. That's how I began doing the PhD at Stanford. And I just continued to take classes, and the Kaiser Family Foundation was wonderful enough to extend my funding to do a 4-year fellowship instead of 2. I was able to do the PhD here at Stanford, and that enabled us to get a faculty position here and then also to continue with Georgette Stratos,[15] whom I had met in 1979, to develop the Faculty Development Program.

"So it's a bit of a roundabout series of serendipitous occurrences which I think almost every faculty member has—wonderful chance occurrences where you meet the right people who help you go to the next step."

The Importance of a "Mentoring Institution"

"I've called Stanford a 'mentoring institution.' One component is a commitment to identify the inherent strengths and the passions of the individual, and what those contributions might become. The other is a recognition that you're at a complex institution that can wrap itself around the person, or at least put them in an environment where others with the same philosophy and a commitment to excellence can help. The concept that Stanford has been a research place has been helpful, not only in the quality of what we've done but also in lending credibility to a new area of research."

Difficulty in Starting the Program

The first difficultly was convincing himself and others that this had merit as a field. "Early on, that was not so clear. Others supported me, but it was not clear that money would be flowing, or that people thought it was a unique thing to do. Many told me, don't do this—there's no career in it."

They struggled to get external funding. "Funding from the very beginning was difficult. Our first grant to Health and Human Services was turned down. It was not a grant program; it was a contract program. We needed money, and what we wanted to do did not match the contract. That was a really difficult time. Wonderful people surfaced and actually influenced Health and Human Services to develop a grant program for general internal medicine, which funded us for 10 years."

Others were essential to his persevering. "One is Georgette. The intersection between our careers has been instrumental in the success that we've had. She has been a selfless, brilliant, analytical individual who has helped us to connect with physicians and teachers in a unique way. The second group is crucial, and that's my family. There were times when I sensed that there was no support for the work I was doing. People really thought that it was not a direction to go in, and some could even be condescending about it. It was at those times that my wife, Linda, who recognized the importance of the work that we were doing, would say, 'Don't stop this. What you're doing is important.' My own daughters, as they grew up, jumped on the bandwagon to recognize the importance of helping others. I think that it's been built into them as individuals. Their support to keep going during the bumps has been crucial."

Professionalism in the Time of Work Hour Restrictions

The Stanford Faculty Development Program enhances how individual teachers relate to learners. The system-wide challenges in medical education that Skeff mentioned were brought up by other leaders in this series, particularly the implications of new Accreditation Council for Graduate Medical Education (ACGME) regulations. "I think it's a real challenge for medical education to perpetuate the professional values that have represented the profession for so long, at the same time taking on requirements that in some cases impede the development of personal characteristics that we all felt were very important."

The new ACGME work hour guidelines pose a particular challenge. "The guidelines are all very valid and have great reason for being; but it has been very, very hard to hold onto flexibility and innovativeness and to run a program that allowed self-discovery. That's been much harder under the current guidelines than it was during the first 15 years I was a program director."

The guidelines come at a time of generational change, and Dr. Skeff related a recent conversation. "I had a medical student not long ago saying, 'Well, I'm just not sure whether medicine is right for me because I think it's going to intrude on my personal life and on other things I want to do as an individual.' The biggest challenge is how to respond to appropriate and meaningful requirements of accreditation councils and the desires of the public, and continue to foster and preserve the types of professional behaviors and characteristics that were in the profession before. The necessity to reconstruct the days, the weeks, the months to meet the requirements has made it very, very difficult to always foster the characteristics that we would want in the profession."

An Opportunity in the Challenge

Dr. Skeff asked, "Now, where's the opportunity inside of this? In the midst of change there's this wonderful thing that's happening, which is a reinforcement of something that we've all believed in. We've all believed in the responsibility one has toward other people, including colleagues. The major opportunity is to make physicians be contributors to the institution where they work, and have that be a set of personal expectations and [a source of] personal excitement."

The task is a redirection of the academic and medical culture. "It's a direct affront to the competitive model that's built into medicine and built into the business aspects of medicine. It's still built into a competitive model that asks, 'Who's on top and who's on bottom?' If we really take responsibility for colleagues, then no longer can we at all have pleasure in saying the delivery of care at Institution A is better than the delivery of care at Institution B."

Changing the Competitive Model

This model operates not just in the business aspects of medicine but in the educational ones as well. "It struck me early on, when we were first studying medical teaching and watching students and residents and faculty, that there was an inherent competitive model built into the educational system, and that when one person failed, the other succeeded. The student who got a good grade received it because it was in comparison to the students who got a bad grade. So I suggest they shift their gratification locus from one in which you're gratified when the person next to you isn't doing things as well as you are, to one in which you're gratified when the person next to you does something better because you happen to be next to them.

"What I tried to do at Stanford is to imbue in the residents a recognition that they are truly responsible for the quality of care delivered by their institution from the moment they set foot in that institution, and that they have an opportunity to let their ideas be known to improve the system and to also try to help, not only the system get better, but each individual in that system. Now this is something that I think is built right into the new accreditation requirements with the idea of professionalism and practice-based improvement and system-based care. But underpinning that has got to be a philosophy that has people really committed and dedicated to the next person."

Accomplishments of Which He Is Proud

As he steps down as the program director, what gives him a feeling of pride? First is the development of the Stanford Faculty Development Center and the multiplier effect it has when trained facilitators go back to their own schools and hospitals. "This has had an opportunity to help so many dedicated faculty help others. One sees the gratification that they get out of helping other faculty, and then I'm just imagining the impact that that has on the people that those people see.

"The other has certainly been to develop a residency program at Stanford where the philosophical tenets that I've discussed with you have become embedded in the program. Even as I pass the baton to others in the next year, I hope that the perpetuation of the concepts of respect for others, dedication to the field, and dedication to your colleagues stays with whatever structural changes are made to this and other programs."

[5]The Stanford Faculty Development Center, created in 1985 by Georgette Stratos, PhD, and Dr. Skeff, has now trained several hundred facilitators from schools around the country.

[6]Edward Harris Jr., MD, chaired the Stanford Department of Medicine from 1987 to 1995.

[7]See his profile in this section.

[8]Robert J. Glaser, MD, was dean and professor of medicine at Stanford. In 1972 he became the first full-time president and chief executive officer of the Henry J. Kaiser Family Foundation.

[9]Harold C. Sox, MD, is editor emeritus of *Annals of Internal Medicine*. He served as chief of the Division of General Internal Medicine of Stanford University School of Medicine.

[10]Norman Kagan, PhD (1931–1994), was distinguished professor of psychology in the College of Education, Michigan State University, Lansing, Michigan.

[11]Hilliard Jason, MD, EdD, was founding director of the Office of Medical Education Research and Development at Michigan State University and the Division of Faculty Development at the Association of American Medical Colleges.

[12]David Irby, PhD, is now vice-dean for education and professor of medicine at the University of California, San Francisco.

[13]Frank T. Stritter, PhD, is professor emeritus at the University of North Carolina at Chapel Hill.

[14]Nathan Gage, PhD, is a professor at the Stanford School of Education.

[15]Georgette Stratos, PhD, is codirector of the Faculty Development Center at Stanford University.

❖ Arthur Rubenstein

"We are here to serve the people who make the place great, which are the faculty and students."

Arthur H. Rubenstein, MBBCh, is dean of the School of Medicine of the University of Pennsylvania and executive vice-president. He graduated from the University of the Witwaterstrand in Johannesburg, South Africa, in 1960 and went on to do important clinical and molecular work in diabetes. He was chair of medicine at the University of Chicago from 1981 to 1997 and then dean of the Mt. Sinai School of Medicine in New York before assuming his current position at the University of Pennsylvania.

South Africa to England to the United States

In South Africa, Dr. Rubenstein went directly from high school to a 6-year medical school, the common practice in countries with an English system. "I had lots of wonderful role models, called registrars, like senior house staff here, and of course, attending physicians and professors. I was also very interested in research and I applied for a fellowship. I wanted to go to London, and South Africans often went to the big teaching hospitals." He went to Hammersmith Hospital. "I worked in the endocrinology division there under Sir Russell Frasier, a great clinical and investigative endocrinologist, and he was a really spectacular role model for me.

"There were few jobs, but luckily, the same person I had trained with in South Africa had moved on to the University of Chicago, and he asked me what I was going to do. I really didn't know because I didn't have a job. He said there was a possibility of getting an NIH [National Institutes of Health] fellowship in America to work with him at the University of Chicago. Interestingly, the fellowship would be in cardiology, and I happened to be an endocrinologist—but as they say, beggars can't be choosers. So, we immigrated to the States, and I took a position as a postdoctoral fellow with Godfrey Getz, and also worked with Murray Rabinowitz in biochemistry, rather than in endocrinology or cardiology. It was somewhat serendipitous but wonderful training. It turned out by chance that I met a great scientist—his name is Donald Steiner. He was working on the biochemistry of insulin, and that was very close to my heart."

Exciting Times

Dr. Rubenstein worked in the daytime with Getz and Rabinowitz, and at nighttime with Steiner. "It was a very exciting time because he was working out how insulin was synthesized in islets of Langerhans in the pancreas. I joined the endocrine division and gave up cardiology studies, and worked with Steiner on basic studies related to insulin, and did more clinical work and teaching, which I always loved. My own expertise was in clinical endocrinology and diabetes, and he was more basic scientist, so I complemented what they were doing. So that was how all that happened. I did the traditional things and took care of lots of patients, particularly those with diabetes, but also in general endocrinology. I guess I made a name for myself, because it was something I loved very dearly. I enjoyed interacting with these colleagues."

Becoming Chair

He was rapidly promoted to associate professor, then professor, and during the late 1970s the chair, Dr. Alvin Tarlov,[16] asked him to become vice-chair and oversee house staff and medical school training. After Dr. Tarlov stepped down, Dr. Rubenstein became the acting chair. "It was all fairly serendipitous because I had not planned any of this, but I said sure, I would run the department until they found a permanent chair. Actually, they offered the job to several people, and for one reason or other it didn't work out. I think that after they got tired of offering it to outside people, they said, did I want to do the job? And I said, 'Well, not particularly, but if the university really wanted me to do it, I guess I would.' So that's how it happened—it was all chance. I took the job in 1981, and I became chair of the department. I remained there until 1997, when I went to become the dean at Mt. Sinai in New York."

Why Move?

"One becomes complacent. One knows everybody, one has connections to the community, to the synagogue, to friends. One always gets comfortable. It was time to look for another position, and successful chairs usually get offered these jobs. So, it seemed a natural transition at that time. I thought I could be there my whole life, but in the end, I think we wanted to be close to family. I understood that we could make it and set up things again, even after 30 years, and we did. So, having a spouse who's a good partner is a godsend, I would say. In my case, it was critical for my success. Totally critical."

The decision to move from Mt. Sinai to Penn was difficult. " I loved it at Mt. Sinai. It is a wonderful medical school and hospital, but in Chicago I had always enjoyed the integration of the school into the university, and it was something I really valued because of scholarship and colleagues and students in the college whom I appreciated. I love universities. The American educational system, particularly universities, is so geared to rewarding hard-working, good people, irrespective of accents or background or training. It's something I value, and, of course, I've been a direct beneficiary of it.

"I've done three jobs, really, at three institutions. Moving from each one of them has been hard because I have enjoyed them, but I think overall, I've made the right decision. In all of these, my wife has been absolutely fantastic, just a terrific partner and I just can't say enough about how she's helped in each of these decisions."

Serendipity
"You know, a lot of the things that happened in my life were serendipitous. Going to America. Getting the scholarship to go to London. Becoming the vice-chair, and then I never imagined Tarlov would choose another job and step down. I never really made long-term plans. Maybe I started to think about the deanship in the last couple years of being a chair, but at the time I became the chair, I was very happy running a big research and patient care program in diabetes. So, would I have been interested in taking a chair at another institution? I had not thought of it seriously until this opportunity came up. So I just can't answer that. Who knows?"

Teaching and Mentoring
Throughout his career, Dr. Rubenstein has seen himself as a teacher. "I loved it. I had been the beneficiary of tremendously good mentors, and I viewed that relationship as something special and wonderful. As I became more senior, I enjoyed having students and fellows and residents in my clinic when I saw patients. They benefited from watching how I dealt with patients, and I loved being able to energize them, and show them the nuances of how you make patients and families comfortable. I was asked to do morning report, even before I became chairman, because I could teach very well to residents. It's a thrilling kind of relationship in working to create a climate where young people thrive."

The Traits of Outstanding Leaders
"I've thought a lot about this over the years. I think there is a certain basic thing that one needs, and that is academic excellence, whether it's clinical knowledge or skill in patient care or the ability to do research. That's a baseline, but it's not nearly enough. The other things are interpersonal skills, integrity, caring for others, and the ability to interact in a warm and empathic way. You also need to believe that you can create a climate where

others thrive, without worrying about your own trajectory. And it's important to understand other people's problems and be able to empathize, and to be a person who, despite challenges and difficulties and adversity, is always thinking through how to do it best, and handle it in a way that one can be proud of. You don't want to lose your temper, you don't want to make snap decisions, you don't want to blame other people. How you deal with challenges and make people around you have confidence in you—these create an institutional climate of excellence."

Accomplishments That Make Him Proud

The first thing he mentioned was having created a climate where people thrive and are able to accomplish their goals to the best of their ability. "So, this means a supportive environment, praise for people who do great things, and support for those who are having difficulty. I'm proud of trying to recruit and retain the very best people. The senior administrator, whether it's a chairman or dean, is there to serve the faculty and students, not to run the place. Now, one does do that in a sense by default, but the goal is to create a climate where students and faculty thrive. People ask, 'Well, what have you done as a leader of the institution?' I'd rather put it another way. It's a privilege to serve as a person who creates a climate for the students and faculty to be successful. Now I don't want to be naive, so let's add in some leadership, but, if one believes the most important people in a medical school or university are the students and faculty, then one doesn't think the most important people are the dean, the vice-president, and the vice-dean."

Difficult Situations and Mistakes

"I think the most difficult thing for me always is what to do about people who do bad things—lacking honesty, doing bad things to patients, being incompetent as an administrator, or abusing students. Those people have to be disciplined. Some of them have to be terminated. I always struggle with that. I think I do it reasonably well, but it doesn't come easily to me. I always try to do what's right for the institution and the team. I always try to be as fair as I can, but it is difficult for me.

"Most of the mistakes I have made are when I've known I have to do something, but I've procrastinated, or consulted so broadly to be sure I was right that it took too long. I've regretted removing people from positions too slowly for incompetence. I've regretted not disciplining people fast enough when it's obvious they've done bad things. Sometimes you know you've got to do something, but you wait 2 or 3 weeks. Nobody is advantaged by that delay. In fact, everyone is disadvantaged."

The Challenges Facing Medical Education Now

Dr. Rubenstein, like others profiled in this section, sees issues closely tied to our national health care system. "There's a lot of money involved today. Some of the value systems are distorted by wrong incentives. So, whereas the care in the best of places is incredibly good, the system itself is flawed, and that ripples through academic medical centers. The science is great and the NIH is one of the great institutions in the world, but I think our challenge is to create the climate in medicine where the patient and their families come first, where money doesn't get involved, and where we have more time in taking care of difficult problems.

"We train students in a real-life setting, and so you've got to change the whole system, rather than just saying we're going to change the curriculum and then it's going to be great. Now, we can still change the curriculum, but, until we move medicine back to its roots with the right incentives and the amount of time one needs to take care of patients, the system is too distorted to be really good."

Opportunity and Privilege

He often thinks about what to advise students, and those considering a career in medicine. "I would just say, this is the greatest profession. It's been like this for hundreds of years, and it's no different now. We may be going through some very challenging times financially and politically, but the ability to take care of patients, to teach the younger generation to do wonderful research, it's an unparalleled opportunity. To be a physician is such an incredible privilege. And if one's given the opportunity to be a leader and influence the profession, whether it's through students or research or models of patient care, it's just the most wonderful thing in the world."

Dr. Rubenstein urges us to see some of these contemporary challenges as temporary distractions. "Whether it's going to be solved in 1, 2, or 5 years, it's a very short-term view of the issues, whereas to be a physician for 40 years, or a physician leader, or a physician scientist, or a physician educator, is the most amazing thing. In the 40 years I've done it, I don't think for one day I've wavered in appreciating what a privilege and opportunity it is. I try to convey that when I talk to young college students or high school students or friends—therein lies the beauty of the profession, which I see with enormous clarity."

[16]Alvin R. Tarlov, MD, was chair of medicine at the University of Chicago from 1968 to 1981. He later became president of the Henry J. Kaiser Family Foundation and director of the Health Institute at the New England Medical Center.

❖ Jordan J. Cohen

"I went to medical school without any knowledge or conception of what academic medicine was. I went, as I guess most people do, just thinking I was going to be a doctor and eventually practice medicine."

As third president of the Association of American Medical Colleges (AAMC) (1994–2006), Dr. Cohen had one of the most "public" roles of any of our profiled internal medicine leaders. He has been a vigorous advocate that academic medical centers be a lever for improving the care of patients in the larger community, he championed racial and ethnic diversity among students and faculty, and he's kept a sharp focus on professionalism at a time when the environment of practice and academics have been increasingly preoccupied by finances. He did not, of course, begin with the end in mind, and in college thought that he would be a physicist. His interview revealed some thoughts for younger colleagues—an openness to uncertainty and career changes that is reassuring, and a quiet humility that comes from seeing one's own work in the bigger picture of society.

"I was one of those medical students who was attracted to virtually every rotation that I went through. In fact, I went around and interviewed for surgical internships early in my fourth year before I came back and did fourth-year medicine, and discovered that medicine was the field that I really wanted to pursue." He graduated from Harvard Medical School and did postgraduate training at the Boston City Hospital. "There was a lot of emphasis on combining clinical activities with research and with teaching, and that appealed very much to me."

A Traditional Academic Beginning

"It felt like a requirement then that one did subspecialty training after general internal medicine. Having done some research work in medical school and in renal physiology I decided that nephrology was probably the best choice for me. I don't think there was much more depth of analysis than that, actually, when I think back on it. But it was a fortunate choice because nephrology was a fairly new field of research and I was fortunate enough to get a position in one of the laboratories that was at the leading edge.

"My mentor was Bill Schwartz,[17] who had the laboratory at the New England Medical Center in Boston, and I spent 2 years as a research fellow.

When I finished my formal training in medicine and nephrology I was extraordinarily lucky to have finished when Brown was just starting its medical school. It had just recruited its first chairman of medicine and was establishing an academic faculty. So, I finished my training, and the next day I was the chief of nephrology at Brown."

Broader Responsibilities at Brown and Then Tufts

At this point in our interview, Dr. Cohen laughed at his situation, and throughout the conversation showed humor and objectivity as he reflected on his career. "It turned out I was the only nephrologist in the state of Rhode Island at the time, so I was not only the chief but also the chief bottle-washer. That was 1965, and it was an extraordinary opportunity to establish a new entity at Rhode Island Hospital, which is still a major teaching hospital for Brown. It was an opportunity to get involved in the early planning of the medical school, too ... because there were so few people there."

His career developed along traditional academic research lines. "Everybody was pitching in to do a lot of different things. I started a fellowship program. I did a lot of teaching for the first years of the medical education program." He spent 2 years in the Army at Walter Reed doing research and some writing. In the meantime, Dr. Schwartz had been named chair of medicine at New England Medical Center, and he asked Dr. Cohen to come back to Boston to lead the renal division at Tufts. He held that position for the next 11 years.

"I had an opportunity to do a lot of research and also to get involved in educational activities. We were responsible for all of the second-year pathophysiology teaching in the renal systems and had a lot of contact with undergraduates. I chaired the selection committee internship program and was very involved in internal medicine training at Tufts."

If Brown had not had a new school, "I'm sure I would have been much less involved. The more traditional career was to begin a lab and simply do research, with the occasional opportunity to round on the service. I don't know that I made that conscious decision, but I certainly found that I enjoyed the teaching aspect enormously. I tended to gravitate towards the teaching role."

To Chicago and Then to Stony Brook

"I became involved in the American Board of Internal Medicine and nephrology exam-writing committee while I was at Tufts, so I developed interest in the more national forum for academic medicine. After being a division chief for 11 or 12 years, I was interested in a broader scope of activities. I had an opportunity to move to Chicago to become chairman of medicine at the Michael Reese Hospital, an affiliate of the University of Chicago at the time, and also associate chairman of medicine with Arthur Rubenstein.[18] I was there for 6 years, and it was a very productive time for me personally and professionally. It was an opportunity to work with a mentor, in the form of Arthur, who was just an exceptionally able and collaborative person. We developed a number of things jointly to bring together a classic academic department at the university with Michael Reese, which was much more involved with the real world of patient care. I think that had the proposed merger between the university, the school, and the hospital and Michael Reese—one of the early attempts at mergers—succeeded, I'd still be there. [Laughter.] It was a very forward-looking proposition, but unfortunately it ran into a number of political obstacles in the two institutions and never came to pass."

Stony Brook in New York was looking for a new dean. "So again, very fortunate. I was selected as the second dean for the medical school, which was also a young medical school. It had just started in the early 70s, and it developed its own hospital in 1980. When I arrived in 1988 it was still very much in the development phase. It was again a terrific opportunity to have an impact on the institution because it was still growing and defining itself."

He recalled an unexpected day in a Seattle hotel room when a flight was canceled. "I drafted a new curriculum for the medical school which we were trying to define, and so I was able to install a substantial modification in the undergraduate curriculum in the medical school." This is an achievement of which Dr. Cohen is very proud. "Stony Brook was a new school, and the only academic medical center in Suffolk County, which had a population of almost 2 million people. It was an opportunity to introduce some innovations in education. Trying to organize the region into a more coordinated care system was a very exciting prospect, and I had a lot of fun doing that."

Moving to the AAMC

Dr. Cohen then became the president of the AAMC when Dr. Robert Petersdorf[19] retired from that position. "I was asked to succeed him, and that was an opportunity I just couldn't turn down. I was having a great deal of fun at Stony Brook at the time. But in 1994, the prospect of health care reform was all the buzz in Washington. That was certainly one of the attractions of the AAMC position, an opportunity to have some involvement in, what looked at the time, a rational approach to health care reform. It turned out that we had a lot of health care reform, but it wasn't very rational. [Laughter.] I was surprised by how politicized Washington is. When I got here, I had never had any previous experience with the federal government. One of the surprises was how special interests were particularly in play, and how difficult it was to maintain the stance of public interest in the face of all the various forces that are vying for attention here."

Working in Different Institutions

How did he feel about the moves in his career? "I can see many advantages of staying at one institution and having the opportunity to develop programs in one place. [There is a] legacy that one can leave in a single institution, an impact that is hard to make when you're moving around from place to place." Dr. Cohen thought that new opportunities gave him a chance to be part of the bigger system. "And as I look back at the institutions where I've been, they would've been perfectly fine without my having been there. [Laughter.] I guess there's no other way to say it."

Was there some specific point in his career that he realized he wanted to move from the academic environment of the medical school to a larger sphere? "Well, I guess that was part of the motivation of going from Tufts to Chicago. I really felt that at that time there was a lot of potential and importance in trying to bridge the academic and the practice worlds. I thought Michael Reese was an opportunity to get a more in-depth sense of what the practice of medicine was like."

Similarly, when he went to Stony Brook as dean, all the faculty were also full-time, and there were few private practitioners on the staff at the university hospital. "I was very sensitive to that gulf that was there, and tried very hard to bridge it because I felt that it was important for the institution to be much more sensitive to and supportive of the local practitioner; it had not been up to that time." This sounds like the theme of his time at the AAMC: "I think maintaining a sense of responsibility for helping to transform the health care system, using academic medical centers as a lever for improving patient care, is an important theme that we tried to play out."

The Challenge Now in the Larger System of Medical Education

"When I look around, I see temptations for physicians to be interested in their own personal interests, particularly financial advantages, to be pressed by the commercialization of medicine to do things that are out of keeping with the fundamental principles of professionalism for keeping patient interest upper-most. That, I think, is the most worrisome part of what's happening to medicine at the present time. I have a firm belief that if medicine loses its trust with the patients and the broader society, we're really going to be in tough shape as a society. I think strengthening students' and residents' commitment to traditional values of medicine, to professionalism as we now call it, is one of the biggest challenges we have."

Another challenge is recognizing that the skills expected of physicians in the future will include new things. "Medical education has got to equip future physicians with the competencies that they're going to need to not only survive but to thrive. We need to be much more collaborative, much more involved in team care, much more cost-conscious, much more interested in quality improvement and maintaining a sense of continuous attention to performance."

Cohen believes that we also need to accommodate the fact that younger generations have different personal expectations, particularly the desire to maintain a broader range of interests, family life, and control of one's schedule in a more predictable way. "These are things that the younger generation has made very clear are part of what they're expecting from medicine," and the profession has to do this in a way that sustains professionalism. "I think we can organize professional activities in ways that don't demand that individuals remain on-call in perpetuity. I think there are ways to manage our affairs that are consistent with those values.

"I would just point out how satisfying it is to have a role in medical education because it is an opportunity to have a broad impact on the future that I think few endeavors really provide. Having been able to influence the careers of young people and equip them to deal with the challenges that they're going to be facing is a pretty gratifying way to go about one's career."

The Qualities of Leaders

"I think we're not always conscious of them at the time, but looking back, I can just recognize how influential a number of people were. Not necessarily any specific decisions about career moves, but just in terms of their commitments to their own activities, their work, and their own careers."

Dr. Cohen mentioned clinicians with whom he worked, such as Walter Bauer[20] at Massachusetts General Hospital and Dan Federman.[21] They didn't have to be chairs, deans, or institutional leaders to have an impact on him. "The values that they placed upon their work and on the people with whom they worked were very, very important to me."

Reflecting on Dr. Rubenstein, Dr. Cohen said, "I think the word 'standards' comes to mind. Maintaining integrity and maintaining a sense of purpose, a broader purpose than just the immediate task at hand, recognizing the context in which the work is done and the importance of maintaining a balanced focus on the overall goal, and not being swept up in the vicissitudes of the moment." Once again he had returned to the idea that seemed to run through all his comments in the interview: placing one's work in a big picture, the larger system from which individual work took its meaning.

[17]Dr. William B. Schwartz was a renowned kidney disease specialist at what is now called Tufts Medical Center. In the 1970s he put himself at the forefront of another line of research: the relationship between economics and medicine.

[18]Arthur Rubenstein, MBBCh, subsequently became dean at the University of Pennsylvania. See his profile in this section.

[19]Robert G. Petersdorf, MD (1926–2006), AAMC president from 1986 to 1994, had been medicine chair at the University of Washington, dean at the University of California, San Diego, and president of Brigham and Women's Hospital in Boston.

[20]Walter Bauer, MD (1898–1963), was chief of medical services at Massachusetts General Hospital and Jackson Professor of Clinical Medicine at Harvard Medical School.

[21]See his profile in this section.

❖ Holly Humphrey

"The quality that I see in the very best leaders is their generosity of spirit." Dr. Holly Humphrey is dean for medical education at the University of Chicago. She has been chair of the American Board of Internal Medicine and president of the Association of Program Directors in Internal Medicine.

"I was a medical student at the University of Chicago, and at the beginning of my fourth year of medical school, I got married to another medical student. The two of us were applying for residencies in internal medicine, and as we looked around the country for medicine residencies, we found ourselves liking very different things. The programs I liked, my new husband was not as interested in, and the programs he liked, I was not as interested in. We came to the conclusion that, as much as we thought we were going to leave Chicago, there actually were very compelling reasons that we should consider staying in Chicago.

"We were very aware of the fact that we were both going to have pretty rigorous schedules, and we knew that our family life was going to be important. Trying to figure out how we were going to balance two careers in medicine and have appropriate time with our family also drew us to Chicago. My family is 2 hours away in Wisconsin, and my husband's family is 1 hour in the far western suburbs of Chicago.

"I was invited to be the chief medical resident. It wasn't on my list of experiences to have, but it was during the year as chief resident that I began to ask questions of myself about why it is that we educate residents the way we do, and how we make decisions about how many months a resident should do on an inpatient oncology service. At the same time, I was confronting the fact that the residents were scrambling to get their work done and simultaneously participate in the core lecture series, and I wondered if a lecture series was really the best way to be teaching residents. It was those kinds of questions that would come to form the basis of the career I ultimately enjoyed."

Whether to Have a Subspecialty Career

Dr. Humphrey completed a pulmonary fellowship. "I very much enjoyed the discipline of pulmonary critical care medicine, and thrived under the mentorship of some of our institution's finest teachers. So, I could easily envision a career path for myself in subspecialty medicine. But it turned out that the person who had been the program director was leaving the position. Arthur Rubenstein[22] was then the chairman, and he asked me to consider being the program director. Should I take this once-in-a-lifetime opportunity to be a program director for a residency program that I love, or should I pursue the traditional subspecialty pathway and build my career in the more traditional manner?"

She chose being the program director for two reasons. "Number one, I would have the chance to work at the foot of a master in American medicine. I would be learning the lessons of medicine and of leadership from Arthur Rubenstein, and that was truly a once-in-a-lifetime opportunity. And two, my love for the internal medicine residency program was palpable.

"That year I had as chief resident put me face to face with the patient care needs as they juxtaposed with resident education needs, and I found that series of inherent challenges to be very energizing. I had a burning passion for the residents and for the residency program that helped me know that I would have the fuel to sustain my career by making that choice."

Becoming Dean for Education

She spent 14 years as the program director, and even at the end she fought off taking another job. "I loved the role as program director and I was not looking for another position. I had a secret hope that I might be able to remain as a program director until I retired. But the retirement of the person who had previously been the dean for medical education led a new dean to invite me to the dean's office. I basically turned down the position three times, and then, ultimately, I agreed to do it. The main reason was that when the dean saw how much I loved being the program director, he said to me, 'Holly, do you realize that the longer you stay in this job that you love so much, you're preventing somebody else from having that same experience?'" Six years ago she became the dean for medical education.

Jobs Born of Crises

"I've had three major jobs in academic medicine—chief medical resident, program director, and dean for medical education. They were all born out of a crisis."

The first crisis occurred when she was chief medical resident. It was 1987, the year of "Black Thursday" in the residency match, when many top programs went unmatched. Chicago was one of them. "Three months into my year as chief resident, I learned that our residency program had three openings. I also learned that my program director was out of town because never before in our history had we ever had openings. It was a day that we hadn't ever paid attention to in the past. With the program director out of town, Arthur Rubenstein called me to his office to help him figure out how we were going to fill these positions. I, of course, had absolutely no idea how to do that, but that was the beginning of Arthur Rubenstein and me trying to solve a big problem. At that moment, it felt like a crisis. We solved the problem and we found three terrific people. That gave me a test of managing a crisis and of trying to take care of the people in our program, as well as the program itself."

Then, 5 months into her chief residency year, the program director announced he was leaving. "The person who was my program director and who had been my advisor during medical school, and who was one of the most influential mentors that I had, was Pierce Gardner.[23] He had been the program director for 13 years. He left in June, just before the new house staff arrived. A new program director was appointed, and I had to help orient the new program director. This gave me a jump start on being the program director, which would happen 2 years hence. So those two crises—having three openings in the match and the loss of the program director midyear—ultimately teed me up for this dream job that I came to have as program director. The person who filled in after Dr. Gardner left had decided to go back to the lab. It was his decision that gave the opening for Arthur Rubenstein to ask me to do the job at the conclusion of my fellowship."

An Unexpected Residency Review Committee Review

More crises were to come. In her year between chief residency and program director, there was a precipitous disaffiliation of a major teaching affiliate, the Michael Reese Hospital, from the university. Now they needed to ask the Accreditation Council for Graduate Medical Education (ACGME) to review some subspecialty programs for which Michael Reese was the primary sponsor.

"The only way the ACGME would review a subspecialty program would be if they reviewed your core residency program as well. We learned this in the May immediately preceding my July 1st start as program director. In order to get our programs accredited in time for our fellowship programs, we had to invite the internal medicine RRC [Residency Review Committee] to come precipitously and review our entire department. I spent my first 2 months as program director filling out all the forms, trying to understand all the rules, trying to get all of the subspecialty programs in shape. Three months into my first year as program director, we spent 2 and a half weeks with an ACGME site visitor, reviewing our entire department. I always felt like that was a real baptism by fire, but I also know that's exactly the time in which I developed my working knowledge of residency programs and accreditation and certification. It was a crash course, but that crisis is what caused me to learn it very, very well."

Very Difficult Personal Situations
Dr. Humphrey has also faced times of great personal difficulty. "The one that left an indelible mark involved the death of a third-year resident. I was a very experienced program director by that point, but experience hardly mattered. It happened that he died one day before my younger sister died of complications of diabetes, and both of those deaths were completely unexpected. That was a very painful time, but it was also a time when I could see the true color of the program coming out, and they took care of me.

"It prepared me well for what would come, several years later. In the eighth or ninth month of my tenure as dean for medical education, one of our first-year medical students was found dead, having hiked the Grand Canyon and run out of water. Taking a whole medical school through the death of a student under just really extraordinary circumstances, and dealing with the family of this student, was an extremely painful experience."

Things To Be Proud of and Regret
"The biggest challenge—and I think as a result of it feeling like it's the biggest challenge, it is the thing that I'm particularly proud of—is that I've been able to be in a wonderful marriage for 26 years and counting, and the mother of three children. But straddling that balance and keeping all those balls in the air with an incredible partner in the form of my husband has required at times what feels like Herculean efforts. But I'm still here, and I would just say that's my biggest accomplishment."

She mentioned the costs of leadership. "At a very early point in my life I was a particularly good cook. My oldest child is now graduating from college, and she was laughing with me about the fact that I had never really taught her to cook. Life has passed in a way that I haven't yet been able to share that with my children, so that's a regret. Another thing that was very important to me in my life was music. In fact I was almost a musician before I decided to go to medical school, and I have been able to teach my children piano, and in the case of my daughters, flute. So, on the one hand I never taught them to cook. On the other hand, I did teach them how to play an instrument.

"In that same vein of balancing one's personal and professional life, I wish I had better understood the skills of delegation. It could have saved me some time and energy. I also wish I had given myself permission to say 'no' more authoritatively early on, [especially in relation] to my time allocation. I'm specifically thinking of travel."

Challenges Facing Medical Education

"If I had to sum it up in one overarching theme, I would say the biggest challenge is public trust in the profession. Public trust has been eroded, whether that's related to conflict-of-interest issues or medical error and patient safety issues. It puts some fundamental principles of medical education into a new context, which can be potentially damaging to medical education, and ultimately to patient care.

"The fundamental balance is between allowing residents, and students to a lesser extent, to gain knowledge and skills, and the general expectation that patient care, and procedures in particular, are best done by the most experienced physician, not the least experienced. This has the potential to push residents and students into a more secondary role with patients than the primary role that they have had for the last many decades.

"As neuroscience helps us better understand how memories are formed, and how those memories ultimately aggregate to form skills and skill reflexes, it's clear that feeling an emotional ownership, or having your skin in the game for patient care decisions, is what makes those memories powerful and sustained. So, to have a secondary role has the potential to have negative consequences on the ownership of learning and the ownership of patient care decision-making."

Advice to Pass Along

To those at the start of their careers, Dr. Humphrey would say the single most important piece of advice is to be very honest with yourself about what you enjoy and where your passion is. "What I mean is that if you can identify where you get your intrinsic energy, the energy that's there when you wake up in the morning and that is in your bone marrow is what's going to sustain you. If you're being fueled from real passion about what you're doing, it feels energizing even in the darkest moments. If you haven't been able to identify where you get that energy, then every day can feel more difficult, and the darkest days can feel unmanageable.

"Any time I spent a half-day in the clinic seeing patients, or I did morning report with the residents, I was energized. What I have come to learn is that even though I have a hugely administrative job, I have to actively plan into my calendar time that puts me in touch with my energy sources. And I would say that the most difficult transition that I've had in this career was the transition from the department to the dean's office. I was actually caught off guard by how different the dean's office is from the department. And so, while my head was in the dean's office, my heart was in the trenches, and I needed to figure out a way to get back to the trenches with enough frequency that I could sustain my heart.

"I feel like the luckiest person on the planet because I've had the chance to work with so many really terrific leaders in medicine and in medical education, and so many terrific students and residents and patients."

[22]See his profile in this section.

[23]Pierce Gardner, MD, is professor of medicine and formerly associate dean for academic affairs at Stony Brook University School of Medicine.

❖ Jack Ende

"I always had a conscious appreciation that there was a gold mine of ideas applicable to medical education that were to be found outside of medicine." Dr. Jack Ende is chief of medicine at Penn Presbyterian Medical Center in Philadelphia. He attended medical school at the Medical College of Virginia and did his residency at the University of Chicago. He was president of the Association of Program Directors in Internal Medicine. He edited this book series and had the idea for this series of profiles.[24]

"In medical school, I don't know why, inexplicably, I just had a natural affinity or inclination towards internal medicine and found myself at the University of Chicago for internship and residency. I was totally taken by a cadre of general internists, teachers, and I just thought that those guys—

they were all guys, no women—were the best thing I'd ever seen. Chicago was an academic program. There were no private practice role models out there. There certainly were a lot of basic science role models, but for some reason I saw myself as a general internist, just like some of those heroes that I was working with."

The Growth of General Medicine in Research Hospitals
The University of Chicago was a high-power research institution. How did general medicine thrive? "There may be some irony in this. They had sub-specialty in-patient services, and by default that created a need: Where do the patients who come from the emergency room go? Where do the patients without a diagnosis go? There had to be a catch-all service, and that was staffed by a terrific bunch of general internists. Through the insight of the chair at the time, Alvin Tarlov,[25] that was the division of general medicine, and it existed there even before this fledging organization, then called SREPCIM.[26]

"Even before then, Chicago had a division of general internal medicine, and while I was chief resident there, we were visited by a couple of people from the University of Pennsylvania, John Eisenberg[27] and Sankey Williams,[28] who were on an exploratory mission. They were trying to convince their chair at Penn that the department of medicine could have a division of general internal medicine. Since that already existed in Chicago, they came out and visited us. So there was something special going on there, and I think that really had an impact on my career."

Chief Residency, A Transitional Year
"I was asked to be chief resident. My time as a chief resident confirmed my interest in general medicine. I felt that academic general internal medicine was the right place for me. That led to a position at Boston University, where, after a couple years, I was 'tapped' to be the clerkship director and eventually the residency program director. I was lucky. I was in a situation where I was able to have some time to think and try to be creative, and that led to some research papers and other papers and eventually national opportunities. I think that's what set me on the track where I am now."

From Boston to Penn
"I was residency program director for 6 years, and I felt that after doing it for 6 years, I wanted to do something different. Penn had a very outstanding reputation in academic general internal medicine. I thought it would be fun to see if I could make it at an Ivy League university. But I didn't want

to be a residency program director much beyond 6 years. I felt that after that amount of time, your creativity wanes a bit, you've seen the same problems. Certainly in some positions, your best work is done during your first 5 or 6 years. So, I had an opportunity to come as the person in charge of ambulatory education, and I moved to Penn in 1989."

A Primary Care Program at Presbyterian Hospital

At Penn, Dr. Ende saw a task that led to his present position. "It was something I just saw as a chance, which was Penn's purchasing an adjacent community hospital, Presbyterian.[29] At the same time, when everybody was really moving forward in primary care education, there was a lot of enthusiasm nationally for primary care tracks. I convinced the chairman, Ed Holmes,[30] that we needed to start a primary care program. He suggested that I move over to Presbyterian as chief of the department to oversee the residency training that we were taking on—we were also sending increasing numbers of faculty to Presbyterian, and we needed a chief there. That's how that came about."

An Affinity for Education

How did he decide upon primary care education as his work? "Aside from the affinity that comes about yourself, that you really can't explain, I do think it was role models. I had not had much contact at all with private practice clinicians. My heroes at a time when I was professionally quite impressionable were all academic clinicians. My mind lent itself to a field like medical education, rather than molecular biology or systems design. And I must say I have enjoyed the instant satisfaction that you get from teaching. I had done some research in college and some research in medical school, and I just wasn't wired to work with a project that may or may not be fruitful 6, 8, or 12 months from now. I liked the 'Ah-ha!' that comes from teaching, particularly teaching informally."

Lessons From Other Fields

"When I came to Penn, my job description included the opportunity to do some development and research in education, and I found myself at a university with a single campus with a school of education. I always had a conscious appreciation that there was a gold mine of ideas applicable to medical education that were to be found outside of medicine. I didn't see many original ideas in medical education, and I didn't see many people really thinking about medical education. It was assumed that it was synonymous with being a great teacher, and being a great teacher was synonymous with being a great clinician. Now that relationship is extremely strong, and I really do appreciate the importance of being an outstanding clinician if you want to be an outstanding teacher. But I just felt that there were so many people knocking their heads against the wall on medical education issues, on things like feedback and curriculum design. Other fields had already wrestled with these issues, and I was fortunate enough to be in situations where I had the opportunity and the time to look into what was happening in other fields."

When in Boston, Dr. Ende had already been influenced by ideas from the business school. "At one of the first SGIM meetings, there was a session on how to lead a discussion by an absolutely wonderful man named C. Roland Christiansen.[31] Christiansen ran a class for the Harvard Business School because so much of their curriculum is based on case discussions, and in order to be on the faculty there you had to take the class. I just made it my business to get to HBS twice a week, and it was spectacular, absolutely spectacular, the way he taught others how to lead a discussion. I became close [to] and worked with him; we spent a lot of time together."

Characteristics of Effective Leaders

Dr. Ende has worked with some renowned leaders. What makes them effective? "When I think of the really incredible leaders I've worked with, Norman Levinsky, the chair at BU [Boston University], where my career really took shape;[32] Jordan Cohen;[33] and Herb Waxman,[34] whom I met through APDIM [Association of Program Directors in Internal Medicine]; and, at Penn, people like John Eisenberg—these people are very, very bright. What stands out is that they're also able to appreciate something about the big picture that others miss. Norman Levinsky was absolutely terrific at that. Long before people were talking about work force reform, he appreciated that there was nothing as important to residents as work hours and lifestyle, and he made sure that his program was always ahead of the curve. The second asset of all the people I've mentioned is that they are great communicators. They communicate so well. I think that is an essential part of leadership; each has his own style. Although they're both nephrologists, Norman Levinsky will never be confused with Jordan Cohen, but they both are excellent speakers and communicators."

Difficult Situations

Dr. Ende and others in our series agree that solving the social context of medicine is essential for the success of medical education, and he had a very close-up perspective. "The difficult situations were the tough times we had back in the late 80s and early 90s when health care reform was being seriously considered, and all the political activity that was happening around the issue of workforce reform. At that point, I was president of APDIM, so I really did have a place at the table. I remember how difficult it was to try to hammer out a consensus within internal medicine about how we were going to align ourselves to solve the nation's primary care shortage. It was disturbing to see how the subspecialists were circling their wagons, and the primary care people were as well; how internal medicine and family medicine were entirely at each other's throats, competing for a larger slice of a very finite pie. That was a difficult time.

"The times that we're in now are very difficult as well. The current financial crisis, as we try to maintain our educational programs, is also difficult. Another common theme in so much of the work that I've done and continue to do is our responsibility for staffing hospitals and trying to make sure that you have enough people to fill all your positions, just trying to get everything covered. Internal medicine has an enormous responsibility for coverage and for the inner workings not only for the hospitals but obviously the medical schools. It's difficult to field a full team at all times, and I think that's not always appreciated."

Interests and Sources of Pride

Dr. Ende has tried to get beyond routine ways of doing things, and he used study of other fields to get beyond business as usual. He found himself "coming up with ideas that just made sense to medicine, that have not been part of the catechism or the standard rhetoric of medicine. One of the first pieces of research I did was on the importance of a sexual history in general medicine practice; that was not mainstream. Probably more germane is looking to other fields for how to answer questions—for instance, how do you provide feedback. There was nothing original that I came up with in that paper;[35] it was all derivative, but it applied those ideas to other fields.

" I took a course at the Penn School of Education on the Theory of Curriculum. Then I was able to talk about it and write about it as it applied to medicine, and I got a couple of interesting projects and initiatives going around curriculum. It was stuff that was already out there, and I was just applying it to medicine. We already talked about how to be a discussion leader. That literature exists. The whole field of adult education and education theory already exists, just waiting. For instance, there's the work of Donald Schön on how professionals think and train other professionals. We certainly can learn a lot of lessons from other worlds.

Advice to Those New in Education

"I think research, publications, and coming up with original ideas are crucial to anybody who wants to develop leadership in medical education. You do have to come up with that contribution that will get you involved nationally. The other thing I would recommend to people who want to get started in careers is to be a joiner, to network, and to be involved with the organizations like CDIM [Clerkship Directors in Internal Medicine] and APDIM. ... Look for the opportunities to answer some of the questions that we're all thinking about.

"The other thing that has helped me is that somehow I was able to come up with the sorts of projects and papers that I was able to do by myself. As a person who's seeing patients all the time and trying to run education programs, it's always helpful to come up with projects that you can do on your own time, alone, rather than having to work with big, unwieldy teams. The research and original contributions that I made in the early part of my career were ones that I was able to do in the quiet of my own study."

Challenges to Role Models and Altruism

"One of the challenges facing us is the paucity of real role models, as well as the limited amount of time to be exposed to role models. What is a role model, and how does a role model impact on others? It's a research question, but it's also a very real problem as we get pressured for time, and move more and more toward shift work. I think the whole notion of shift work and hospitalists and the pace that we're under is another challenge for medical education. I'm very concerned that the doctors of tomorrow will not be the same as the doctors of yesterday, given the environment that they're being trained in.

"Who knows? Maybe they'll do better. They certainly know how to use a lot more resources and access information, but all of us have to be concerned first and foremost with the doctor–patient relationship, and that is something that is becoming more challenged. So, I think that that's one of the major issues facing medical education. How do we train professionals who first and foremost have the understanding that the major tenet of professionalism is altruism and putting the patient first? I think that's something we're really going to have to address."

---

[24]Dr. Ende did this interview to help me try out my interviewing protocol, but I decided to include it because it contains some perspectives not heard in other interviews.

[25]Alvin R. Tarlov, MD, was chairman of medicine at the University of Chicago (1968–1981), and later became president of the Henry J. Kaiser Family Foundation and director of the Health Institute at the New England Medical Center.

[26]The Society of General Internal Medicine (SGIM) was founded as the Society for Research and Education in Primary Care Internal Medicine (SREPCIM) in 1978.

[27]John Eisenberg, MD (1947–2002), was chief of the Division of General Internal Medicine at the University of Pennsylvania (1986–1992) and subsequently chairman of medicine at

Georgetown University (1992–1997) and director of the Agency for Health Care Policy and Research (subsequently renamed the Agency for Healthcare Research and Quality).

[28]Sankey Williams, MD, was chief of the Division of General Internal Medicine, University of Pennsylvania.

[29]The Presbyterian Hospital of Philadelphia became a member of the PennMedicine System in 1995.

[30]Edward W. Holmes, MD, was then chair of medicine at the University of Pennsylvania and was later dean at both Duke University in North Carolina and the University of California, San Diego.

[31]C. Roland (Chris) Christensen (1919–1999) was professor at Harvard Business School.

[32]Norman G. Levinsky, MD (1930–2004), was Boston University's chief of medicine from 1972 to 1997.

[33]See his profile in this section.

[34]Herbert S. Waxman, MD (1937–2003), was a national leader in medical education and senior vice-president for the American College of Physician's Medical Knowledge and Education Division.

[35]This report (Ende J. Feedback in clinical medical education. JAMA. 1983;250:777-81) is one of the most frequently cited medical education papers in the past few decades.

❖ Lawrence Smith

"Undergraduate education and graduate education will never be better than the practice model that they're immersed in. We can't put learners into a completely dysfunctional practice model, and think they're going to come out altruistic, humanistic caregivers." Dr. Lawrence Smith is founding dean of the Hofstra University School of Medicine in New York, which in partnership with North Shore-Long Island Jewish Health System will admit its first class in 2011. He is thinking a lot about curriculum and how to design a medical school.

"Why does medical education always seem to be looking for new curriculum? Each and every step in medical education, probably since the Flexner Report, probably produced, in its time, pretty good doctors, and so why are we always changing the curriculum?

"Part of it is that change engages people, and when people are engaged and excited, they do a better job, and some of the benefit of constantly pushing the envelope of curriculum is to get people excited and engaged. But many of the settings that we have taught in, especially the acute hospital, have radically changed."

What's Not Working Now

Dr. Smith had an example from surgical training, but it also applies to medicine and other specialties. "The decision-making occurs before the patient gets to the hospital, and virtually all the postop care, except in the handful of really major surgeries, is done as outpatients. And so you, the student, never do the thinking in deciding whether to operate and how to do it, and you rarely see the patient postop, when they're recuperating. How can we teach someone the field—not just the skill set of using tools in an operating room—but the real field of surgery without that continuum?"

Even on medical services that happens now. Patients rarely get admitted to the hospital without a diagnosis and anticipated decision. "That's maybe less dramatic than in surgery, but it's just as devastating in terms of teaching people how to think through a problem. It's really hard to train someone when they never participate in the thinking from the very beginning."

What Could a School Do Differently?

Dr. Smith is now designing a medical school for a very large, successful hospital system. "I'm thinking of clerkships where you link the student to the doctor, not to the ward." He began with the kind of teachers that are needed. "There are people who love being doctors, and we have to find them, reward them, and plead with them to make time for the learners to be part of their lives. We praise the person with the NIH [National Institutes of Health] grant, and we praise the person who's the super-duper quaternary proceduralist. We've got to take the people who are the real master clinicians, not promote them into administrative roles but keep them out on the floors of the hospital and in the practices, where the young people can rub shoulders with them. Well, I am an optimist, and I believe that there are actually lots of people who still love coming to work to be a doctor every day."

Deciding on Students and Curriculum

We might find different students who will eventually become a different kind of physician. This includes nontraditional students. " I think that we have to be much more open to expanding the pool of people who become physicians. Admissions committees are usually staffed by individuals who like to reproduce themselves, and so, whoever you pick on your admissions committee is likely to search out your applicant pool for people who look just like them."

He is considering newer models for clerkships, like the longitudinal model that integrates multiple specialties. "I don't have an intuitive feel of what the weaknesses are yet, but we're going to try to learn what we can, from Cambridge City Hospital and UCSF[36], and see if we want to make that part of the menu that we offer students. I'm much less wedded to processes than to outcomes. And so, if it produces outcomes that are closer to where we really want to go, I have enough varied hospitals in this health system to try something like that on a modified basis, and see how it compares to more traditional clinical rotations."

What Was His Own Training Like?

He went to medical school at New York University and did his residency in Rochester. "I was at Strong Memorial, where there was an overt dedication to education. You could taste it, feel it. That gave me a set of role models, and a picture of medical education that really changed how I approached everything about practicing medicine, and how I always knew that I wanted to find the job that would let me be the perpetual chief resident."

He was drafted, and after 2 years in the Army he joined a large, multi-specialty private practice group on Long Island. "I took a position in a group of really well-trained doctors, and immediately volunteered to do some teaching at the local medical school, which was Stony Brook. I was spending 2 half-days a week teaching third-year students. I would go to the local VA and teach in the clerkship. I was 9 years into practice, I had the busiest practice in the group of some 50 doctors. At that point, the chairman at Stony Brook called me up, and he made me an offer to come and run the residency program."

He was a little bit shocked. "I think the words of my wife were probably the best advice: 'You know, all I hear all the time is, I love teaching, I love teaching. So, now somebody made you an offer you can't refuse. Either take it, or shut up.' And so I left a booming practice to go full-time at Stony Brook, and ran their residency program as well as their clerkship."

Undergraduate Education at Mt. Sinai

After some years, he was recruited to do the very same thing at Mt. Sinai in New York City. "I was a vice-chairman of education. And having raised my hand every time anyone ever asked 'Would you like to volunteer for this or that committee?', I chaired the curriculum task force at Mt. Sinai. The dean tapped me and said, 'Would you like to be the dean of education for the medical school?' That was a big step for me.

"The world of medical students was definitely different than the world of residents. It took me a while to learn the culture and lingo, but I spent the next 3 and a half years running the 4-year curriculum at Sinai. Then, I got a call from one of my really good friends, who said, 'Come on out to Long Island and be the senior physician for this huge health care system.

It's now 10 years old, 15 hospitals that survived merging cultures, 8000 doctors. If you can teach residents and you can teach medical students, let's see if you can actually teach practicing doctors.' The timing was right. We had had a number of changes of leadership, and I was ready for a new challenge."

A New Set of Challenges

He moved back to Long Island and the North Shore-Long Island Jewish Health System as senior vice-president of academic affairs, and then as chief medical officer. There was one caveat: "When I was interviewed for the position, I was not allowed to ever talk about the possibility of forming a medical school. That was off the table. This was a chief medical officer job, and don't ever mention medical school. Okay, no problem. I came in and sunk my teeth into quality and practice models and styles of care and quality indicators, and really was having fun with a whole new set of challenges. Changing already established behaviors is way more difficult than changing students. And lo and behold, Hofstra University came tapping at our door and said, 'You know, we've gone from a local to a national university, and you've gone from a bunch of disparate hospitals to one of the most successful health systems in the country. Isn't it time for us to form a medical school together?'"

Experiences and People That Prepared Him

He was asked to establish a new school as the founding dean, and his career was a gradual preparation for this. First was the model at Strong Memorial Hospital, but as important to him at the start was an individual. This was not a typical, full-time faculty mentor mentioned by others in this series of profiles but someone in private practice. "When I was in practice, the most senior of the internists in the group, Dr. Reese Alsop,[37] really took me under his wing, helped me learn a lot of the real side of ambulatory medicine. Helped me block off time for teaching, and encouraged me when the opportunity came to leave the practice and go full-time at the university. When everyone else in the group was offering me psychiatric care for even thinking of such a crazy idea, he was telling me, this is the right thing to do, just go ahead and do it.

"At Stony Brook, the man who was the vice-chairman of the department, Marty Liebowitz,[38] was the epitome of the experienced, grandfatherly person who just really showed me the ropes of academic medicine. I was 10, 12 years out of training but completely inexperienced as an academic physician. I was thrust into the program director role, but without the experience of having grown up as a full-time faculty member. And Marty really showed me the ropes, helped me get into the culture, and was critical in my not self-destructing as soon as I landed.

"Then when I was at Mt. Sinai, I had the incredible opportunity to work under a chairman, Barry Coller,[39] who was one of a handful of visionary people I've worked for. He showed me that there was always another way to look at every problem, and that until you've exhausted every perspective, don't make a decision. Never do secret deals. Every decision should be something that you can stand up in public for and proclaim. When in doubt, do the right thing! The wise ways he taught me were lessons that I think few people have."

Lessons

What do you do to develop your career? "One is being open to recognizing great mentors, and I don't think you necessarily have to work for them. Mentors must be at the stage of their career where it isn't about them anymore. I think it's really hard to have a mentor who feels threatened if you succeed. You need a mentor who absolutely cares that *you* succeed."

The other lesson had to do with taking on available jobs. "Recognize the opportunities that are key to success and grab them every time someone offers them. That doesn't mean getting so diffuse that you don't do anything well, but to recognize when people are looking for someone to *own* something; for instance to run the medical student free clinic, or run a piece of the curriculum. When you can have anything that you can own, where the success of it is identified with your own efforts, you want to raise your hand and say, 'I'll do that.'"

The Importance of Expertise in Education

One needs some formal training. "You can't lead education and be influential just because you're a good teacher. You have to transition from being a good teacher to being a true educator. Setting goals and objectives, mapping curricular items, and talking the lingo of assessment were all things that did not just come to me, even though I thought myself a pretty effective teacher. They eventually became intuitive, but in the beginning it seemed burdensome, and if anything, a distraction from what I imagined was just pure, good teaching. I had to learn the value of those things.

"Although I was never going to rival a pure researcher in scholarly output, I wrote papers, made presentations, and tried very hard to convert my education work into some degree of scholarship. I tried to build a credible portfolio that at least was recognizable to others in the medical school. They certainly weren't going to put it up there with *Cell* and *Nature* publications, but at least they understood that I was approaching education from a scholarly bent, and that was very important."

Participating in sessions at Association of Program Directors in Internal Medicine and especially a month at the Stanford Faculty Development Center were critical to his development, and how he became respected by his medical and scientific colleagues at Mt. Sinai. "As I got more expert in education, I could challenge them, the science and specialty faculty, on their own ability to understand what works and what doesn't work in what they're doing in education, and how to assess it. They began to recognize that I possessed an expertise that would help them. Others quickly compare you to their benchmarks of scientific expertise. I think you can return the favor and show them that, in fact, each of you has expertise that the other doesn't have, and as a team you can help each other."

The Kind of People He's Looking for

As he again mentioned the importance of team work in fostering acceptance, and in reforming the curriculum, it brought us back to starting up a new school. What is he looking for in the people he recruits? "Number one, energy and enthusiasm and number two, the ability to work as a part of a team. I like people who are passionate about what they want to do, and fit into a team seamlessly, so that everybody likes coming to work and likes working with each other. I think that being a superstar is only a positive quality if it's equally matched by being a good team member."

[36]Longitudinal, interdisciplinary integrated clerkships are being tried out at the University of California, San Francisco; the Cambridge Hospital of Harvard; and other schools.

[37]Reese Fell Alsop, MD (1913–2006), was chairman of the Department of Medicine at Huntington Hospital and a founder of the North Shore Medical Group in Huntington, New York.

[38]Martin R. Liebowitz, MD, is professor emeritus at Stony Brook University Health Sciences Center, Stony Brook, New York.

[39]Barry Coller, MD, currently vice-president for medical affairs and physician-in-chief at the Rockefeller University, was chairman of medicine at Mt. Sinai School of Medicine from 1993 to 2001.

❖ James Woolliscroft

"If I did not pursue medical school, I'd probably be a teacher now." James Woolliscroft is dean of the University of Michigan Medical School, a prestigious post, and he got there through a career in medical education. This profile addresses his personal growth in responsibility through 3 decades at the same institution and reflects the passion for teaching we see in all our profiled leaders.

Jim Woolliscroft received his MD degree from the University of Minnesota in 1976 and did his internal medicine residency at the University of Michigan. "When I got into medical school, I realized that you could still continue to teach and be a physician. When I was in residency, I was chosen to be a chief resident here at Michigan, and during that time period was enlisted by Faith Fitzgerald,[40] who was one of a group of committed educators revising how basic clinical skills and bedside diagnosis would be taught. Faith was, in many ways, the ringleader of this change, and I was part of it.

"When I came on faculty, Bill Kelley[41] brought me on as a 'primary care internist,' but at that time we didn't know that name. Very early in my career, Bill asked me if I would take over leadership of the clinical skills course, which was, at that time, a major course within the medical school. And so I did that, and as part of that process, I continued to try to figure out if there was evidence for a lot of the things that we taught our medical students. That was the root of my interest in medical education research, as I tried to get data on whether or not things like interviewing skills actually made a difference."

Education or Basic Science Research

During this time Dr. Woolliscroft continued his ongoing investigations in free radicals and high-energy adenosine triphosphate breakdown products. He realized that it would be difficult to continue along both an educational and a more traditional research path. As a result, he decided, relatively early in his career, to focus on education.

This was an important decision. "Kelley, whom I looked upon as a mentor, encouraged me. But I had some very memorable conversations with leaders in internal medicine who were chairs at other institutions, telling me that was absolutely the kiss of death for an academic career, and that I was being very foolish to pursue such a route. Nevertheless, I decided that I would go where my passions were, the things that got me really excited at that time, and so I really dove into the whole area of medical education, medical education research, and medical education administration. Very early on in my career, within 2 or 3 years of taking over the clinical skills [course], I was also responsible for what was called the 'Introduction to Clinical Sciences' course, the biggest course in the medical school." And so Dr. Woolliscroft assumed administrative responsibility, and very importantly, used it as a laboratory for studying medical students' educational process.

"Along the way, early on, I was able to partner with some very talented PhDs in education that really were very formative in my career, introducing me to how to ask an answerable question in educational research, how to pursue a study, how to design a study, so that you had appropriate control groups."

Weekly Meetings of the Chair's Cabinet

After this early phase, Dr. Woolliscroft became the medicine clerkship director, and an associate chair for undergraduate education in the Department of Internal Medicine. He mentioned one very formative experience under Dr. Kelley that he recommends to other leaders in medical education. It's worth describing in detail. Dr. Kelley had appointed several talented medicine faculty members who had specific areas of responsibility, such as clinical education, the graduate medical education program, and the research program. "We would meet every Saturday morning, beginning at 9, and usually going until 1 or 2 in the afternoon. We'd have incredible discussions, incredible strategic planning, as well as practical planning. [It involved] all sorts of different areas administering the whole department, planning for its future, et cetera. This was an incredible education for me in administration, as well as in leadership, and probably was the most important leadership training I've ever had … it made me think about a whole department, and internal medicine departments are big departments."

This was Dr. Kelley's "cabinet." All of the associate chairs would bring news of what was happening in the university, and what was happening nationally would be brought back to the group as a whole. Then people would toss out ideas. "And oftentimes … as I recall, … an idea would be tossed out, or a plan of some type, and people would respond to it on the first go-round based upon their assigned responsibility. After that, it would be a free discussion, so that people could chime in from any perspective. But the discipline about trying to think of the various aspects of the department and the faculty and the school was very instructive. That was clearly a pivotal time in my development."

What Path to Academic Leadership?

"Early on, I really had thought that what I want to do is be a chair. And so I had that more or less as a career direction, but it wasn't a single-minded thing, simply because I recognized that I was taking an incredibly aberrant path to even be considered for a chair position. That was a conscious decision of mine, going at a very early stage, investing in education, rather than a much more traditional 'rational route,' because … no NIH [National Institutes of Health] R01s or anything like that were being given out for education. Clearly, that was the mark of success. My division chief told me there was absolutely no way I'd ever get tenure at the University of Michigan. You didn't get into ACIS [the American Society of Clinical Investigators][42] by trying to figure out how to enhance learning in medical students or residents, or how to affect competency. So I knew that."

Dr. Woolliscroft was a trailblazer in medical education research. He became a founding member and president of the Clerkship Directors in Internal Medicine, chair of the Association of American Medical Colleges (AAMC) Group on Educational Affairs, and chair of the Research and Medical Education Committee. He became the first Josiah Macy Jr. Professor of Medical Education, and later was given a second endowed professorship, the Lyle C. Roll Professor of Medicine, for enhancing medicine through education. Then, he advanced into higher levels of administration as chief of staff of the University of Michigan Hospitals. "[I realized that] first, the most powerful educational context is the clinical setting, and … in order to really take our whole educational programs to that next level, we'd need to get involved in making certain that the clinical context in which our students, whether residents or medical students, were learning was an optimal clinical context."

What One Learns as Chief of the Medical Staff

"I had thought that I knew a lot, but when I moved over to the chief of staff role, I realized there were huge gaps in my knowledge base, things that I didn't have a clue about, and so, I learned about the hospital, and I learned about JCAHO [Joint Commission on Accreditation of Healthcare Organizations]. At that time, the chief of staff was also the designated institutional official and so had to learn about GME [graduate medical education] from a whole different perspective, but this too was an incredibly powerful learning experience. It introduced a whole other level of oversight, of regulation, that I now recognize was important for somebody in an administrative role to really pay attention to. [I had to] make certain that I understood how to not only accommodate but also how really do our best to make sure it did not interfere with the whole educational process."

After he stepped down as chief of staff, the associate dean for graduate medical education position was created for him. "I transitioned for the very first time into a more active role in the dean's office, and so had moved from being primarily hospital-based to now having the dual-report to the dean and to the CEO of the hospital." Dean Allen Lichter then asked him to be executive associate dean. "And, once again, it was enlightening to see aspects of all of the missions at a school level that I just wasn't as familiar with, based upon my prior experiences. That then led, when he departed, to being interim dean, [and then] to becoming dean. So, in a nutshell, that's how I ended up where I am."

A Career in One Institution?
Dr. Woolliscroft has had a series of jobs with increasing responsibilities. They have all been at the University of Michigan, where he has worked for 33 years. "One of the things that I also learned, a long time ago, is that if I'm doing the same thing for 7 years, whatever it is, I need a new job, a new challenge. I've been very, very fortunate in that most people I know, in order to have these four fundamentally different careers, would have had to move multiple times. And ... I haven't had to do that. The institution's afforded me the opportunity to do very interesting, very stimulating, and quite different things here at Michigan. Therefore, I really think that graded responsibilities from multiple different perspectives [are] probably the most educational or most powerful education programs you can have."

Some leaders feel it's good to move around to get broader experience, and others feel that remaining in the same place is needed to learn the institutional culture. "I think there's wisdom in both. Indeed, you can bring things from other institutions that can be informative. However, I am quite different from a lot of people—I think overall, the higher you go in the institution, the better it is for the institution to take somebody from an internal rather than an external vantage point. Some of the worst misfits, as I've looked across the nation, have been external hires, where the individual coming in didn't really understand the culture of that institution. [In those cases] the institution frequently does a poor job of articulating what it really wants from a leader. So it's almost incumbent upon the leader to figure out what the institution wants. That's very difficult to do when you parachute in from someplace else; you just have to take people at face value."

Progressing up the academic ladder took training and mentorship. "For me, I would guess that the vast majority, probably 95%, was self-study, but there were also important mentors along the way, like my first chair, Kelley, encouraging me to do what interested me and not forcing me into a mold. You know, a lot of chairs wouldn't have picked a second-year faculty member to lead big chunks of the department's responsibilities. At the same time, people like the PhD educators that I mentioned were really willing to work with me. I could teach them about medicine and they taught me. It opened my eyes early on to the importance of a team, and so they too were mentors in that way."

Dr. Woolliscroft mentioned the characteristics in his mentors and leaders that helped him most. "Passion. Seeing that level of commitment, that level of just striving for excellence. Understanding that it was something, if you will, bigger than us individually that we were all participating in."

Getting Through Barriers to Change

What barriers has he encountered in his work? "Speaking specifically about medical education, the most common difficulty I've encountered is an unwillingness to try something different. I can't begin to recall all the times I've heard, 'If it's not broken, why change it?' There was this perception that our educational process was perfect, and everybody was very comfortable doing what they were doing, so why should we do something differently?" One way he addressed this was by treating educational innovation as research. "This is an experiment, and we're going to collect data and, very importantly, if it doesn't work, we'll shut it down. Pretty early on, people who were above me recognized I was truthful about that. Because we had things that failed, we had the data, and we stopped doing it. And we collected the data all along."

Educational Challenges Right Now

In describing the challenges facing us right now, he returned to the theme of how the way care is delivered affects the educational process. "A friend of mine describes his worries that we're now in the cultural revolution of medical education, and what he means is that docs are going to wake up at some point and realize we've lost a generation. In many of our institutions, payers like Medicare have changed the rules on payment, and they have taken medical students from playing integral roles in the care of the patient to being increasingly marginalized. If your patient progress notes don't count, if you're not looked upon as doing important work, then the motivation to really learn and contribute is decreased. I worry about the unintended consequences of well-intentioned actions with all of the regulations on duty hours for our residents. Increasingly it seems like the attending knows more about the patients than anybody else on the service. Are we really creating a situation where people can, under directed supervision, put in that 10,000 hours of directed practice that seem to be a recurrent theme for the development of expertise? I am concerned that we've lost sight of the profession through some of these regulations, and the impact it will have on the next generation. I don't think anybody is out to impede the development of expertise. In fact, they want to enhance it, but they haven't necessarily thought through what might be the downside. Certainly, with CMS [Centers for Medicare & Medicaid Services] and the financial regulations, I don't think there was ever an intention of negatively impacting medical education, but it has had that effect at a lot of our institutions. We don't quite know what direction we're going."

Advice for Aspiring Educational Leaders

"Find something that really excites you intellectually, that you're passionate about, that you approach not as a job but actually as a privilege to be involved in. And I know that may sound corny, but I truly believe that if you enjoy getting up every day, and actually even enjoy thinking about what your responsibilities are, that goes a long way to helping you through some of the unpleasantries associated with every single job. In a leadership position, it's not always pleasant to be the one that has to talk with a student and tell him or her that they're not doing well, let alone taking all the actions required to dismiss them. Every leadership position has negatives like that. So, you need something that really engages you on all of the plusses.

"The vast majority of leadership is about personnel and personal interactions. You have to invest the time in developing your skills in working with people, and then develop the tool kit for personnel and human resources. All of our institutions are 100% dependent on people, and so you've really got to invest the time and understanding on how to work with your people, on what makes them tick. It's not the same thing for everybody.

"I think that leaders, great leaders, are a product of the circumstance with the right persons, so I think that the requirements for leadership change. Let's just talk about internal medicine. Back in the 70s and 80s, you could hire a cardiologist or a procedural gastroenterologist and pay for multiple faculty to be working in the lab. Those days are probably gone. An individual who was a great leader then may or may not be a great leader now. I think there's this real interaction with the times, the needs of the institution, and the individual. I don't think there are any absolutes to any of these things, and coming up with a cookbook recipe is very difficult.

"Similarly, I think one of the [biggest challenges], in any leadership position, and we see this at the national level all the time, [is] becoming insular in your thinking because you may be surrounded by people who don't tell you the truth. You think, 'I have the right answer,' when indeed you might. But oftentimes you might not, and people just don't tell you that. So a leader needs to have a much greater ability to reflect and do the metacognitive activities than other folks."

Educational research has become a viable pathway to academic recognition. "What makes me feel incredibly good is that when I go to AAMC or to CDIM [Clerkship Directors in Internal Medicine], I see now hundreds of incredibly talented, committed, young or even midcareer physicians who are similarly dedicated to education. It seems like the profession has once again embraced the critical importance of studying the ways for passing things on to the next generation, other than just standing up and lecturing. That creativity, that passion, that I see is the most rewarding thing."

[40]See her profile in this section.

[41]After being chair of medicine at the University of Michigan, William N. Kelley, MD, became professor and dean at the University of Pennsylvania School of Medicine.

[42]Entry into this prestigious group was a mark of academic success.

❖ Faith Fitzgerald

"The office of a teacher is to stimulate and inspire young people to want to know more than you do, and to be better than you are, and to ask questions that you haven't thought to ask, and to keep exploring all these things." Dr. Faith Fitzgerald is an internist and teacher. She was board-certified in internal medicine in 1973 and has been teaching medical students and residents ever since. She is professor of medicine and associate dean of humanities and bioethics at the University of California, Davis, School of Medicine.

"I did my house staff and medical school training at University of California, San Francisco. Then, having a peculiar and irresistible affection for patients who were hospitalized at San Francisco General Hospital, whom I found rich in their experience and challenges, I was chief resident there in medicine. It was as chief resident that I found the greatest pleasure in teaching at the bedside and exploring the histories and physical exams, diagnoses, and therapies of a wide variety of patients, and watching the eyes of medical students and junior house officers lighten at how much could be done without modern technologies. And I just continued to do that for the next 40 years or so."

From California to Michigan and Back

Dr. Fitzgerald remained in San Francisco as assistant chief of medicine. There were frequent strikes by the unions and shortages of essential supplies. "It suddenly came to me that I could not in good conscience admit a member of my family to my own hospital because of the uncertainties of care." Then her chief and teacher, Hibbard Williams,[43] left to become chair at Cornell. About the same time she received an inquiry from the University of Michigan. "They were looking for a chairman's helper, somebody who would round with the house staff and teach the students and take care of patients, and I said, 'Sounds like me.' So I went there and then met Bill Kelley,[44] who was then the young chair of the department of medicine at Ann Arbor. I rounded with him and he offered me a job, which I took. It just was time to move. So, off I go to Ann Arbor, have a wonderful time there for 2 and a half years teaching and seeing patients and directing the third-year clerkship and the ICU [intensive care unit] as the clinical director, and seeing a lot of patients.

"Two and a half years later I got a call from Hibbard Williams. He said, 'I've just accepted the dean's slot at UC Davis and I want you to come and be here.' And I said, 'I'm really happy in Ann Arbor.' He said, 'Please.' I said, 'Okay,' because he was my teacher and my friend. 'What do you want me to do?' 'I don't know. We'll find something.' She went and has remained at Davis for 29 years.

"About 3 or 4 years after I'd accepted the dean of students slot, I found myself dealing principally with first- and second-year students, and I missed the bedside rounds with third- and fourth-year clerks and with interns and residents. I asked Hibbard to relieve me of the office, and I went over to the department of medicine. There I went into full-time teaching and ultimately became program director in internal medicine. [I] spent the next 10 to 15 years recruiting a new house staff and getting everything organized."

What happened after that? "Much the same thing on my part. I kept doing all the same things, the system changed around me, and ultimately I wound up sort of old and venerable. A new dean assigned me this title as associate dean for bioethics and humanities, which covers everything. I'm a free agent to teach that and to integrate the humanities with medicine, which is easy to begin with."

"A Mutual Dependency, Students and I"

"I was one of the first, along with a colleague of mine in San Francisco, Larry Tierney,[45] to be allowed by a generous and wise chair, Holly Smith,[46] to do this. When I was a house officer people kept telling me I had to go into fellowship and subspecialize, and do either translational or, better yet, bench research to make it in academic medicine.

"I had actually been in practice for a short while by virtue of an exchange with my co-chief resident at San Francisco General, who had gone into practice in Eureka. He and I had agreed to exchange 1 month a year, and in that 1 month I enjoyed myself tremendously up in Eureka. The patients were marvelous, the challenges were marvelous, the community was welcoming. But every time I came across something exciting or interesting or wonderful, I would turn around to tell somebody, and there was no one there. No students, no house staff. It is as if we have a mutual dependency, students and I."

"My Job Was To Be Faith"
"Holly Smith was the first to say, 'You know, the bedside is your laboratory. That's what you do well, you go ahead and do that.' After exploration of other possibilities, I said that this is worthy stuff to do, and it seems to fill a need—you need at least one of me, and here we've got two in San Francisco, me and Larry. I think we were the first general internist teachers that ... officially [had that role]. There were of course wonderful teachers at the time, but we were the designated people."

In the same way she was supported in Michigan by the chair, Bill Kelley. "We're talking about a man who hired me for just that, to serve as the 'permease' between the two worlds of academic medicine and the students. I was hired to be a teacher at Ann Arbor, and Kelley protected me. When Hibbard hired me back, that was also my job. In a sense, my job was to be Faith."

The chairs at Davis supported her "being Faith"; she mentioned Joseph Silva[47] in particular. "[He's] the embodiment of goodness. I recruited him here from Ann Arbor, and that's probably the best thing I ever did in my professional life. He built the department of medicine and the colleague-ship, and had this sense that the well-being of the entire system was important, but not at the sacrifice of the individuals within it. Bless him."

Mistakes and Regrets
"You know, that [question] gave me a lot of thought. I was thinking of all the medical mistakes I've made. The thing I regret most now, and that I probably couldn't have done otherwise, is that when as a medical student, house officer, and even junior faculty member, I had this inculcated sense of disdain for the PMDs, the men and women out in practice, who referred their patients because they couldn't take care of them or were too ignorant

or too behind the times. I had, without knowing any other world, accepted that the more you know, the smarter you are, and that the more you know of the latest thing, obviously the better doctor you are.

"There was a certain arrogance that I really regret now—had I not been that way, I might've earlier learned a lot more that was more enduring. Here at Davis I've had patients for whom I have been a personal physician for a quarter of a century. No one could have told me when I was young how rich an experience that was, how extraordinarily expansive it is. It's something that I think can't be taught, can only be learned over time. So that's my big regret, that I didn't know that sooner."

How to Have a Career Like This

On this topic Dr. Fitzgerald was as clear and explicit as she is on nearly everything. "They should never allow themselves to be separated from patients, students, and the bedside, or the clinic. Their teaching must be in the presence of the actual patient." Simulations and standardized patients have some uses, but learning medicine requires the presence of the "unpredictable, unforgivable, ever-changing, totally unreliable patient. There is an absolute need to have a patient there as the central teacher from whom you draw and distill the lessons in a public place. 'Public' [is] the students around you, and you should show them not what a great teacher you are but what a great teacher to the prepared mind the patient can be. Because that'll be their teacher from now on.

"The other thing I would tell people planning to go into teaching is that you have to accept that the thing itself is its own reward. You know that if you help craft a student into a curious, kind, compassionate, and confident doctor, you have done a valuable thing, no matter what the academic structure says. My worth is something that I have to presume and feel confident in, rather than being constantly reassured by titles or money or promotion. Once you get rid of the need to be externally defined and recognized by others, you are freed. You can do whatever you like."

Current Challenges in Teaching

"The difficulty is ... the system as it is now constructed, and the emphasis on efficiency, which is a necessary thing for system survival. But it is not good for any teacher, if only because knowledge is evanescent and the efficient delivery of knowledge, particularly with the Internet, bless it, is extraordinary now. It's information. T.S. Eliot had this wonderful line: 'Where is the wisdom we have lost in knowledge? Where is the knowledge we have lost in information?' There's a lot of information out there, but knowledge is better than that—it's the judicious use of information as applied to this circumstance, now. And wisdom as to whether to use that to effect any change is even rarer.

"I am also struck by the idea of rapid throughput. There's a current common situation that we don't think about very much, the 'ROMI to MIRO' phenomenon. ROMI is the admission diagnosis in the emergency room that means 'rule out MI.' The patient stays 24 to 36 hours, troponins don't go up, EKG is stable, they're discharged with a diagnosis of MIRO, 'MI ruled out.' Well, there seems to be something missing, which is, 'Why did this guy have chest pain or shortness of breath or begin to have problems?' It really doesn't matter. We've done our job, right? With two acronyms, we have focused on that single issue. And the patient is now discharged, often into the abyss. We're done with him. We have changed ourselves from diagnostic and therapeutic instruments into the users of diagnostic therapeutic instruments. I don't like that."

Because of regulatory requirements from accrediting bodies, she feels that the job of program director has also become more difficult since she had the role. "At that time program directors felt as if they were actually entrusted to know what to do, which is certainly not the case now. People keep telling you what to do. I look at my current program director, this marvelous young man, and I'm thinking, 'You poor sot.' And there are these predicate assumptions by the regulatory agencies—one is that if they don't tell us what to do we won't know, and two is that you have to learn everything before you get out of residency, otherwise you're lost."

Tasks for the Next Generation of Teachers
"Their job is to inspire young people to understand how richly rewarding it is—not to know the algorithms or the practice pathways, because those will change; not to know what to do in the way of procedures, because those will change even more rapidly—but to somehow model what a good doctor should be. And that can be learned only by witness. Only by witness because it's watching interactions, it's watching physical diagnosis. It's seeing how other people do it well. I know that I can't remember much of what I learned from syllabi and lectures and textbooks when I was a medical student, which is just as well, because it's all changed.

"What I remember, though, is the patients and patient stories and what they taught me, and teachers who showed me things that I didn't quite understand then, but seemed to work. If that's the enduring memory of an older doctor like myself, then there's something probably valuable about it. And that cannot be reproduced by anything other than doing it for my students. Maybe when they're old they'll remember me and what they learned. Not what I taught them, but what they learned by watching me."

[43]Hibbard Williams, MD, is dean emeritus and professor emeritus of internal medicine at the University of California, Davis, Medical School.

[44]William N. Kelley, MD, was chair of the department of internal medicine at the University of Michigan (1975–1989) and dean of the University of Pennsylvania School of Medicine (1989–2000).

[45]Lawrence Tierney, MD, is professor of medicine at the University of California, San Francisco, School of Medicine and associate chief of medical services at San Francisco Veterans Affairs Medical Center.

[46]Lloyd H. "Holly" Smith Jr., MD, is former chair of the Department of Medicine at the University of California, San Francisco, School of Medicine.

[47]Joseph Silva, MD, was chair of medicine and then dean of the University of California, Davis, School of Medicine.

❖ W. Dale Dauphinee

"I'm concerned that a lot of people in education and the management side of medicine haven't got a strong enough background in social sciences." Dr. W. Dale Dauphinee has spent his career thinking about the larger context in which medical education works, and which it should serve. From 1993 to 2006, as the executive director of the Medical Council of Canada in Ottawa, he was responsible for the certifying competence of Canadian physicians. At McGill University he was associate dean for medical education, director of the Center for Research in Medical Education, director of the internal medicine program, and chair of the Department of Medicine. He is currently a Senior Scholar at the Foundation for the Advancement of International Medical Education and Research.

Beginnings

Dr. Dauphinee received his undergraduate and medical degrees from Dalhousie University, Halifax, Nova Scotia. "In the mid-1960s, Dalhousie graduated 45 to 50 people a year and then traditionally sent people away, specifically those regarded as potential faculty members. Some went to Boston; some went to Toronto; I was sent to McGill, with my full agreement." At the end of his chief residency he was considering a career studying gallstone formation, but the chair of medicine called him in: "'I don't have a sense you're really interested in laboratory research, but you sure have a lot of interest in what's going on in the emergency room and in teaching. Why don't you go away and learn something about those issues, because I think that's where you'd be better academically?'

"Programs for Clinical Scholars were starting about then. So, I went to Johns Hopkins for a year as a visiting fellow in the Clinical Scholars Program, paid by Canadian money. I was with Bob and Sue Fletcher, Bob Brooks, Randy Barker, and Tom Inui. What a crew! When I came back, I had a mentor at McGill, Sidney Lee, who was really the professor of 'social medicine.' He was preparing McGill for the consequences of the switch to universal health insurance in 1970. He and I decided that we would apply for funding to one of the new Robert Wood Johnson [RWJ] Foundation Clinical Scholars programs. With his good advice, we got one, and I can remember sitting one morning, I think it was on Park Avenue in New York, tears running down my face. A man came up and said, 'What's wrong?' And I said, 'Well, someone gave us a check for a million dollars!' I ended up running the RWJ Foundation Clinical Scholars Program at McGill and having to develop the curriculum with several social scientists brought in to teach the scholars."

Always the Bigger Picture

Behind his relaxed conversational style you sense the social system churning in the background, the idea that education and medicine are part of a big picture, with both a social context and a social impact that are always on his mind. "If we don't pay attention, the patient's own circumstances may outweigh the doctor's training and actions. I don't think we pay enough attention to social context in medical school or in training programs, because in the end, it's what determines health, not simply the doctor. This is important and accounts for most of the variance in health, so we had better understand it." Medical education should focus not on justifying what the doctor is doing but on trying to understand what is going on in the patient's world. "When we started the RWJ Clinical Scholars program, that's what we were trying to do. We were trying to change the health outcomes of populations."

Dr. Dauphinee cited examples of things that had fostered his seeing the 'system context' in terms of medical educational issues. "One of my best teachers was a clinician. I'll always remember the first time I saw him do a consultation, and he said to the patient, 'Tell me the story of how you got here,' not 'What's wrong'—because the patient would have said 'I've got a pain in my gut.' He said, 'Tell me the story of how you got here,' and he let the person describe what all the problems were. After that he had an amazing scope of understanding of what the issues were for this person, because it wasn't just biology."

Moving Into Educational Research at McGill

After several years back at McGill, a new dean invited him to be undergraduate dean. "Sam Freedman[48] at McGill picked me out. I said, 'Well, I'm worried. I've been running all these programs and my publications are limited.' He said, 'Funny you should mention that. We've got this Center for Medical Education, and I don't think it does enough research about education. Why don't you fix it?' It was just administering curriculum at that point. He recognized that if I was going to succeed, I had to have academic output. He also needed me because the folks that had run the center before ran it as an administrative operation. That really should have been in the dean's office, not in a center. Centers are for new thought, assessing better ideas, which was in keeping with the McGill philosophy. That's part of what Sam was trying to do. So, I suspect I was one of several people whom he put into leadership positions in various fields and told them, develop better ways and new ideas. That was very enabling.

"And that's how I got into medical education. I played it the standard way. The people I recruited had to go in tenure track. They had to do original research, and we didn't allow excuses for things like 'there's no research funding in my area.' Every person I ever recruited in that center got tenure.

"I did that for about 6 years. Later I stayed as director of the center, but I didn't want to do the deanship work anymore. I became the physician-in-chief at the Royal Victoria Hospital, and eventually chair of medicine at McGill. After 7 years as a chief, I said, 'That's enough.' I went to Medical Council of Canada because I just wanted to do something different. I didn't want to be a dean, and I didn't want to be a chair anymore. It didn't have enough interesting opportunities for me at that time in my life."

Leadership

In addition to his leadership positions at McGill, he was asked to be a trustee of the American Board of Internal Medicine, a member of the Executive Board of the Association of American Medical Colleges, and president of several Canadian professional organizations. What is leadership like for him?

"I never thought of myself as a leader, but as I looked back on it years later, it was there—I just didn't recognize it. There are people who self-assess well, but most of us struggle, either by underestimating or overestimating. I think there are lots of areas where I was overconfident. But in the area of education, I never saw myself as somebody who would play a leadership role, except when I look back in retrospect. It just sort of happened, and I never thought that much about it until many years went by."

Characteristics of the People Who Helped Him

Visiting many other academic centers early on in his development had an effect on his perspective. In those days, the role of the chief residents included going to important meetings. "As chief resident, you traveled with the chief. So I knew the chief residents at Duke, Hopkins, Case Western, and other places. There were a lot of connections, so I knew other young leaders fairly well. And I also learned that when chiefs gave you responsibility, they expected you to try to develop a plan for your program. You had to know your people well." Leaders have to figure out who will stay with a task until it's done. "I had a medical school classmate[49] who organized a lot of things, both in the arts and sports. He was the best person I ever saw in organizing projects and people. He'd have an idea, and I'd say, 'Well, do you think it will work?' and he'd say, 'Dale, let's see who shows up.' And by 'shows up,' he meant 'came and stuck with it.'

"It's an important quality to be able to read people, recognize [those] who are really interested, why they're interested, and try to fit them together. I think I learned a lot that year as chief resident because I realized that I could lead a group. I recognized that there are a lot of smart people out there, a hell of a lot smarter than I am, and you better talk to them to get an understanding, by listening to what are they trying to tell you."

Two Useful Strategies in Running Things

The first principle he mentioned was to realize that not all new ideas will work until the time is right and people are ready. "I had what I call my parking lot. You make a note of everything; you don't forget about the non-priority items, but you park them until there's a better opportunity to address them. Later, you actually know when it is a good time to do something. And I would sit with a young guy, and think, 'He could do this' or 'That woman really has a natural interest.' It may take a while to find the right person or the right time. Some ideas are worth parking as they may become better ideas with a better champion or opportunity."

A key lesson for him was trying to understand what the comments of others really meant and what they were feeling. "I learned this from my dad, who was really bright, trained as school teacher, but was a successful businessman and eventually was cabinet minister and later a senior civil servant in Canada. He used to say to me, 'Dale, don't attribute to other things and other people some problem you've got in your own heart or your brain.' The notion is not imputing motives to people before you understand what is really going on, what the influences are, and why she or he behaves that way. This is really important in terms of leading and keeping out of trouble. Once you start to point fingers, you're probably wrong [in] being reactive—even on thin ice—and life is a lot more complicated. You're not in a position to try to do something proactive about it, because you're externalizing blame to someone else."

Difficult Moments in His Career

"I would never say I have regrets because I don't think you can look at it that way. Rather, there are certain difficulties or challenges in every situation that you need to see as an opportunity to learn something. Let's think about it—what would you do differently next time to recognize the situation sooner? How are you going to manage it?

"Most of us can't fire our bosses; we can't fire our problems. You must manage them somehow. So in that sense, I think every time you're in a difficult situation, you've got to think strategically—for the longer term."

Like others in our series of profiles, he emphasized not putting off difficult actions. "I've made that mistake several times, particularly in an academic institution when you're chief of a department, and you've got some really difficult people. I sometimes had some hard situations that I delayed dealing with, and they did not get better. You have to manage them it. You might not be able to move somebody outside or move them out of the way, but you've got to figure out how to manage it."

He emphasized that leaders must see the big picture for their own people, including the social and family context of how they function. "I think the issue here is the importance of family situations. If you are recruiting somebody to your group, accommodating their social situation is very important, especially now when both spouses work. This was especially true for me because I'm married to a 'physio,'[50] who understands the professional issues," and whose own career was important.

A Caution About the Academic World

Dr. Dauphinee added a perspective not heard elsewhere in these profiles: caution for leaders themselves. "I'm worried about the same things I'm always worried about, which is 'doctrinairism,' trying to justify opinions, rather than trying to clarify what the issues are. This is a perennial problem—we tend to say, 'This is the answer,' and of course it isn't."

He related this to his comments about attributing motives to people, and reacting to ideas in predetermined, fixed ways. In the academic world, he feels it's important to keep trying to understand the issues and keep explaining why things happen rather than continually justifying your present position. "I can remember once, one of the secretaries when I was in the dean's office said, 'You've seen so many similar problems with students by now, you tend to tell them "here's what to do" before you let them work their way to what the real question is.' It's like a doctor not letting the patient finish, as in my friend's approach, 'Tell me how you got here.' If you hear it, and you've heard it before, and if you think you know the answer before your colleague or student finishes telling you about it, then you've been there too long. It's time to move on. You are now part of the problem."

[48]From 1981 to 1991, Dr. Samuel Freedman served as McGill's chief academic officer. Along with Dr. Philip Gold he discovered a carcinoembryonic antigen.

[49]Lou Simon, a classmate of Dr. Dauphinee and former chief of staff at the regional hospital in St. John, New Brunswick, known for its innovative use of technology and design in Canada.

[50]Sharon Wood-Dauphinee, PhD, is a physical therapist and an epidemiologist at McGill University who conducts studies of rehabilitation after stroke.

❖ Thomas Nasca

"We need constantly to remind ourselves that the only reason we exist is to help others. It needs to play out in the way that we educate people to participate in the structuring of the healthcare delivery system, as well as delivering the best care within that structure to each of our individual patients."
Thomas J. Nasca, MD, MACP, is chief executive officer of the Accreditation Council for Graduate Medical Education (ACGME). He received his undergraduate degree from Notre Dame University and attended medical school at Jefferson Medical College. He is former chair of the Residency Review Committee for Internal Medicine and president of the Association of Program Directors in Internal Medicine. Before going to the ACGME, Dr. Nasca was dean at Jefferson Medical College. We had the chance to discuss how junior faculty might prepare for this kind of position.

Preparation for Being a Dean

"The path to becoming a dean is most typically through one of two doors. The first door is the successful department chairmen, usually research-based, well-funded from an NIH [National Institutes of Health] perspective, with a background in a department of reasonable size. They have administrative experiences that would allow them to conduct the business dimensions of the work of the dean. The second most frequent path would be the associate dean's promotion to dean. This most likely occurs within an institution, so it's unusual to be an associate dean at one institution and then become the dean at another institution. Those institutions frequently are less driven by the research agenda than either the educational or clinical agendas of the faculty."

He emphasized, however, the need for deeper preparation. "I would caution anyone who is aspiring to be a dean to ask a fundamental question. Why would you want to do it? What are you really trying to accomplish in becoming a dean? I wanted to dramatically transform the educational program at a major medical school to have an impact, not only on the cognitive and technical development but also on the personal, behavioral, and professional development of medical students. I wanted to re-elevate the importance of medical education of students and residents to the level that it should be in the minds of the faculty, and I had to create the appropriate recognition and reward systems to make that happen for the faculty. The role of the dean is so complex and so challenging because of the fiscal and competing needs and the kinds of challenges that you face—if you're only doing it to have been the dean, you will most likely be short-lived in the role."

Reasons To Be Dean

After his nephrology fellowship at Brown University, he returned to Mercy Hospital in Pittsburgh where he had been a resident. "I was chair of medicine at 34, as well as residency program director. It became clear to me that I was observing behaviors and attitudes in young residents that were counter to what I thought should be present. Despite attempts to modify those behaviors, it became clear that many of them were formed at the medical school level. The next realization I had at Jefferson was, despite the fact that I was responsible for about 20% of the medical school curriculum, despite being on the curriculum committee, and having significant influence over the specifics, I was not able to influence the environment sufficiently. The informal curriculum and the activities, behaviors, and attitudes of the faculty were not controlled by the educational leaders. They were moved in particular directions based on the structure of the reward system for faculty; not just the financial reward systems, but especially the academic reward systems, which at that time did not recognize education and educational scholarship as the equivalent of research productivity as commonly measured in most academic medical centers.

"I realized that I had to move higher in the administrative chain to have a significant influence. I decided to return to the medical school environment to attempt to modify the values and behaviors that I was seeing. This was about the time that Linda Blank, John Benson, and Harry Kimball[51] had led the development of humanistic attributes, and this began the discussions around professionalism in internal medicine. That's when I decided that I would move towards becoming a dean. I never really believed that I would have been the dean at Jefferson, but thought that if I prepared myself well, I would have the opportunity at another institution. When Joe Gonnella[52] stepped down, I was named the interim dean, and there was a national search. There were 25 deanships open that year. I applied for and interviewed at two, and actually was offered two on the same day, and then chose to stay at Jefferson."

Influences and Mentors
We discussed a few of the people who helped shape his view of what the right environment for learning was. "The first was Frank Luparello, who was the chair of the department at Mercy in Pittsburgh, a classic bedside diagnostician, and what we would now call a master clinician educator. I chose to do my residency there because of my experiences with him as a medical student, and then had the privilege of eventually being a chief resident with him. This instilled in me this desire to become an educator, specifically at the graduate level, not at the undergraduate level.

"I then went to Brown [for nephrology] and my division chief and program director was Serafino Garella,[53] who instilled in me the combination of academic excellence, superior clinical skills, and ethical and professional behaviors in a complicated environment. Caring for patients with end-stage renal disease opened my eyes to the importance of medical ethics and professionalism. ... Making difficult or life-changing clinical decisions with patients was a transformative experience. These mentors gave me a set of fundamental values that have remained with me to this day.

"My third key mentor, Joe Gonnella, I knew as a medical student at Jefferson. He was an associate dean at the time, and we spoke at a fortuitous meeting. A week later I had a phone call. The chair of medicine at Jefferson asked me to come back and be the vice-chairman for education in the Department of Medicine. And I went back. My wife and family moved to Philadelphia. We embarked on this path to try and improve the values of students in what is still the largest private medical school in the United States.

"They were all models of academic excellence as well as professionalism and clinical excellence, because I have always wanted and aspired to be a superior clinician in addition to a superior educator. They were all good family people who were able to somehow manage the demands of positions of significant authority and responsibility, yet be personable and committed to their families and their friends, as well as their work."

Colleagues and External Mentors

Dr. Nasca introduced to our series of profiles the notion of "external mentors," valued peers from other institutions who worked with him in national organizations or on committees.[54] He named Jordan Cohen[55] from the Association of American Medical Colleges, David Leach from the ACGME, Linda Blank and Dan Duffy from the American Board of Internal Medicine, Holly Humphrey[55] from the University of Chicago, Henry Schultz from the Mayo Clinic, Ray Mitchell from Georgetown University, Tom Blackwell from the University of Texas Medical Branch, Galveston, Robert Wright from Scranton, and Herbert Waxman from the American College of Physicians. "These are colleagues who taught me so much, not by actively teaching me or opening doors, but just sharing their thoughts and opinions, their challenges and how they cope with them, and entering into dialogue around difficult issues. In that process, they also provided support during difficult decision-making times. These are individuals that you have the privilege of working with along the way who, just by their behaviors, model the kinds of behaviors and thought processes that *you* aspire to have."

Leaving the Role of Dean for the ACGME

After 15 years Dr. Nasca left Jefferson. "I was able to make the changes that I thought would result in the outcomes that we pursued, and most of the things that we attempted to do, we actually demonstrated. The great fortune of being at Jefferson was that the longitudinal study[56] and the research enterprise there allowed me to document that we had actually achieved the outcomes we were attempting to achieve. After about 7 and a half years or so as the dean, the realities of all the other dimensions of that job wear on you. It was a long, circuitous route—it really began with my recognition that I was not happy with the values and professionalism that I was seeing in residents, and now I've come full circle. I hope to have a positive influence on that dimension of their career development and personal development, regardless of specialty, in this role."

Challenges for the ACGME

As head of one of the stronger forces in medical education, Dr. Nasca must respond to the challenges now being faced by professional training. He came to the ACGME during a controversy prompted by the Institute of Medicine's report[57] on residents' work hours, which he sees an issue of balancing professional values. "This is a much more complicated issue than how many hours people work. If we tell them that they can't stay with their patients, or if they do, they have to lie about it in order to satisfy some external body's rules, what are we doing to the fundamental fabric of medicine? I'm on record as having stated that we don't have it right, that if anything, we are fostering unprofessional behavior in our residents by forcing them to lie, forcing them to choose between satisfying duty hours and satisfying the needs of their patients as they perceive them."

At the ACGME, "we're placed in a situation as an accreditor where we have to prioritize among goods. We are debating competing goods, as opposed to debating rights and wrongs. We have to make the decisions and set the rules. All other things being equal, would one want an ideally rested individual caring for them, whether that be a resident or attending physician? The answer everyone would give is yes. But, faced with the choice between doing that and providing potentially less than ideal care—because the rested caregivers don't know the patient, and errors are introduced in providing that care by multiple individuals through … multiple handoffs, regardless of the data systems used—we have an ethical tradeoff. We have to choose something that is less than ideal."

Searching for Underlying Values

"What is not frequently recognized is the implicit trust that must be present among physicians. Each physician must trust that when in need for the care of their patient, their colleague will come to the aid of their patient, regardless of what time of day or night it is, regardless of the patient's ability to pay." There may be pressure to copy other countries where restriction on work hours fits into a society-wide mechanism for minimizing unemployment, and there is a risk: "When that honor, that trust, among physicians frays, we are unable to deliver on our individual and group promise to society to serve their needs above our own and the profession is doomed."

Difficult Moments in His Career

"The transitions have been difficult. I've been fortunate only to leave institutions because of new opportunities, but the transitions away from the group of people who become your second family, your colleagues and friends and students, at every juncture in my career have been difficult. The second was an administrative challenge that I would certainly consider a failure. I was attempting to create an educational consortium and failed to recognize that my efforts were being used by my superiors to accomplish another goal. They were willing to jettison the consortium, which would have improved education for residents and students, in order to accomplish other goals. That was a tremendous sense of disappointment to me, and it was also a lesson, a political lesson, in learning how to watch one's flank and anticipate resistance from unexpected sources in making change."

How Do Junior Faculty Avoid Pitfalls?

"There are some general thoughts that I would give. The first is that it's always important when you're pushing the lodestone to occasionally stop and look around; another analogy would be, when you're out leading the troops in a particular direction, every once in a while, look over your shoulder, and make sure that they're still there. One of the most difficult things, I think, for young people who are thrust into leadership roles where change is warranted is understanding the pace of change, and understanding how far, and how fast or how slow, you should or should not push a group. We need to learn to use the skills that we as internists have at the bedside to understand and to anticipate the political realities and the political environment in which we live. We need to recognize that there are other systems acting in what superficially appeared to be independent realms that can have an influence on what you're trying to accomplish.

"Don't push—lead. Always forcing issues will predictably result in some failures; whereas if you create situations that have multiple alternatives, you're most likely able to get things accomplished. We in internal medicine are often willing to sacrifice the good in pursuit of the excellent. One infrequently achieves perfection in solutions to complex problems. The drive to achieve perfection, at the expense of an incremental positive outcome, often dooms people to failure because you get the reputation as a win-lose negotiator. In other words, *you* have to win and somebody has to lose, as opposed to creating the compromise that allows things to move forward.

"When I first became dean, a mentor sat me down and said, 'You need to have some small wins.' And I said, 'I don't need small wins. I have big problems here. We have to have big wins.' And he said, 'No, no, no. Slow down. You need to demonstrate to the faculty that you can solve problems, so solve some small ones, solve ones that you're not going to have opposition on first, so that you build consensus, and you build a team that believes in you.'"

Placing Values at the Heart of the Matter

"Twenty years ago I had a vision of what I would like to accomplish if I were successful, and what I wanted to do was to help start a medical school at Notre Dame. About the time I recognized the issue of values in residents and decided to return to the medical school environment, I decided that I would prepare myself, in case Notre Dame ever wanted to start a medical school. I would be eligible to be the founding dean.

"Values are a gift given to us by those who have gone before us. There is a set of values worthy to be an essential element in the discourse of American medicine. If I don't have the opprtunity to start a school dedicated to those values, then I can think of no position in American medicine more opportune to express those values than head of the ACGME. I have the ear of everybody, and the interesting, mixed blessing of the duty hours discussion and the Institute of Medicine report is that everybody's listening. I'd better get it right."

[51]Leaders at the American Board of Internal Medicine.

[52]Joseph S. Gonnella, MD, is dean emeritus and founder and director of Jefferson Medical College's Center for Research in Medical Education and Health Care.

[53]Serafino Garella, MD, subsequently became vice-chair and residency program director at Michael Reese Hospital in Canada under Dr. Jordan Cohen.

[54]Others in this chapter also paid tribute to such colleagues, but we list these here because Dr. Nasca's recognition suggests the richness of collaboration in an academic career.

[55]See profile in this section.

[56]The Jefferson Longitudinal Study of Medical Education is a comprehensive database of academic and long-term career follow-up data on all medical school classes since 1964 (over 24,000 students and house staff).

❖ Charles Griffith

"I can't image doing anything else in my life. It is a joy and a privilege to be taking care of patients, to be teaching students and residents, to try to inspire them to be the best doctors they can be. To be the person who is taking the responsibility for educating the next generation of physicians is a great legacy to have." Charles "Chipper" Griffith was president of the Clerkship Directors in Internal Medicine (CDIM), where he is honored for his humanism and respected for his educational research. CDIM named its annual research award after him.[58] He was medicine clerkship director at the University of Kentucky College of Medicine for 15 years and recently stepped down to become the residency program director. In 2004 he won the national Alpha Omega Alpha Robert Glaser Award for teaching. He is a leader who has remained, primarily, a teacher.

"My dad was a pediatrician. He is the best doctor I have ever known, but I was never going to be a doctor. Actually I was deluding myself into thinking I was going to play baseball. For a while I was toying with being a writer, and maybe an English professor." But he did go to medical school, at Vanderbilt University. "I drifted into med school. The first 2 years of med school I didn't enjoy that much. We had very little clinical exposures and so it was all memorization and regurgitation. But then the third year came around and everything just clicked. I think I really decided to become a doctor in the *third* year of medical school.

"Looking back now, I can't image being anything besides a doctor—being involved with patients and getting to hear their stories, and people trusting you for care and counsel. For a little while I actually toyed with being a surgeon, of all things. But when I did my clerkships the old ways resonated with me, and I thought I would do pediatrics because my dad was a pediatrician. So, I ended up doing a meds/peds residency. I'd been at Vanderbilt for 8 years, and it is not a primary care–focused institution. I thought I would go to Kentucky and become a primary care meds/peds doctor, and probably go back to work with my dad in Alabama, where I grew up.

"I enjoyed the academic atmosphere. I loved morning reports; I loved conferences; I loved the teaching and learning that was going on, especially when it came to the upper-level resident. I used to get excited for rounds each day. I would think the night before [of] some questions I could ask the students and interns. I even made little hand-outs and quizzes and things like that. It was just a lot of fun—taking care of patients as you're teaching and learning.

"I didn't really have a good sense of what academics was, but I wanted to teach. I was naive as to what that entailed, and was greatly influenced by Gene Rich,[59] who transformed our general medicine division. He talked about how one could always have students and residents in your clinic, and that being a role model is a very valued form of academics. But, he also said that if you want to be a leader in educational programs, you need to have academic credentials; that people are chosen to be residency directors not based solely on their being great teachers, but on academic credentials. That's just the way it was.

"I did a -2-year general medicine fellowship under Gene. You have got to spend some time focusing on learning academic skills, including administration, and including research, scholarship, and teaching skills. We had to limit my clinic time during the fellowship, and that was hard because I enjoyed being in the trenches with the students and residents."

Getting Started in Educational Research

"I started asking questions about the residency and how patient outcomes are affected by the program, not necessarily bad outcomes but also good patient outcomes. I truly believe that the team concept—multiple eyes taking care of the patient—is the reason outpatient care is better in teaching hospitals than we find in non–teaching hospitals, in the literature. We did studies on workload and how that might affect some outcomes like patient satisfaction.

"To probably my surprise I enjoyed it a lot. It brought in some of the creative aspects I enjoyed when I was contemplating being a writer. You could use your mind, be creative, and ask thoughtful questions, and that was fun. To be both a teacher and a doctor, and to do creative things, this was like a dream job."

Clerkship Director, Then Program Director

During Dr. Griffith's second year of fellowship, the clerkship director left for a different position, and Dr. Rich advocated for him to be the clerkship director. "He convinced our chair, Dick Glassick.[60] He was a great chair. Among all the clinical and research priorities of the department, he always made sure we had a focus on education. His faith in Gene Rich, who in turn had faith in me, allowed me to be the clerkship director early on. It was quite a testament to the faith he had in someone who was fairly junior.

"Through the early 90s, things that helped my career development were organizations like CDIM. I went to the early meetings and met people like Rhee Fincher[61] and realized that being a clerkship director could be a career. Being involved with people with similar passions and interests is restorative. When you have the day-to-day challenges of one's job, you get to see the big picture by coming to the CDIM meeting. I feel very blessed to spend time with those people.

"Some people talk about networking as an academic skill, and I was always turned off by that a little bit. But what I found at CDIM, especially, is that you met people because you wanted to, because you enjoyed being in their company, and it was fun. Through CDIM … and SGIM [Society of General Internal Medicine] and AAMC [Association of American Medical Colleges] as well, I guess I got to know a lot of folks. I got to be on national committees and had leadership positions. I guess that's the way I was able to get a national reputation. I could see myself as being a clerkship director my entire life, as several folks have done, like Gary Ferenchick, Cyril Grum,and Tom Painter.[62] I've been doing this for 15 years, and colleagues would say, 'Why you would keep doing clerkship director? Why not consider associate dean for education, or residency director?'"

He thought about this. "Why remain clerkship director for so long? First, if you are enjoying what you are doing, it is hard to think of anything else to do; it is rewarding. There are always challenges, including some practical, daily ones; the curriculum does not stay stagnant, there are always innovations, creative things one can do. If one gets a reputation for being an energetic teacher, the student's expectations of you are pretty high. You must always be on your 'A' game, and it's a challenge, but it certainly keeps you improving."

Dr. Griffith became the residency director 2 years ago, and his decision to leave a job he loved is instructive. "Our long-time program director was Steve Haist,[63] and he left. He'd done pretty much everything one could do at the University of Kentucky in education, and so the residency director spot was open. From the department's point of view, I was the natural person for it, but it did give me pause. It was something I had not planned on doing. The deciding factor was that I had a co-clerkship director, Andrew Hoellein. And he really could run the clerkship on a day-to-day basis as well as I could. The need was greater in our residency program than in the clerkship program. The clerkship was in good hands with Andrew, so I agreed to do it."

Lessons From Being Clerkship Director
"The important skill for a clerkship director is to inspire. I hope my students and residents want to be the best students, the best residents, the best doctors that they can be, and I hope that they want me to be proud of them. They are going to look at us as examples of how to comport yourself with patients, ancillary personnel, staff, and students, and so have courtesy in everything you do, value others when you're interacting with them.

"It is easy for some residents and students to just scrape by, and just do the minimum, and many do despite my efforts. But if you can, hold before them an example of truly wanting, of always wanting, to be better. But I think almost everybody can rise to a higher level. The Socratic method, at least as embodied in Plato's *Republic,* was that Socrates took people from one level of thinking to a higher level. You can always take someone to a higher level. So taking the below-average student or resident and bringing them to at least average is an accomplishment. The below-average will still pass; they'll still hang a shingle somewhere, but they won't be the best doctors they can be. And to me that is the business we are in, trying to make people the best doctors they can be, for themselves and not just for their patients."

Now more than ever he thinks that we need to support and inspire trainees. "The workload of the residents and the medical students can be overwhelming. We have work hour restrictions now, and on one level they are working fewer hours than we did in the past. But the volume of work and the pace of the work are greater than ever. I think that in most academic systems, the residents do more in the hours they are asked to work than ever."

Role models can counteract the risks to the house staff. "They lose some of the ideals that attracted them to medicine in the first place. They see the work as doing these forms and filling out these discharge things and getting the patients out of the hospital. Sometimes they are so focused on just getting the tasks done that they lose sight of their education, in terms of reading and learning. I am also afraid they become more cynical. The common thing you hear about is that the patient is almost viewed as the enemy. They all need our help. And so I try to role-model that you can't lose those ideals, and you always have to treat every patient's needs as almost holy, not to be too religious. You are the best doctor you can be to your patient. They expect nothing less; they deserve nothing less."

Challenges Facing Medical Education Right Now

"It's described pretty well in Ken Ludmerer's book, *A Time to Heal*. He doesn't just talk about education, but about medical practice. Even though the work hours for residents are less, the volume of work is greater. It is the same for people in practice. There is so much pressure to see more patients, to meet one's RVU [relative value unit] targets. How do you convince community-based faculty to take a student or resident into the clinic when [trainees] slow them down and impact their revenue? The pressure to see a patient in 10, 15 minutes is just crazy. How can you attend to people's needs in just a few minutes like that, plus teaching? An ideal would be to see the patient at the bedside and then all talk about what we just saw for 10 minutes. It would take changes on a global scale to change things."

Do You Have Advice for Clerkship Directors?

Dr. Griffith's advice for those who are or would be clerkship directors is simple. "Try not to take yourself so seriously, but take what you *do* very seriously. I think the best leaders are people that can laugh at themselves; you are comfortable around them and you don't feel that they think they are the most important person in this room.

"We are in the business of training doctors to take care of people. That's a sacred profession. In terms of academic careers and perhaps target the leadership is. Take the long view of your career. In any job, there [are] going to be good times and bad times. There will be times when you don't agree with the leadership. But, if you like being in the trenches with students and residents, if you like directing your clerkship or your residency, you are building a legacy—a legacy of all the students and learners and the people you have worked with through the years. And that is something to look back on as an accomplishment. When I think of Georgia, I think of Rhee; when I think of Vermont, I think of Lewis First. To be the person who is taking the responsibility for educating the next generation of physicians is a great legacy to have."

[57]Resident Duty Hours: Enhancing Sleep, Supervision and Safety. Washington, DC: Institute of Medicine; 2008.

[58]The Charles H. Griffith III, MD, Educational Research Award, known affectionately as the "Chipper."

[59]Eugene C. Rich, MD, chief of the Division of General Internal Medicine and Geriatrics at the University of Kentucky College of Medicine and then chair of the Department of Medicine at Creighton University School of Medicine.

[60]Richard Glassick, MD.

[61]See her profile in this section.

[62]Dr. Ferenchik is clerkship director at Michigan State University, Dr. Grum is clerkship director at the University of Michigan, and Dr. Painter is clerkship director at the University of Pittsburgh.

[63]Steven A. Haist, MD, joined the National Board of Medical Examiners as associate vice-president of test development services in 2008.

❖ Ruth-Marie E. Fincher

Early in her career she was asked a critical question by a chair who cared about her future: "Why do you want to throw your career away doing medical education?" She was not deterred, and Ruth-Marie Fincher, MD, is now vice-dean for academic affairs and professor of medicine at the Medical College of Georgia School of Medicine (MCG). She was a founding member and served as president of the Clerkship Directors in Internal Medicine (CDIM), and is considered the "mentor of mentors" by her colleagues.

After earning her MD degree and doing her residency in internal medicine at Emory University School of Medicine, Dr. Ruth-Marie Fincher—"Rhee" to the American medical education community—and her husband, Mike, were both paying back their commitments to the government. "I spent the first 2 years after I finished residency paying back a scholarship to the Public Health Services—the only doctor in a little town in South Georgia."

Detours or Building Blocks

"When you look at someone's career pathway as a whole, activities that at the time appeared to be detours or dead ends actually end up being building blocks to the whole career theme. It was an important building block because it taught me that I didn't want to be a small-town rural practitioner for my whole career. It gave me an enormous appreciation for people who do practice, and practice well, in isolated, small areas, and it became important in my ability to talk with learners about various kinds of career opportunities and to talk about primary care."

She started a private practice, which she turned over to someone else when her husband began an endocrine fellowship. "I followed him to Tacoma, Washington, and I was very fortunate to happen upon a job as a general internist at the American Lake VA Medical Center. We had a small inpatient service with a team from Madigan Army Hospital. We taught physical diagnosis to students from the University of Washington, and I spent my clinic time teaching and working with nurse practitioners, and PAs [physician assistants]. I discovered that I loved all of those venues of teaching. I decided at that point that I wanted a career in teaching and not in private practice as I had previously thought."

A Fortuitous Beginning: Becoming the Director of Education

"I did not start out a good teacher. I still remember a talk I gave to two residents. I had prepared the old 35-millimeter slides on an arcane topic and turned the lights down as they struggled to keep their eyes open. In retrospect, I couldn't think of anything good about it and learned a whole lot from my disastrous experience, but by the time I left, I had decided I really wanted a career in academic medicine and was fortunate that the Army sent Mike to Eisenhower Army Medical Center in Georgia."

Their plan was to stay 2 years until he fulfilled his commitment to the military. Mike did get out of the military, but they stayed there. "Within a month after I got to MCG, the person who directed the clerkship, the course in physical diagnosis, and the fourth-year electives was leaving. I gathered my fortitude and went to the chair of the department and told him that I really wanted to be the clerkship director. I had no background, no reason to think I was qualified to do it, but I felt passionately that was what I wanted to do. He said to me, very seriously, 'Rhee, I thought you were a bright young faculty member. Why do you want to throw your career away doing medical education?' He asked me to think about it. I returned the following day and told him I wanted to do it, at which point he looked very relieved and said, 'Thank goodness. Nobody else wants to do this.' But it was fortuitous and exactly the right thing for me to do."

Lesson for New Educators

"I also did things that, in retrospect, were wise. I talked with the clerkship director who was leaving and asked him why. He felt he had done—and he had—a very good job and had made major contributions to the department, but he had not been promoted. So I took guidance from his experience, and I read the promotion and tenure guidelines. I made a timetable for myself of what I needed to do to be promoted and to earn tenure. At each step I met my expectations, and the biggest challenge for me was to have some accomplishments in scholarly work and also earn a regional and national reputation."

Through the courses for new clerkship directors that she initiated at CDIM and the Association of American Medical Colleges (AAMC), and through her *Guidebook*,[64] Dr. Fincher has helped many of us who are educators to achieve success. In our interview she offered some condensed advice. "Medical education is an absolutely marvelous career path assuming you feel really passionate about some aspect of medical education. Key elements include becoming the best teacher you can be, incrementally gaining experience in educational leadership as a course or clerkship director, to earn an excellent reputation as an outstanding teacher and an educational administrator. It's also important to become involved regionally and nationally through groups like the AAMC Group on Educational Affairs, CDIM, the ACP [American College of Physicians], or the NBME [National Board of Medical Examiners]."

Finally, it's important to become engaged in scholarly work: "Ideally, scholarly work in medical education. You will have a deeper appreciation of medical education and innovation, of where medical education is or should be going, if you actually become involved in scholarly work in education yourself. I think it also opens doors in getting to meet colleagues who are the visionary thinkers in medical education nationally, and to engage in discussions and possible collaborations with them."

Remaining at Medical College of Georgia

At MCG, Dr. Fincher took on broader roles, moving from medical student director to associate dean for curriculum and then to vice dean. "I have dreamed about different kinds of opportunities within the broad domain of medical education, but I have found that my own professional needs have always been fulfilled by the joy of helping other people. I guess the other people have primarily been medical students, but in the last decade or so, also faculty who are more junior than I—now many of the faculty—helping them get to do what they want to do."

She reflected on remaining in one institution. "This is one area that Mike and I together have probably struggled with the most over the last 25 years. On the side of staying in one place, I have had a very fulfilling journey for 25 years, growing in the jobs I've had, and having multiple different responsibilities. There are advantages in doing a job like mine, which is predicated on individual working relationships with people, and if one moves from place to place, it takes time to develop the new personal working relationships. I think one of the important reasons we haven't moved is because—I don't quite know how to say this—but I felt a certain lack of confidence as to whether I would really be able to fulfill the expectations in another position."

Particular Mentors

While she is now recognized by colleagues as the mentor of those who mentor others, she recalled her own influences. "I have to start with my own parents. My mom was a high school teacher and my dad was a dean at the University of Connecticut. They both ingrained in me a deep appreciation for education itself, and they were so pleased with their own choice of careers as educators. I think they both felt that education for them was more of a calling than a job they chose to do."

Another influential person was Kenneth Walker, the clerkship director at Emory. "I knew Ken from when I was a third-year medical student on the medicine clerkship, but his influence really came from an afternoon I spent with him after I had been appointed clerkship director. I realized that I had no idea how to be a clerkship director. I needed a crash course. Since CDIM didn't exist yet, I called him, the only person in the world I knew who was a clerkship director, and said, 'I need to come over and talk with you about how I can survive this first year.' And the notes I took that afternoon became the outline for the precourse for new clerkship directors at CDIM.

"I've worked for seven different deans. One of the longest duration was Darrell Kirch;[65] he created the position of vice-dean for academic affairs and offered me that job. His style of mentoring was to include me in aspects of his own decision-making, and to use evolving case studies in decision-making as a way to teach me skills as an administrator."

Traits of Outstanding Leaders

"It's important to have a broad vision that you convey to the people you work with, and sometimes to the larger community. But it's also very important to be willing, even eager, to discuss aspects that are in evolution, and to involve additional people in the decision-making. Having said that, another key characteristic is to know when you've got enough input and, particularly when the input is diverse, to know when it's time to make a decision and move on, and not drag out a decision-making process too long.

"It's important to set expectations, to agree on desired outcomes, but then for a leader to get out of the way, and not to micromanage. Leaders also celebrate others' contributions, and don't feel the need to shine the light on themselves, but would rather acknowledge the other people around them who really make things happen.

"Strong leaders are honest and candid and model the highest ethical standards. They surround themselves with talented people with diverse interests and perspectives. They want real input from people who may not share their view. When something goes wrong, they take responsibility. Strong, effective leaders don't look for a scapegoat, but rather analyze what went wrong, learn from it, deal with it, build upon it, and move forward."

Challenges Facing Medical Education Right Now

"I was thinking about this while I was pulling weeds in the garden yesterday," she said without irony. "The challenges in medical education are intertwined with challenges in health care that we are experiencing nationally. The broken remuneration system in health care has a direct negative impact on students' career choices and on the maldistribution in the location of physicians. Restoring the level of respect for medicine as a profession, as a calling and not as a business of providers and consumers, is a challenge not only in health care but also in medical education.

"There are important generational differences, and the goals of professional life and work ethic, the balance of work and family time, are different. And I don't say that in a judgmental way, saying that one is better than the other, but they're different, and I think we need to understand that as we teach the next generation."

Then there are curricular issues within schools. "We have a great tendency to pack more in, to build curriculum by accretion without implementing an excretory system. This is a substantial challenge. We also need far more integration of the foundational sciences with clinical practice. For students to appreciate the value of, to understand, use, and remember foundational science, it needs to be taught nearly always in the context of how it's important for taking good care of patients. To that end, I think we need increasingly to get away from simple transfer of information and to have students become more responsible for their own learning through collaborative work in groups as well as independently.

"Finally, another challenge is identifying protected time for faculty to devote what is necessary for helping students learn, in light of what I think everywhere has been increased demand for generating clinical or research dollars."

Sources of Pride in Her Career

She did not mention recognitions or awards[66] but rather her work in mentoring colleagues around the country, for which she has earned their respect and love. "Tremendously gratifying to me in the last 10 or 15 years is the opportunity to work in mentoring junior faculty. What I really cherish most is helping other people accomplish their own goals and playing a role in the development of new programs in schools locally or nationally. Playing a role in the visioning and founding and growth of CDIM started fairly early in my career. The organization and the people in it have exceeded my dreams for a clerkship directors' organization, and I really feel very proud of the growth of the organization and the people who've made it that way.

"It's really pretty easy. The thing that makes me the *most* proud is being able to look back on probably now 4500 medical students and feel I played a role in helping them get to do what they really want to do. Watching students mature and celebrating their successes—sometimes having to deal with their disappointments or at times their misbehaviors is less fun—but celebrating their accomplishments is probably the most gratifying thing I have done."

[64]Guidebook for Clerkship Directors, now in its third edition. Fincher RM, ed. Alliance for Clinical Education; 2005.

[65]Darrell G. Kirch, MD, president of the AAMC since 2006, was then dean at the Medical College of Georgia.

[66]She has received the Alpha Omega Alpha/AAMC Distinguished Teacher Award and the Daniel S. Tosteson Award for Leadership in Medical Education from the Carl J. Shapiro Institute for Education and Research.

❖ Marshall Wolf

"All the years I did the job, I thought I had the best job in American academic medicine." For almost 3 decades, Marshall Alan Wolf, MD, was program director for the medical residency at Brigham and Women's Hospital in Boston. He is now emeritus vice-chair for education in the Department of Medicine. In our interview, he reflected on dealing with change, on initiating change, and on the tension between growing regulatory requirements and the internal process of innovation and quality improvement process in which he believes. "As program director, you have to just keep looking at your program constantly and asking the trainees who really know what's going on as well as your faculty. What are the problems? What do we do to make this better?"

In the interview he looked back from his present emeritus status. "I'm now a senior physician. Mostly what I do is I teach, I practice, and I mentor a lot of young people, including the people who run the training program now." His conversation is direct and quick; giving diplomatic answers is not his style. We began with the question, How did he get to be the program director?

The Beginning of the Story

"My parents were both immigrants. I was lucky because school came easy to me. I got to go to Harvard College and went to Harvard Medical School, and I met my bride at the foot of our cadaver on day one. That was the best thing far and away. "

He expected to be a medical scientist. "In medical school I worked with a guy who was in bilirubin metabolism, and I did research with him on porphyria and I liked that. He moved to Chicago, where I had 800 relatives, and my wife said, 'We're not going there.'"

After residency in Boston at the Brigham he went to the National Institutes of Health for experience. "I picked the lab of biochemistry because I was really still interested in organic chem. It was wonderful because I wasn't working weekends and I had more time to spend with my wife; but it was disappointing in that the lab I chose was interested in technology more than science, and it turned out I wasn't a very good experimental scientist.

"I came back to the Brigham, and I decided I would be a clinician. We were working with all these incredibly gifted cardiologists, so I decided to do cardiology. I came back to work with Bernie Lown[67] because I was interested in arrhythmias and sudden death. As a second-year fellow I would help out at the Harvard Community Health Plan, which had just gotten up and running. By moonlighting, I was their 'cardiologist,' and I also did a general medicine clinic. I found out that outpatient medicine was a lot different than what I'd been trained in. I hustled around to improve my skill set. I had time off, so I'd spend half-days with a dermatologist and half-days with a rheumatologist, and half-days with an endocrinologist. So I became a better doctor."

In a few years he was looking for a job, and Dr. Eugene Braunwald[68] was just announced as the new head of medicine. "He was interviewing everyone to see how they fit in to his vision, and he called me in and said, 'How'd you like to take Gene Eppinger's[69] old job?' Dr. Eppinger was the program director. I said, 'Yeah, I'll take it.' He said, 'Don't you want to talk about money or anything?' I said, 'No, that's fine. Why don't we talk about what we're going to do together?' And that's how I got that job. The negotiation was about 2 minutes.

"In the old days, people who were program directors usually did it as a favor to the chief for a few years and then moved on, back into some specialty and up the academic ladder; and this was just something they did part-time. It never occurred to me that it was something I should prepare for. Who told him to ask me, I don't know. But I was very glad he did, and after about 6 months he figured out I wasn't psychotic and we had a lot of good years together."

Working Closely With the Residents and With the Chair

"When I first started my job, I continued to do medicine and cardiology, and I also started a primary care program to train people in the skill set I didn't have when I started. I mentioned how I'd improved my skill set, so that was really the origin of our primary care program. Bill Branch[70] and I sort of set it up. So I did 'cards,' medicine, primary care. I was an attending both in the CCU [cardiac care unit] and the MICU [medical intensive care unit]."

As program director, he thought that it was important to experience what the trainees did firsthand. "I think it was very important that I be there and practice with the house staff. So I gave up cardiology rather than give up medicine. I figured I'm running a medicine training program on how to do medicine and not 'cards.' That was very important because it allowed me to be on the floor with the interns and know what was going on because I was there taking care of my patients.

"It was the best job in academic medicine. I had the best boss. I had the best senior staff because once Braunwald had recruited, we had the best senior staff. I had the best house staff in the country as well. Braunwald said, 'By the way, you have the most important job in the department.' And I said, 'Why is that, Dr. Braunwald?' And he said, 'Because you're going to hire my future faculty.' And I did. After we'd been doing this for several years, Braunwald said to me, 'You know something, we're like one of those old vaudeville acts where there are two guys inside a horse suit, and I know which end of the act I am.'"

Leaving the Best Job in Academic Medicine

"You know, I trained a lot of people who could have done my job better than I did, but I wasn't leaving. Then there was a moment in 1999 when I decided I'd had enough. Braunwald had retired. The new chief and I had different styles and different visions, and I thought maybe 28 years is enough. In addition to running the program, I had a very busy internal medicine practice at the Brigham.

"And the other thing was I really didn't like what the Residency Review Committee was doing; and they didn't like me. So it was good that I stepped down. I'd done it long enough." Yet, he was philosophic about changing requirements. "If you take over a program, you think, 'Well I'm going to run it just the way it was run last year for the rest of time in memorial.' You're going to have a problem because the realities of life change."

Unanticipated Changes

Dr. Wolf mentioned some of the changes in the educational setting in the last few decades that were not expected. First, he mentioned the length of hospital stay for most patients. "When I took over in '72, the average length of stay was probably about 10 days. Did I expect there to be a time when it would be 3 and a half? No. Next, did I think that there would be a time when ambulatory medicine would be a third of the program? That wasn't on my horizon. Did I think that oncology and cardiology would grow so that they dwarf the rest of the hospital in terms of inpatients? No. When I took over the program, every inpatient had an intern, and only the interns were allowed to write orders. I never expected to have a third of the patients in the Brigham covered by a nurse practitioner. I can't imagine that what we have now will be what we'll have 20 years from now. It will be different."

The Difficult Situations

Dr. Wolf felt that the biggest difficulty he has had was adjusting to increasing regulations and requirements from the Residency Review Committee, which he referred to as "the Board." "Dr. Braunwald and I were experimenting with our program all the time. We would always try new things. The Board would come and say, 'You're supposed to do this.' And I said, 'I tried that. It doesn't work as well as this, what I'm doing now.' They didn't like that.

"The bane of my existence was the Board, and I think I was the bane of their existence. I had among the most outstanding training programs in America, and we always drafted first in the intern match, but they were always unhappy with me, because I wasn't dotting every 'I' and crossing every 'T' just as they liked.

"The problem is they're rigid without data. And I was always doing things differently. I was always after them and they were always after me, and threatened to take away my accreditation. The thing that's going to make it tough for the next generation of program directors is the rigidity of these regulatory boards."

Dr. Wolf felt that he had a record of adjusting to problems and what his residents were telling him, and described an incident that far preceded newer regulations. "One of my residents said to me, 'When I'm in the emergency room more than about 16 or 17 hours in a row, I begin to resent the patients, instead of feeling sorry for them.' And that's wrong. In those days we had 60-hour shifts. So I brought in 15 residents and interviewed them, and they all told me the same thing. About 2 days later I shortened the shift in ED to 16 hours. We were doing things that had to do with hours and workload a long time before the board came along."

Pride in Improving the Program

When asked about making mistakes, Dr. Wolf felt that "mistakes" could be a necessary part of the improvement process. He felt that he did a few things that were really smart, and one sounds a lot like teaching systems-based practice and practice-based learning and improvement. "I empowered my residents to make the program better, and I would meet with them every week and they'd tell me what was broken. And they would come up with wonderful things. So when I wanted to do something new, I would meet with them. We'd discuss it. And then if we tried and it didn't work, it was something we had done together. They helped me figure out a better way of doing stuff.

"The second smartest thing I did was I put house staff on the intern selection committee. They would say, 'Well, so and so's got very good grades; but I don't want to be around alone with them at night.' And we wouldn't take that someone in the program. People visit our program say, 'How come your house staff's so happy?' And I'd say because we pick people who are happy and we don't harm them.' So that was the other thing I did that I thought was unique."

Key Advice for Junior Leaders

He learned some lessons that he thought worth passing on. "Dr. Braunwald let me do my thing, but he was there to help me. He would say to me, 'Do you want to show everybody how smart you are, or do you want to change things?' That was very useful to me because it made me realize what I needed to do … I saw the world as a very black and white place, and he taught me there's some gray. And you could afford to give people a chance to live in the gray area."

He feels that programs directors need flexibility, such as to help individual residents do research projects. Through generous patients he was able to develop an education fund to support his trainees' projects. "I thought my job was to help my trainees identify and pursue their dreams and to enable them to do that, whatever they wanted to do, as long as it wasn't immoral, illegal, or fattening. And through my patient's generosity, I had the wherewithal to do that so that."

In finishing the interview, he returned to the importance of discussion and feedback within the family. "I was lucky that my wife was very supportive of my career, because I could have made a lot more money as an academic cardiologist than as a program director, and her feeling was 'Do what gives you joy.'"

[67]Bernard Lown, MD, professor emeritus of cardiology at the Harvard School of Public Health, invented the direct-current defibrillator.

[68]Eugene Braunwald, MD, was then chair at Brigham and Women's Hospital. Generations know him as editor of *Heart Disease* and as coeditor of *Harrison's Principles of Internal Medicine*.

[69]Eugene C. Eppinger (1903–1980) was clinical professor of medicine and retired in 1969.

[70]William T. Branch, MD, was vice-chair for primary care and director of the Division of General Medicine at Emory University School of Medicine.

❖ Steven Weinberger

"I found that my day-to-day gratification came from my teaching interactions with residents, students, and peers, and my ability to convey concepts to trainees and work with them to help develop their skills." Dr. Weinberger began his career as a pulmonary researcher, and his textbook, Principles of Pulmonary Medicine, *remains one of the most successful in the field. Before his present job at the American College of Physicians as deputy executive vice-president and senior vice-president for medical education and publishing, he directed the Shapiro Institute for Education and Research at Harvard Medical School/Beth Israel Deaconess Medical Center and was professor of medicine and faculty associate dean for medical education at Harvard.*

"After my training I was thinking of a standard type of academic career with a heavy research base, along with some clinical and teaching responsibilities. My hope was to be a triple threat." And his training at the National Institutes of Health and initial research made him successful. I asked him about how careers change their focus, and he showed the candid self-reflection that is seen in all these profiles.

Moving From the Laboratory to Education

Although Dr. Weinberger remained an active clinician, his focus switched from research to medical education. When and how did that come about? "Over the course of my first few years on the faculty, I realized that I was not the most creative researcher in the world. As I looked carefully at my own talents and skills, I realized that I was not the kind of person who would end up making major contributions in research, and at the same time, I had always really liked teaching. Just around that time, Harvard was also recognizing that more needed to be done to support clinician teachers and provide academic pathways for them. Fortunately, a clinician-teacher pathway was being developed at the right time for me, and I was able to have that as an acceptable form of academic advancement that felt right for me."

"My first educational leadership role came when Dr. Eugene Braunwald[71] called me into his office. Whenever he called you into his office, you had no idea whether to be trembling or not. But it turned out to be fine, because his intent was to ask if I would run the fourth-year medical student clerkship. That was not at all what I had expected, but I was pleased by the offer and decided to say yes." Although Dr. Braunwald was always well-known for his commitment to research and had more than 1000 publications in cardiology, he "was totally committed to developing people in whatever way their talents appeared. For me it was an opportunity to try out an educational leadership position and demonstrate whether I was good at it."

Progressing in the Same Institution

Dr. Weinberger remained at Harvard for more than 25 years. "Over time I was able to get more and more in the way of educational leadership positions. The fourth-year clerkship was the first of my educational administrative jobs. And then things just snowballed to a number of other leadership opportunities, eventually including positions as vice-chair of the department in charge of education; as education director for the Shapiro Institute, which was focused largely on medical education; and later as the executive director of the Institute.

What would he advise younger people who are right out of their chief residency? Did he make the decision to remain at one place, or did it just happen?

"I really liked where I was working. Actually, there were some very good job opportunities I was asked to explore at other institutions, such as chief of medicine positions, and one of them involved moving to a place that I thought my family would find quite attractive. I went home and talked to my wife and kids. Much to my surprise, my kids' response was, 'Dad, we have no interest in moving.' And that just stopped the discussion right there."

The Fun Stuff

"When I was a student and a house officer, it seemed to me that a chief of medicine was more involved in teaching and modeling clinical expertise, and over the years I saw that type of position evolving more into a business role. And that part to me was less attractive. I'm a traditionalist in the sense that, for a chief of medicine position to be really attractive to me, it would have less of the business aspects and more of the teaching and role-modeling aspects. One of the things that I found particularly enjoyable about being a vice-chair is that I got to do a lot of the fun stuff without having the ultimate financial buck stopping at my desk.

"I think getting the first administrative position is always critical. The other boost to my career in medical education was the first time I won a teaching award. When I started my career, there was much less in the way of formal feedback from students and house staff, so the first time that I won a teaching award was an emotional, very touching experience for me. Quite frankly, when I was called about it I really got choked up, because it was the first external validation of what I had been doing."

Success in an Academic Setting

"The other thing that was important for my development was recognizing that to be successful as a clinician-educator, you had to have an impact outside of your own institution. This in part means figuring out how to get involved in writing and publishing. That aspect of my career evolved fortuitously."

In his early years on the faculty, Dr. Weinberger took care of a young, pregnant asthmatic patient, who ended up being admitted to the hospital many times during her pregnancy with apparent exacerbations of asthma. "I decided to scour the literature, and I realized that there was nothing particularly good in the way of a review article on pregnancy and lung disease at the time. So I decided that I would try writing a review article on pregnancy and the lung. And much to my surprise, it was accepted.

"Shortly after it was published, my division chief was asked to write a book chapter on pulmonary disease and pregnancy. He said to me, 'You've just written a review article on this. Why don't you write the chapter?' It was a good opportunity for me to write a book chapter for a major medical publisher. They liked the chapter, but even more important, because they liked my writing they subsequently asked me to write a textbook on pulmonary disease."

Role Models, Mentors, Colleagues

"One person I admired tremendously was Dan Federman,[72] starting back when I was a second-year medical student and hearing what were probably the most beautifully crafted lectures that anyone could ever deliver. Then I had the good fortune to have him as one of my attendings in my third-year medicine clerkship. Dan often served as a mentor for me later on during my time on the faculty, and he was always the role model for the ultimate clinician educator.

"But there were other people as well. When I was a medical student, a wonderful educator, a pathologist named Harvey Goldman,[73] could explain the most difficult concepts so simply and beautifully, and his skill was something that I really emulated." As a high point in his own career, Dr. Weinberger recalls "one time when Harvey, years after he became chief of pathology and a well-respected professor nationally, snuck into the back of one of the lectures that I was giving. I found it touching and gratifying to have one of my role models come specifically to hear me teach."

Later in his career, when vice-chair for education and then executive vice-chair of the department, he worked closely and had a wonderful working relationship with Robert Moellering,[74] chair of medicine at Beth Israel Deaconess Medical Center. This experience added a new dimension to his thoughts on working relationships with leaders and mentors. "A chair and a vice-chair, or a dean and a vice-dean—the two people in those roles really need to be thinking alike, so that one automatically knows what the other is doing and thinking, and each can very much act for the other based upon the trust that has been established in a seamless leadership relationship."

Sources of Pride and Difficulties

"I'm probably most proud of any impact that I have had on the professional development of other people, particularly as I've seen them go on to become leading clinicians, clinician-educators, or administrators. The most difficult situations I have had as a leader were those times when I had to give negative feedback, or in the most extreme cases, actually fire people. I find it very hard, very difficult to give negative feedback, even in a constructive way, and then in rare cases take the ultimate action of letting someone go. Fortunately, over many years I've only had to do this twice, but on each occasion I found it to be very painful and difficult."

Advice

"I would certainly try to find a mentor, and the type of person that I would look for is someone who is very good at listening and skillful in understanding other people. At the same time, ideally it's someone that you consider a role model, someone that you emulate." How do you do that if you've just finished being chief resident or are new on staff? "Finding an unbiased person who will listen and who will have your best interests at heart is the critical issue. And then there is the intangible aspect of getting a sense of the chemistry—how you relate to a potential mentor."

In asking for advice or seeking a mentor, Dr. Weinberger cautioned against assuming that leaders are too distant to approach. He learned this himself when asking Dr. Braunwald for guidance. "Everyone feared him. But yet, as much as everyone feared him, everyone really respected him." So, when Dr. Weinberger had to deal with an issue of someone plagiarizing from an article he had written, he decided to seek the advice of Dr. Braunwald, his department chair at the time and one of the most prominent names in American medicine. "As a very junior faculty member at the time, I had no clue what to do. So I went to Dr. Braunwald and basically said, 'Please give me some advice. What do I do in this type of situation?' He took my question very seriously and suggested what I felt was a good approach. I think it worked out well overall, and his thoughtful guidance was incredibly helpful to me."

In retrospect, Dr. Weinberger would do one thing differently. "I actually never received any formal training in either medical education or in leadership. As a result, I needed to pick everything up through observation and imitation of role models. I think it would have been helpful to have more formal training in these areas. And although I picked up a lot of good ideas, knowledge, and skills along the way, I often feel that there may have been times when I could have been more effective if I had gotten that type of background."

Challenges Within Medical Education

Although self-critical of his own lack of formal training in educational methods and research, Dr. Weinberger was chosen as leader of the Shapiro Institute and directed the first three Millennium Conferences on medical education and innovation. He addressed the challenges facing medical education, and he has continued to do so as the educational leader at the American College of Physicians..

"One challenge now is the need to train and develop teaching faculty in a changing environment where ever-increasing pressures for either clinical or research productivity make it more difficult to devote the time necessary not only for teaching, but also for helping trainees with their own professional development."

At the same time, there are complicated new topics and skills that faculty have to teach, areas in which they have had little experience and no formal training. "Newer educational priorities such as quality improvement and the competencies of systems-based practice and practice-based learning and improvement—these are areas that are new to most faculty. To be successful in training the next generation of people, the faculty have to be up to speed in getting trainees to understand and gain skills in these unfamiliar areas.

"A third challenge is that there has been an erosion of the culture of medicine as a calling. Although adoption of duty hour requirements has been important in allowing residents to balance their professional and personal lives, an unanticipated consequence has been some erosion of the sense of professional responsibility for patients. I think it's a challenge for us to regain that sense of professionalism at the same time that we adhere to the requirements."

Challenges in the Health Care Environment

"We now have a healthcare system that is under tremendous pressure, particularly financial pressure. A real challenge—from undergraduate through graduate medical education—is linking what we do as individual physicians with the broader perspective of the overall system for delivering health care. The profession must work closely with legislators to solve the problem of spiraling health care costs. Unless we somehow build an understanding of financial and other societal issues relating to health care into our educational system, the profession runs the risk of losing control and being at odds with the federal government and the payers of health care. We must teach students not only the scientific and humanistic components of medicine, but also some of the more practical aspects of medicine and societal expectations for health care and health care costs."

Receiving "The Prize"

Shortly after his fellowship and as a new faculty member at Harvard Medical School, Dr. Weinberger got a call from *Science*, asking if he would review an article. "I was really quite flattered and asked 'What's the article about?'" They said, "Well, the article is on proton beam weapons." This seemed like a topic more appropriate for a physicist than a pulmonologist, and the call was in fact the first of a series of mix-ups with Steven Weinberg, a professor of physics at Harvard.

Dr. Weinberger has received many teaching awards, but that's not all. "Very early in my career I received the Nobel Prize. The problem is, I didn't *win* the Nobel Prize." Professor Steven Weinberg, not Dr. Steven Weinberger, won the Nobel Prize in Physics in 1979. "Shortly after he won the prize, however, I got a package from the Karolinska Institute in

Stockholm, which was intended for Professor Weinberg but kindly readdressed and routed to me by the Harvard mail office. When the package was opened, we saw the bronze replica of the Nobel Prize, which I delivered that evening to its rightful owner. So after 'receiving' the Nobel Prize, I figured I had made it to the pinnacle of a research career, and I could now focus my time on medical education."

[71] Eugene Braunwald, MD, was then chair of medicine at both Brigham and Women's Hospital and Beth Israel Hospital. Two generations know him as editor of Heart Disease and as coeditor of Harrison's Principles of Internal Medicine.

[72] See his profile in this section.

[73] Harvey Goldman, MD (1933–2009), taught pathology at Harvard Medical School for 40 years and was faculty dean for medical education.

[74] Robert Moellering Jr., MD, is the Shields Warren-Mallinckrodt Professor of Medical Research at Harvard Medical School.

Index